Master
Of The
Abyss

A Journey Into The Unknown

Lee Ehrlich

First Edition:
First printing

Lee Ehrlich

PUBLISHED BY HAUNTED ROAD MEDIA, LLC
www.hauntedroadmedia.com

United States of America

Dedicated to
Spencer F. Ehrlich

My Father. My Hero.

Acknowledgments

This book, and the adventures within, wouldn't have been a reality without the friendship and support of a great many people. I thank all of those who have stood beside me, manning the trenches and holding the line, as we've fought the good fight, until to this very day.

I owe a great deal to a great many, notably, my wife, Diana, and daughter, Alyssa, whose belief in who I am made this book a reality.

Nor could I have done any of this without the tutelage and support of Solvej Jordahl, a dear friend who stood beside me through thick and thin while teaching me everything I know about a magical thing called writing.

And last, but certainly not least, I owe a special thanks to Susan Coker, The Mayor of Arcadia, whose friendship and kindness nudged me in the right direction, lighting the path all the way to the finish line.

Table of Contents

Prologue

By the time I heard the flamethrowers, things had gotten totally out of hand. And when the screaming started, I realized they were about to get a whole lot worse.

Maybe the pockets of methane gas bothered me the most. Or maybe it was the way grown men were running for their lives. But regardless of which, I knew it was time to run.

With my back to the mine's rotting timbers, I watched as half of our team ran into the darkness. "Live to fight another day," I thought, as they ran for the tunnels. Then, wishing I'd joined them, I put my hand to my face, as the first of the chemical blasts went off.

The flash was nearly blinding, blurring my vision to a dull, muted glow. I couldn't see anything at first, but then, as my senses returned, I saw the shadow of something huge, as it drew closer.

"FALL BACK!" I yelled, as the shadow moved toward us. "GET THE HELL OUT OF THERE!"

I tried to warn them that the thing was on the move, but despite my urgent calls, all I could hear was shouting, and the sound of whooshing flame.

"It's time to go," Charlie said. "We need to go… NOW!"

I looked at him, his face barely visible in the flickering light. We crouched amid the stench of burning ether, and as he tugged on my jacket, I knew it was time to go.

As I rose to a knee, I looked far down the shaft to where fire reflected on the wall. The flames danced like fiery imps, and as their ghostly arms flailed wildly, a cold chill ran down my spine. "One more reason to leave," I thought, as the flames danced about. Then, just as the fire seemed to be coming alive, there was a flicker, as the lights went out.

Clicking on my tactical light, I looked at Charlie as he crouched beside me. He'd heard something, and as he tilted his head with an ear to the shaft, we both held very still.

There was a rumble in the distance... a scuffing roll of muted sound that was nearly indiscernible. The sound was soft at first, until it built to a roaring crescendo as it thundered down the mineshaft.

First we heard the sound of heavy boots, then raised voices from afar, just a second before our friends bolted from the darkness like The Devil was chasing them.

"RUN!" Mark yelled, as they blew by like a freight train. "IT'S COMING!"

We paused a moment, staring into an inky void that flickered with random embers. There was a sound... and a roar... before we ran for our lives, as something beastly brought up the rear.

Running wildly into the darkness, I followed my friends at nearly a full gallop. It was a crazy run, over a rough-cut floor that was heavily littered with debris. All I could hear was the sound of our boots, while knowing that one false step could end the game forever.

"It's just a matter of time before someone cracks his skull open," was all I could think. And then, as if on cue, the sickening sound of a brutal face-plant echoed through the tunnel.

It sounded like someone had put their boot through a rotting pumpkin, and I cringed at the implications of what I'd heard. I suppose it was bound to happen, especially with an errant railroad tie here and there. So, as expected, my friend Jason had taken a header, like a human lawn dart.

He easily could have killed himself. But then, as several others gathered around, Jason popped to his knees like a Jack in The Box, with a hideous, blood-soaked grin.

"Get your bloody ass up!" I yelled, as the Shadow-Thing drew nearer. "Get up or get EATEN!"

Jason paused a moment, probably due to shock. Then, as the birds stopped chirping, he leaped to his feet like nothing at all had happened.

"That way!" I yelled. "That way down the shaft!"

We were about to run, when an errant flash of a light beam froze us in our tracks.

"Oh my God… look at that!" Mark said, as his light illuminated the ceiling.

"OH, MY, GOD…"

As we clustered together, we stared at the cut in the rocks where Mark's light was pointed. In the soft part of the light, I could see something quivering on the ceiling. But until it spread its wiry legs, the horror of the moment hadn't fully set in.

It took a moment for our eyes to focus. But then, as the tap, tap, tap, sound of Jason's dripping blood echoed through the cavern, the spider's legs unfurled . . . And we all gasped as one.

"Holy Crap!" Mark rang out. "THAT JUST CANT BE!"

But it was… And as we stood beneath the giant spider's web, in the shadows to my left, something else clicked and stirred.

Within an instant of hearing the sound, we swung our lights in its direction. And with a group-wide gasp, we illuminated a cluster of spiders so large, they simply should not have been.

"My God!" Was all I could think, as death crawled all around us. We were surrounded by spiders nearly the size of my hand. And as they pulsed with the smell of freshly let blood, they positioned for the swarm.

"This place crawls!" Mark said loudly. Then, as he swung his light to the left, we saw for the first time just how close to death we were.

Looking down, I could see the lower half of the web, and the series of trip-wires that were anchored to the floor. There were spiders in every portion of the web, so close to us, that our skin began to crawl.

"GET AWAY FROM THE WALLS!" I shouted, "The bastards are moving in on us!"

And that they were, until their eyes reflected the pilot-flame of Mark's handy-dandy, home-made flamethrower.

"GET BACK!" he yelled, as he turned up the primer. "WAY

13

back."

We stepped back as far as we dared, before Mark painted the web with a wall of flame that was nothing short of hideous. Flaming spiders fell to the ground like leaves falling from a tree, and as they flailed around like freakish demons, I began to wonder if we'd found our way down to Hell.

Whether or not we had, there were other things to consider, such as the thing that we'd awakened, and the ever present notion that it was drawing nearer.

I called out to Mark as he torched the cavern, his shadowy form back-lit by a crimson wall of flame. "GET BACK!" I yelled, "The thing's still coming for us, and we've got to get a move-on!"

Mark looked nearly insane as he rolled off one more round, then, as he stared down the corridor, he heard something just around the bend.

"IT'S COMING!" Mark yelled. "IT'S STILL BACK THERE!"

That was all I needed to hear, for now that I'd seen the spiders, I knew there was nowhere to hide.

"Run to the culvert and get to the rope!" Charlie said. "Once we're in the pipe we can better defend ourselves!"

I wasn't nearly as concerned with that, as I was getting to the rope and climbing my ass out of Dodge. Half of our team was already topside, and if they were waiting by the ropes as planned, they'd be able to pull us to safety in a heartbeat.

The tunnel narrowed, bringing us to a split corridor with two auxiliary shafts. We'd come in on the left, through a narrow corrugated pipe, that originated at the base of the oil-fields. It was a narrow tube, barely five feet tall, and its century old walls were heavily rusted from the elements.

Charlie entered the pipe first, switching to his head lamp as he led the way. We shuffled like a centipede, down the center of the shaft, until Mark yelled "STOP!" as we were barely half way through.

"What is it?" I asked. "Why did you tell us to stop?"

"Because of the growling," he said, in nearly a whisper. "Don't you hear it?"

At first I didn't, until the guttural sound rolled through the pipe like a hellish bellows. "That's not a growl," I said, as we all began to run. "IT'S A ROAR!

We ran as fast as we could, while hunched over like a group of freakish elves. The thing was coming, and as we saw the first sliver of moonlight, I began to hear its feet on the rusted metal floor.

Ahead of us was a light, a bluish circle of light where the tunnel ended and the rest of our lives began. Down the center of the circle was a fine white line, a thin thread of hope that hung down from above. Charlie hit the rope first, holding it with one hand as he craned his neck skyward.

"WE'RE HERE!" He called out to our friends above, then, as they yelled back, he locked in, as they pulled him up the sheer rock wall.

One by one we swung out over the chasm, until just two of us remained. Mark was last in line, and I tapped him on the shoulder as he pointed the flame-gun down the corridor.

"You go," I told him. "Give me the gun, and get the hell out of here."

"Thanks man," he said, as the rope dropped down again. "If the thing comes your way, light him up for me!"

I shouldered the gun as he locked into the rope, then, with a slap on the back, he swung out over the abyss.

I stood at the edge of the tunnel, where the drain pipe ended, and a sheer drop began. I don't know how far it was to the bottom of the abyss. But I do know there was death in that hollow, and whatever it was that stirred below, was already making plans for me.

"Not today," I muttered, to the shadows. "You're not going to get me, and this thing isn't either!"

Facing the darkness, all I could see was the dancing glow of the gun's pilot flame. It was being pulled into the tunnel, as if invisible hands were drawing it long and thin as it stretched into the darkness. I watched the flame flicker and jump as the tunnel seemed to breathe, then, as it nearly went out, I heard a hissing sound, as something dark drew nearer.

The thing knew I was alone, and I could feel it pulse as it crept closer. It growled like a bear that had just been awakened, and as it approached, my   hair stood on end, as if I'd been cloaked in a veil of darkened static.

I could see a shift in the darkness, where a shadow slid toward me like ink had been poured from a well. The beast had come, and as it rose up like a curtain of death, I squeezed the trigger, sending a crimson ball of flame down the corridor.

The beast reacted with frightening speed, compressing itself against the floor as the flame rolled harmlessly by. I rolled off blast after blast, but no matter where I pointed the gun, the shadow just danced with the flame.

"It can't be killed!" I thought. "It shape-shifts somehow, avoiding the fire altogether."

That thought was frightening, as was the notion that with each missed shot, the thing was getting closer. There were only seconds before it pounced, and as it took form once again, I grabbed the rope, swinging out into the night.

As I arced out over the abyss, I looked down into the darkness, where the mossy pulse of a thousand hands tried to draw me closer.

"Not today," I called out down below. And not tomorrow either, because there's still much work to do, before I return to The Abyss, where it all really began...

The Dock

Weekend summer days were my favorite days of all. Because on each and every one of them, my father would join my mother and I at our beachfront cabana, on a leeward, Long Island sound. Those summers way back when, were a magical time for all of us. And as the long, beach-going days passed, a sense that life was good permeated the air, along with the sound of seagulls, and the hiss of the bay's still waters.

I must have been in a fools-paradise to think there wasn't something sinister lurking behind the brightly colored beach umbrellas. And for the most part, I turned my back to the flapping canvas that blew noisily in the wind. But then one day, I saw the far-off look in my father's eyes, and I realized that our perfect little world was really just a dream.

The day my father walked to the water's edge shouldn't have been different from any other. Yet for some unexplained reason, everything felt so wrong. For those like myself with a keen sense of intuition, there was a "feel" in the air that something wasn't quite right accompanied by an undertone of dread, whose grip was unmistakable.

As my father walked toward the bay, I looked up, just in time to see him pause at the waterline. He stood there like a sentry, and as the oily sand oozed around his feet, a chill ran down my spine.

I jumped to my feet as he stood there, as if a genetic alarm had warned me that something was terribly wrong. I ran to him as the alarm rang in my head, knowing right then and there, that I needed to be by his side.

As I ran, I glanced back at our beach umbrella where my mother was sitting with the other ladies. She hadn't bothered to notice that I'd run toward the water, or that my red pail and shovel lay unattended beside a small tidal lagoon. Perhaps that was because bad things never happen on vacation. Or maybe, it was because on weekend days, it was Daddy's job to watch the children, and her responsibility to work on her tan.

I tried to catch her attention, before stepping slowly into the oily, clam bed water. My skin crawled at the water's touch, as I waded knee-deep into what felt like cold diesel fuel. I moved tentatively, grabbing hold of my father's hand as I looked up at him. He knew I was there, but he stared straight ahead, as if he'd seen something he didn't want to lose sight of.

We stood there silently as we stared at the sound. And even though I hadn't seen what had caught his eye, I could tell from his silence that its relevance would change my perspective forever. "What is it Dad?" I asked. "What did you see?" He could have answered, but rather, he just squeezed my hand, while raising a finger to his lips, as if to tell me to be very, very quiet.

I looked toward the horizon, seeing nothing but what my mind was pre-programmed to see. For a moment, it looked like the same old bay. But then, as I looked to the heavens, I gasped, as I realized what he'd seen.

It was a wall, a gigantic gray wall, blocking out all things far and wide. And from the way it towered toward the heavens, while plunging deep into the sea, it felt like we were standing at the edge of the world.

"What the hell is THAT?" My father said, in a strange whisper. "It looks like we're inside a giant box, and the walls are closing in on us."

I didn't know what to think other than time and space seemed to end just a few hundred yards off shore. Something definitely wasn't right, and I knew that whatever the solid gray wall was made of, it certainly wasn't fog.

As we stared at the insanity of where the world seemed to end, it looked as if our reality had been projected onto a giant drive-in movie screen. I looked up at the wall, half expecting something to appear, but just as if the projector's bulb had burned out, all I could see was futility.

I was about to say something, when my father scooped me up in his arms, pulling me from the water. He carried me onto the sand, then, as we were half way to our umbrella, we turned to look at the wall, one last time.

The wall stared at us, leaning forward a bit just to show us how tall it really was. We stared back like a couple of frightened kids, and at that very moment, I think my father realized what I'd been trying to tell him all along...

The beach was damn creepy.

That was the beginning of it all, or, at least, the beginning of my father's realization that there was definitely something odd about the sound. Also, I think he finally realized there was a hell of a lot more to the strange stories I'd been telling him, than he'd previously given me credit for.

One such story was about a strange icy chill that crept along the beach. I'd be playing in the sunshine, on the hottest days of summer, when an ice cold rush of air would run the length of my spine.

Each time this happened, it always seemed as if the cold breeze had come from the bay. But with the air being so hot and still, it just didn't seem natural that there could have been so much coldness to it.

The breeze itself was creepy enough, but what made it even worse, was that every time I felt the phantom chill, it always seemed to have come from the direction of an old floating dock that was anchored just offshore.

I'd stare at the dock, as its rusted metal drums creaked and groaned with the tide. The thing was a menace in every way, but what I hated most about the rusted monstrosity, was the way it pulsed with death, as it grinned with the Cheshire Cat's smile.

At first, I thought the whole "creepy dock" thing may have been nothing more than a figment of my fertile imagination. But then, after speaking to some of my friends about it, they all agreed that there was something odd about the rusty, old platform. It seemed to beckon in a strange way, and although some of my friends didn't care to admit it, there was also a sense that somehow, someway, the creepy old thing was calling out to you.

Because the dock was so damn creepy, I did everything I could to stay away from the sound's oily waters, choosing instead, to sequester myself to the large estuary tide pools that had formed in the deep sand areas a few hundred yards down the beach. These pools were shallow, bright, and filled with all manner of small sea creatures, providing a safe, oasis-like play-land for small, world-class waders such as myself. I spent nearly all of my beach-going time in and around those tidal lagoons, and by immersing myself in their safe haven, I was able to temporarily turn my back to the bay, and the dock's siren song.

During the mid-summer months, some of the older boys would come out to the beach and show off for their peers. In what was nearly a rite-of-passage, these boys would wade into the murky water as if on a dare. Then, those who were brave enough, would hazard a swim to the dock. I'd watch them laugh and rough-house as they dove into the bay. Yet for all their bravado, I couldn't help but wonder how long it was going to be before one of their laughs turned into a scream.

Perhaps I was being a bit morbid, or even a tad morose. But with rumors of huge sharks in the bay, and the recent sighting of a giant dorsal fin very close to shore, I knew that before the season was over, one of those boys wouldn't be coming up from the bottom.

Being isolated from it all, I didn't let any of this affect me for the most part. Especially since the summer season was coming to an end, and fewer people were joining us on the sand each day. That suited me just fine, especially because the smaller crowds meant less teenagers running up and down the beach, which ushered-in a noticeable resurgence of wildlife that I appreciated most of all.

It was during one of those late-summer days when I experienced an event so bizarre I still can't figure it out. It happened while I was sitting waist-deep in the lagoon's bath-like waters, lost in the thoughts of an eight year old boy. Beside me was my favorite beach toy, a red and white plastic sailboat that was floating calmly in the sun-drenched shallows. Several small minnows swam around the boat, their bodies sparkling brightly in the mid-day sunshine. The day was beautiful, and everything was so peaceful and serene until something unsavory came to call that had no business disturbing the serenity of my idyllic little wonderland.

In retrospect, I suppose the minnows noticed it first, because, as I watched them dart around in the inch-deep shallows, suddenly, for no apparent reason, each and every one of them bolted for deeper water. I leaned forward to see where they'd gone, and as I did, a fierce chill ripped down my spine that seemed to come out of nowhere.

As I shook off the chill, I looked toward the bay, where a weird, orange mist was sliding across the water's surface. The mist moved slowly at first, as if it was creeping up on something. Then, as it reached the floating dock, tendrils of orange smoke caressed its edges with long, skeletal fingers.

I looked away, while pretending that none of this was really happening. "Just look at the happy water," I told myself. "Look for your fishy friends."

I stared into the shallow pool searching for salvation, but instead of seeing the reflection of the clear blue sky, all I could see was gray. That took me by surprise, as it had been quite sunny throughout the entire day. But now, as I looked deeper into the water, something began to change, as the first of the wavelets appeared.

It began as just a shimmer on the surface, then, within seconds, the water began to whip and boil as waves were driven upward by an unseen force.

The first of the waves rolled toward me, breaking against my body with remarkable force. I was knocked to my back, baffled by how a wave of that size could have come out of nowhere. Sensing danger, I tried to stand up, just as a second, more powerful wave slammed against me, sending a stream of eggy, salt water up my nose.

The waves came in rapid sequence, each of them slapping my body with palpable conviction. The water had turned deadly, and as I floundered to gain a foot-hold, I could feel it course with malice and intent. The fish were right, something evil had come, and now, if I was to survive, I needed to follow their lead before it was too late.

Sensing an ever-growing presence in the water, I struggled to get to my hands and knees, but the breakers slapped me down one after another. As I rolled side to side with each relentless blow, I could see my toy being pummeled in the waves of the mini-maelstrom. I felt sorry for the toy, and despite my need to save myself, I fought against the chopping waves, to where the sailboat now floundered.

"Come here Boaty, COME HERE!" I called out to the toy. "LET ME SAVE YOU!"

I didn't think I was going to be able to grab it, but then, with the slap of a breaker, the boat's plastic sail came within reach, and I pulled the toy to my chest.

We rolled in the wave-pool as the mist crept closer. And as we did, I hoped dearly that someone would pull us from the hell. But nobody came, and no one heard my cries, even as the sailboat and I were battered violently to shore.

The last wave had tried a bit too hard. For instead of it being content to simply slap the air from my lungs, it wanted more. It pushed too hard for its own good, sending me rolling into the shallows, where I quickly scampered to my feet.

As I clutched the sailboat to my chest, I tried to make sense of it all. Something unnatural had happened, but being a small boy, I couldn't imagine what that was. I only knew that the lagoon had changed somehow, and while all of this had transpired, the strange, orange mist had crept up onto the sand.

I stared into the mist, feeling a sense of dread that was nearly overwhelming. There was something very wrong about all of this, and wanting nothing more to do with it, I picked up my towel, before heading toward our cabana.

I'd begun to walk toward safety, when suddenly, out of nowhere, a strange voice spoke to me.

"Don't go in the water!" The voice said, in an odd, metallic tone. "DON'T GO IN THE WATER!"

I nearly jumped out of my skin when I heard the voice. Then, as I quickly spun in place, I yelled, "WHO IS THAT?"

There was no answer. Nor could I hear anything at all, but the whistle of the wind.

The phantom voice was unnerving, and seeing that there wasn't a living soul on the beach, I began to get a big-time case of the creeps. Flags blew in the distance, where now, through the encroaching fog, I could see my mother waving to me from afar.

"Weather's gone bad," I thought. "That's got to be it. And it's also got to be the reason why the lagoon had gotten whipped into a frenzy." I was happy with those explanations. So, pretending the voice hadn't really spoken, I ran back to our cabana, after a quick glance at the dock, one last time.

The months had been long, and between the sea-turtle migration and the crazy-crab happening in the parking lot, much had transpired that summer. By season's end, we'd spent a great many days at the beach, and over time, I'd begun to notice that the highly coveted cabanas were becoming vacant one by one.

Sometimes, when I'd journey to our cabana, the long, dark shadows cast by the narrow, wooden structures seemed almost menacing. There was a feel of emptiness in those rows, combined with an unmistakable presence that was nothing short of alarming. I'd listen to the wind blow, while shadows shifted behind me . . . And as I pushed aside a chill, I knew far too well that we'd overstayed our welcome.

Now, in the eerie orange glow of the late-summer sun, the time to pack up was almost upon us. We should have left long ago, but I guess that like many other New Yorkers, giving up on summer, and giving in to winter was a hard thing to do. We were there for the long-haul, so, with no say in the matter, I sat on the beach with my mother and her hair-salon friends, listening to the colorful flags of the cabana rows snap a desperate warning for us to go home.

Knowing what I know now, we should have packed-up and gone home long before our friends had. But since we'd paid for the cabana through the last week of summer, we foolishly overstayed our welcome, rather than listening to what the voices had been telling us all along.

It was the week before Labor Day when it happened. And as it always seems to be when death comes to call, there wasn't a living soul around to save me. That's just the way it is, I suppose. The way it's always been when there's something deadly afoot. So naturally, as I walked alone beside eerily calm waters, my mother knew nothing of what would transpire that day, nor of the oncoming storm that would soon beset her little boy.

As I walked the wet sand, there wasn't a person to be seen. That alone should have warned me to turn-tail and run. But I kept on walking, shadowed by something sinister that hid behind the smell of rotting clams, and the din of buzzing sand fleas.

With nothing particular to do, I meandered down the beach to a place where a wood-slatted fence marked the border between the beach and the nearby sand dunes. On my side of the fence was a clam flat, comprised of the gray, oily sand that clams love to live in. But on the other side, was a place I dared not go, a place called the Dunes, where according to many, including my father, the dreaded Mole Men lived just below the surface of the sand.

I feared the Dunes, and I especially feared the Mole Men, for whom I was told, would reach up and grab the legs of any child who dared wander their way.

The story did scare me, but being a bright little boy, I had my doubts about the whole Mole-Man thing. Knowing my father's sense of humor, I was pretty sure it was all a hoax, but given the unusual occurrences of late, I wasn't about to take any chances. With that in mind, as I reached the fence, I stared at the forbidden dunes for a moment, before doing a quick about-face just in case something was planning on grabbing my feet.

The tide was unusually low that day, and because of that, the clam-rich mud flats were within easy stepping distance. I had nothing to do, so I figured it would be fun to dig up a large clam or two just to see what they looked like. I ventured out onto the oily mire, as the smell of rotten eggs wafted up with each tentative step. It was icky and gross the way my feet sank into the ooze, but knowing there were some pretty big clams for the taking, I stayed my course, while treading lightly just in case the Mole People were listening.

As I slogged along, I wondered how anyone could possibly eat the clams that lived in that eggy, oil-soaked sand. The whole concept seemed really gross to me, tantamount to eating something that had been cultured in the bottom of a portable toilet. I imagined that some people liked the things, and that there was no accounting for taste. But for me, they were far from food, and more of a curiosity than anything else.

I knew the clams were there, now all I needed to do was find the dimples in the sand that gave away their positions. I imagine I was lost in thought as I was searching for one of those dimples, when suddenly, the phantom voice rang out, stopping me dead in my tracks.

"LEE... LEEEE..." the voice called out. And as it did, I spun around, seeing only the rusted dock, and its evil, crooked smile.

As I looked down the beach, I could see the colors of our beach umbrella far off in the distance. I called out to my mother, somehow rationalizing that she had called my name. But all I could hear was the buzzing of sand fleas, as they raced in and out of a dead crab's shell.

I coursed with goose bumps as I faced the bay's oily waters. Then, as loud as I could, I yelled in the direction of the dock, to where the strange voice seemed to have come from.

"IS SOMEONE OUT THERE?" I yelled. "IS SOMEBODY THERE?" I waited for a reply, but there was no answer, save for the distant buzz, and the undeniable feeling that I wasn't alone.

I was completely perplexed, especially since there wasn't a living soul in or around the water. It stood to reason that if someone was out there I'd have seen them. And besides, I was just a little kid, so why the heck were they calling out to me?

None of it made any sense, and as I listened for a voice I hoped I'd never hear again, the voice in my own head told me it was time to get moving… And fast.

"Maybe it was a seagull," I thought. "Or maybe I'm just too far down the beach for my own comfort."

I knew better than that, but seeing that no one was there, I ignored my gut, as I scanned the mud-flats for the percolating bubbles that were a dead give-away that a clam was hiding out. As I walked along, I could have sworn something was moving just offshore. But every time I looked up, all I could see was the dock, and its jagged, steel-toothed grin.

I blinked several times, wondering if I was seeing an eyelash out of the corner of my eye. The clam hunt was growing creepier by the minute, and as I stood in the oily ichor, I took a moment to sum things up. The strange voice had been creepy enough, but now that I was seeing things, my inner voice knew that the beach was empty for a reason. "Listen to your intuition," my father always said. "A good, little woodsman ALWAYS listens to his intuition."

Dad was right, as was my intuition. For regardless of whether I'd seen the tip of an eyelash, or the tip of the fin of the world's biggest shark, it was definitely time to run.

I looked to my left where far down the beach I could see the domino-like rows of cabanas lined up in the distance. Atop the cabanas were brightly colored flags, which hung limply, like deflated wind socks, in the still, early-morning air.

Walking along a step or two, I took one last look at the mudflats before deciding to call it a day. "Maybe Mom will make me a sandwich," I thought, "And maybe, I'll be able to talk her into going home early." I liked the sound of that, but before I was able to take a step toward the umbrellas, the voice from nowhere spoke once again.

"Run for the flags!" It shouted. "RUN FOR THE FLAGS!"

I spun like a top when I heard the voice, seeing, once again, that no one was there.

"WHO ARE YOU?" I called out. "WHO ARE YOU?" But as always, there was no answer to my call.

I should have run, and there was no good reason not to. Except that thinking this through took time, and I needed to do it standing still.

"What the hell?" I thought. "Why is a voice talking to me? And why did it call me to the water one moment, while urging me to run away the next?" I pondered that for a moment, until, in a flash of revelation, something occurred to me that I hadn't considered before.

Two voices had spoken, two distinctly different voices that seemed to have come out of nowhere. One of them sounded evil, while the other voice had a more desperate ring to it.

"There will be plenty of time to sort this out," I thought, "But right now, it's time to run!"

I really did try, but just as I did, a shrill voice called out from the water.

"Help me! ... Help Meeee!" It said, with a mewling cry. "Help meeeee!"

"Oh God!" I thought, as the voice called out. "Not another voice!"

I really wished it wasn't. But as I listening to the cry grow in both intensity and conviction, it became quite clear that someone really was in trouble.

There had to be someone out there, and I was determined to find out who. I wasn't losing my mind, and now that the voice had called out so clearly, I was certain that the distressed swimmer was close by.

As I looked out onto the bay, I couldn't see one sign of a swimmer in distress. The bay seemed completely devoid of life, and I began to think that the distressed swimmer may have slipped beneath the surface.

As horrible a thought as that was, I was starting to believe it was true. Right up until something large boiled to the surface with a resounding, sloshing "Splash!"

When it first popped up I was both shocked and relieved at the same time. I knew all along that I'd seen something out there, and now that there really was an object floating in the water, the whole scenario began to feel a lot less dream-like.

As I stared at the bobbing mass, I could see its general shape, but it was too far away for me to identify it clearly. At first I thought it might have been a half-inflated inner tube or some type of floating buoy, until the thing jerked wildly, leaving no question that it was alive.

All I wanted to do was run. But I couldn't do that, as something about the thing in the water was drawing me closer to it. I strained my eyes to see what the thing was, but all I could tell was that it was close to the dock, and it was jerking around like something was picking at it from below.

"What the hell is it?" I wondered. "What the hell?"

It looked as if I'd never know, until, as suddenly as it had appeared, the thing rolled over, looking very much like a man, in a faded red life-jacket.

"Oh my god!" I muttered. "There really is someone out there!" Horrified, I didn't know what to do. Sure, I could have run all the way down the beach in a vain attempt to find help, but I knew that none of the mothers could swim well enough to save someone's life. So, given that there was no one around to help me, it was up to me to save the swimmer's life.

With no time to waste and no help in sight, I was tortured by my dilemma. "Should I swim out into the sound?" I wondered. "And if I did, could I possibly save a man's life with my limited swimming skills?"

I wasn't sure of anything, other than a good little woodsman never leaves a man behind, and it seemed like I was this man's only hope. Knowing that, I had no choice but to attempt the swim, regardless of the sharks, or the voices, or the hideous dock that had threatened me all summer long.

Like a robot, I stepped into the sound, where I was immediately shocked by how cold the water was. It felt nothing like my happy, little lagoon, with the water being at least fifteen degrees cooler than what I was used to. Hating every muck-filled step, I reluctantly waded deeper, while shuffling my feet in an attempt to shoo away the large horseshoe crabs that littered the bottom of the sound.

After reaching swim-depth, I slid through the water like a muskrat, while hoping to keep my face high and dry. I tried the best I could, until a wave slapped my face that filled my mouth with a sharp blast of sulfur. "How could the older boys swim in this stuff?" I wondered. "How could anyone swim in this rotten-egg flavored ooze?" There was no rational reason for it, I supposed. Other than the bigger boys may have lost their senses when they got older, or maybe they never had any sense to begin with.

That thought kept me occupied, as the water grew deeper and colder by the second. Ahead of me, I could see the jacketed man floating near the dock, and now that I'd reached the half-way point in the swim, the headless form was beginning to splash around a bit. At first he seemed to be moving toward me, until he abruptly changed course, slipping from view as he rounded the corner of the dock.

That's when I should have turned-tail and headed home. But he had called out to me, and for that reason only, I forged onward, in the direction of a partially submerged boundary fence that ran perpendicular to the edge of the dock.

The fence was long, extending from the land of the Mole Men to the footers of the dock's deep anchor points. As I dog-paddled with my head above water, I chose to stay close to the slatted fence, as its presence offered a sense of comfort. That's because my father had told me that sharks never swam near anything they could get caught-up in, and the low-slung wire fence was just that sort of thing.

My plan was to swim to depth on the fence-line, then, once

29

parallel to the dock, it would be a short swim to where the man was last seen. As I slowly made headway, I could see several pieces of floating debris that were flushed-up against the fence. The debris consisted of small chunks of Styrofoam that had most likely come from a derelict beach chair or a broken-up beverage cooler.

As I swam past the mess, I began to hear a weird screeching sound, which I attributed to the foam rubbing against the boggy wooden slats of the fence-line. The sound was eerie as hell, sort of a combination between a howl and a cry. I didn't know what it was, nor what was causing it, but as I swam past its origin, an eerie vibration filled the water that felt far from normal.

I had no idea what was creating the sound, but I knew instinctively that I needed to put some serious distance between myself and the cause of it. Sensing danger, I panicked a bit, dog-paddling as quickly as I could in the direction of the dock.

"What am I thinking!" ran through my head, as I swam toward the grinning menace. "There are sharks under the dock, and you're probably swimming right toward one!"

Ordinarily that would have been enough to send me racing toward shore, but as the screeching intensified to a near fever-pitch, the dock from Hell began to look less like a monster, and more like safe haven. I was half way to the rusted beast, when suddenly, near the fence-line, a huge boil crested, as something huge rose to the surface.

I gasped and blinked as the thing approached, its massive bulk pushing a displacement wave nearly two feet in either direction. Drawing my knees to my chest, I froze for a second before my survival instincts kicked in, telling me to swim like I'd never swam before.

Face-down, I swam like a madman, reaching the rear portion of the dock within seconds. Now all I had to do was grab hold of the ladder and pull myself up to safety. It was a great idea. One I felt was really going to work. Except for one very important detail…

There was no ladder.

It all came rushing back so clearly, the way I'd seen the older boys pull themselves onto the dock like gymnasts and how some of them had never climbed aboard the dock at all. It all made perfect sense to me now. How only the biggest, fittest boys, had been the ones atop the dock. And how little-old me, a child one third their size, didn't stand a chance of pulling himself topside the way they had.

Summing up the situation, there was no question that it had been a really bad idea to swim out there in the first place. Especially now that my arms were beginning to tire, and the cold water was sapping my strength. I began to panic, but with no ladder or foot-hold to be seen, all I could do was pull myself from one rusted floatation drum to the other, hoping to find some way to climb aboard before the thing in the water consumed me.

As I floundered beside the dock, a couple of things became readily apparent. For starters, the dock's orange, demonic grin, was actually a row of rusted, steel drums that were welded to a frame beneath the dock's upper platform. The make-shift float tubs were so badly corroded that most of them were partially flooded, giving the dock its bent, Cheshire Cat smile. Atop these drums were pieces of plywood that formed the dock's upper deck, while raggedly strewn over the rotting wood, was a layer of carpet that must have been there since the Truman administration.

Pulling myself from one drum to another, I began to feel the tow of a powerful tidal current that was passing beneath the dock. The current pulled at my legs with surprising ferocity, and try as I might to hang on to the floats, I soon found myself neck-deep and in big trouble.

I fought for a hand-hold as the oily water slid around my neck, but the current's pull was too strong a foe for the arms of a little boy. I was about to let go, when to my surprise, the dock pulsed with the tide, and my feet pressed against something soft beneath me.

It felt like I was standing on a sand-bar, possibly one that had formed around the deep footers of the dock. I wasn't thrilled by the thought of my chicken legs soaking in the water column, but for the moment, I was too tired to fight, and too tired to swim. Besides, as I rested my weary limbs, there was much to consider. First, there was the sea monster, which had momentarily disappeared. And then, there was the man in the life jacket, who seemed to have disappeared as well.

"Where the hell is he?" I wondered. "And what madness brought him out here in the first place?"

I couldn't fathom a guess, nor did I care about anything other than saving my own hide. Something monstrous was out there somewhere, and although it seemed to have swam off to God-knows-where, I knew I had to climb aboard the dock, if I was to save my own life.

I'd just begun looking for hand-holds, when the phantom voice chimed in out of nowhere.

"Get out now!" The eerie voice said. "Get out of the water NOW!"

"OKAY, OKAY!" I yelled back. "I'M MOVING!"

Maybe I should have swam, rather than test the bottom with my toes, because as I did, more and more, something just didn't feel quite right.

With slow, kneading steps I felt my way along the sand-bar. It was soft, but not in the way that sand should have felt. It rebounded in the oddest way, and as I stood there, I could feel a strange, rubbery texture to the sand. That was weird as hell, as was the way the bottom had appeared out of nowhere, right underneath me too.

I didn't dare consider what I already knew, until the ground began sliding to one side, as something monstrous swam out from beneath me.

I freaked, freaked-out in a way that I'd never freaked-out before. I kicked and screamed, and did God-knows-what, while all along my cries were muffled by the strange, orange mist that was growing thicker by the minute.

Floundering in horror, I knew the thing could come for me at any moment. And I also knew that when it did come, there was absolutely nothing I could have done about it. I hated how helpless that made me feel, and I hated the fact that I was being made to wait. But those feelings only lasted a moment, as the monster rose up behind me, body-slamming me against the dock.

The beast crushed me against the drums, before turning to one side as it enormous body steamrolled by. It had hit me hard, but aside from a few scrapes and bruises, I weathered first-contact without as much as an injury. As the creature turned with a giant wake, I clamored for my life, crawling onto the rusted drums like a lizard on a screen door. What bag of tricks that move came from I'll never know, but for the moment my entire body was out of the water, and in a pinch, that suited me just fine.

Perhaps the creature wasn't too bright, for just as I pulled myself out of the water, the monster dove deep, in search of where I had gone.

I was safe for the moment, but with my arms holding the lion's-share of my body weight, there was no way that I could hold on for long. Looking around for something sturdy to grab hold of, I saw the tail of a ripped carpet remnant teasing me from above. It looked fairly rope-like to me, and with few options left, I grasped it like a horse's mane, pulling against it with all my might.

It held fast, supporting my body weight well, but with no foot-hold to be had, my legs dangled in the water like a couple of meaty fish-sticks.

"Pull harder!" I cried. "Pull yourself up before the damn thing bites your legs off!"

I pulled as hard as I could, until the waist band of my bathing suit came out of the water. I kicked and squirmed, but given how exhausted I was, waist-high above the waterline was the best that I could do.

Completely sapped of energy, there was no possible way that I could climb up any further. I held on a moment, then, as my arms gave out, I released my grip, plunging downward like a guillotine blade. I fully expected to spear down like a lawn-dart, but to my surprise, the waist-band of my bathing suit snagged on a jagged tooth of steel, momentarily tacking me to the side of a drum.

I hung there for a moment, as the waistband stretched with my full body weight. Then, with a "Snap!" the waistband tore loose, plunging my abdomen onto a spike of rusted steel that tore deeply into my flesh.

A cold sensation rushed over me as I floated there in shock, accompanied by the strange, intuitive feeling that something necessary had been torn loose. As I lifted my hand to my stomach, the salt water burned like fire, and I gasped as a rush of warm blood washed all around me.

In a panic, I grabbed hold of a rusted D-ring, while pressing my free hand against the torn flesh. I could feel the rush of warm blood streaming from my abdomen, and I instinctively balled-up my fist as I pressed it against the wound. The harder I pressed the less it stung, so, without knowing why, I pushed as hard as I could, while choosing to disregard the things that swam around me.

Because the water was so dark, there was no telling how badly I'd been injured. I had no desire to see my intestines splayed out in the water, but as bad as that would have been, somehow the sight of seeing it would have given me the resolution to carry on.

There was a long, loop-like flap hanging from my abdomen. And I couldn't tell if it was a segment of my intestines or the drawstring of my waistband. I tried repeatedly to roll to my back, but every time I did, the current pulled downward, causing the ripping pain to intensify.

I was bleeding-out, and I knew that if I wanted to stay alive, swimming back was my only option. With my free hand I pulled myself from float to float, while wondering just how long it was going to be before a hungry fish grabbed hold of my intestines, before pulling them from my body as if I was a giant ball of yarn.

That was a cheery thought, something to occupy my mind as I backtracked around the perimeter of the dock. Once I reached the end closest to the fence, I looked around the corner, to where the sea monster had come from. The swim was the shortest on that end, and I figured that with any luck, I could make it to the shallows before the monster grabbed hold of me.

With my head down and my eyes closed, I thrashed my way toward shore, while the fleshy loop flapped against my side. My abdomen burned like fire, but despite the pain, I was starting to believe that I might actually make it back to shore alive.

Things were going well… Right up until the moment when something monstrous grabbed me around the torso, nearly crushing me in two.

"SNAP!" went the thing's jaws as it grabbed hold of me. Bearing down with a force so great, it felt like I'd been grabbed by a giant pair of pliers.

I thrashed wildly, but regardless of how hard I fought, the thing held me like a vise. I fully expected to feel the snout of a giant shark around my waist, but when I punched my fists into the darkness, I felt something that made absolutely no sense at all.

I'd been grabbed by some kind of cable. As if in some crazy way, I'd ventured into a trap. I was wildly confused, not knowing what the thing was, other than it felt like it was cutting me in two. I floundered as the cable dug into my wound, then I felt a sharp tug as the cable-thing dragged me under…

I gulped in a half-breath as it pulled me below, never expecting to see the surface again. "This is my last breath," I thought, as I clawed the slick, black water. "The very last breath I'll ever take."

That might have been true, had I not looked up to see a yellowish glow that looked a whole lot like sunshine. It was the Sun, and somehow by the grace of God, I was being pulled toward the surface by the same thing that dragged me down moments ago.

I gasped for air as I broke the surface, knowing only that somehow, the cable-thing was cycling up and down. I cupped my hands as I dog-paddled in place, until seconds later, the cable pulled downward, dragging me below once again. "Wait, just wait," I told myself, as I stared into the inky darkness. "You'll come back up, just like last time!"

And a moment later I did, as if the cable-thing was dipping me in and out of the water like a giant tea bag.

I had to do something, as the vise-like grip of the cable was squeezing the life out of me. Each surge of the tide cycled me under the surface, and as I was pulled up and down I wondered if I'd been caught in some kind of mooring line. Nearly desperate, I looked toward the slatted fence, where I caught sight of my first clue. Near the fence's end, far down the line from the floating debris, were two rusted, steel cables. They were fastened to the pickets somehow, and as a wave rolled under the dock, I could see them tense up, as if they were fixed to something.

"Oh my God!" I thought, as I realized what had happened. "I've swam into the cables that hold down the dock. And now the hellish thing is going to drown me!"

And it would have, had I not felt something in the vise-like cables that made a bit of sense.

The thing that gripped me was twisted somehow, almost as if I was caught in a huge strand of rusted DNA. I mapped the twists with my feet, and as I did something inside my head told me that I too needed to twist… like a big human corkscrew.

I timed the surge as it pulled me under. Then, as the cable lessened its grip, I twisted wildly, writhing free of its grasp, before floating to the surface.

As I broke the surface, I had only one thought. "Get back to the shore, NOW!"

Even as a child, I could tell there were way too many curves being thrown my way. Some unseen force was trying to kill me, and if I had any hope of staying alive, I needed to swim fast, and I needed to swim now.

Taking my own advice, I put my face in the water as I began to hammer home. I swam like The Devil was chasing me, doing the best I could to hold my guts in place, while they slowly pickled in the sulfurous water. I probably should have looked where I was going, but because I was so confused, I inadvertently swam in a sweeping arc, straight toward the fence, and the floating debris.

When I opened my eyes, I realized I'd made a fatal mistake. The Styrofoam chunks were all around me, floating aimlessly like little icebergs on a jet black sea. I paddled between them, navigating through the lot as if I was piloting an icebreaker. But as Styrofoam always seems to do, the smaller pieces clung to my skin like iron filings to a magnet. There was debris all around me, but I chose to ignore it, wanting only to reach the shore, where hopefully my mother's love could save me.

Following the fence-line was the straightest run to shore. Knowing that, I damned everything else, choosing to follow it straight onto the sand. I was half way to shore, and half way toward believing that I was actually going to survive, when right in front of me something bobbed to the surface that nearly made my heart skip a beat.

It was the man in the red life jacket, floating face-down, like a drowned airman whose chute hadn't opened. As I drew closer, I could see the wrinkled leather of his jacket pouching in and out as the water washed all around him. Something was wrong with him, dead wrong. And although I had more than my share of problems to deal with, I felt the need to at least tap him on the shoulder, just to see if he was alive.

Seeing that his face was in the water, I cautiously reached out in an effort to flip him face-up again. Grabbing hold of what looked like a waterlogged Airman's jacket, I pulled as hard as I could, and as I did, I was immediately surprised at how heavy he was.

Something was wrong, for no matter how hard I tried, I wasn't able to roll him upright again. It seemed strange that I couldn't move him, so I swam a little bit closer, hoping to grab him by the torso, and flip him over that way.

As I approached his side, I kicked my legs beneath me. Yet for all of my kicking there seemed to be nothing beneath him. No legs, no body, nothing at all...

My blood ran cold, as something horrible crossed my mind. "Maybe he's been bitten in half by a shark!" I thought. "And maybe the shark has been bobbing his torso up and down like a hideous finger puppet!"

That could have been, had I not seen the leathery skin of the man's back twitch as I pulled against his shoulder. He wasn't dead, he was alive plain as day. And as his irreverence to my presence began to anger me, I reached out and touched the skin of something that was far from human.

At first I thought it was skin. But as a thin veil of flesh scraped over a rough, bony plate, I reared back in horror at the implications of what was beside me.

I tried to swim away, but as I did, the leather jacketed thing spun around, unhinging eight spider-like legs from beneath its leathery carapace.

Back paddling like a wild-man, I could barely comprehend what I was seeing. The thing looked like a nightmarish horseshoe crab, with a long, leathery shell and the legs of a spider. I screamed as its spindly legs danced on the surface, and as it closed in on me with frightening speed, I could hear a screeching, crying sound coming from within its bony carapace.

I stared in disbelief, while my mind snapped pictures of the hellish crab as if it was a camera. I remember vividly how large it was, and how its spider-like legs skipped and clamored all at once. They looked like the oars of a Roman ship, protruding from both sides of its shell as they sculled deep into the water. I'd never seen anything so horrifying, and as it rowed toward me with its boney, sculling oars, I felt like I was doomed.

None of it seemed real. Not one thing that had transpired since the voice had called out from the water. I swam for my life, and as I did, I began to wonder if everything that had happened was all just a dream.

"Maybe I'm dreaming," I thought. "And maybe, I'm back at our beach umbrella, with my face in the sun and my toes in the sand."

That thought was nice, but it was rudely interrupted by the *clap, clap, clap* sound of the crab's spidery legs. I swam as fast as I could, but within seconds the thing with the faded, red jacket climbed onto my back like a giant spider.

It moved way too fast, and despite my violent thrashing, it wrapped its legs around my torso with relative ease. I tried to pull it off my back, but every time I did, its spindly legs tightened their grip until they'd nearly dug into my flesh.

I faltered for a moment, as what strength I had left seemed to have been pulled from my body. The thing shifted its weight as it leaned to one side, and as time stood still, we slipped beneath the surface, until the light of day faded from view.

We sank downward amid a serenity that's hard to describe. And as we did, I felt like I was in the womb, with a comforting presence nearby. "Who's there?" I thought out to the darkness. "Who's out there?"

There was no reply. Save for the muffled sound of water, and a rhythmic whine that emanated from the crab-thing's leathery shell.

I should have been scared, nearly to death I imagine . . . But at that moment I felt nothing. No fear at all. Not even for my own life.

I was pondering just that, when out of the darkness came the voice I'd heard on the sand.

"You are the one to be feared!" the voice said. "YOU ARE THE ONE TO BE FEARED!"

I listened to those words like I'd never listened before, and as I was empowered by something greater than myself, I was overcome with a sense of strength that nearly overwhelmed me. Whoever had spoken, he had sent me more than words. He'd sent me something that catalyzed a power... something within me that I'd never felt before.

It shot into my body like a lightning bolt, re-wiring nearly everything inside of me. I don't know how it happened, but somehow I'd been turned into a killer, and in that moment of crystal clarity, being a killer suited me just fine.

"The thing is going to die," I thought. "I'm going to kill it because that's what I do!"

From where that came, I don't know. Nor did I understand its meaning... until seconds later, when we hit the bottom, and all hell broke loose.

I remember how it screamed, as I punched its legs with the design of splintering them all. I hit its legs with both fists, and as I attacked, the crab thing loosened its grip, perhaps to get a better hold.

That was a BIG mistake... For its miscalculation allowed me to spin around, raining down with a salvo of punches that was nothing short of hideous. There was a fury within me that I'd never felt before, and as my fists found their mark time and time again, the thing screamed like a cat, as I splintered its spindly legs . . .

What happened next, I don't really know. Other than somehow, I made it to shore alive. When I finally came to my senses, I was hunched over the sand on my hands and knees, with strings of bloody drool dripping from my mouth. Everything seemed muted, like my senses had been dulled, and as I desperately tried to regain control, my body felt like it was on auto-pilot.

Minutes passed as I lay balled-up on the sand, while the sand fleas buzzed all around me. I shook violently from shock, until several minutes later, when the lights began to come on. First my heart-rate slowed to normal, then, with the steadiness of breath, all of my senses soon returned.

The wind blew loudly, and as I came back to life, the little boy inside of me needed his mommy very, very badly. I tried to stand up, but the checks and balances of self-preservation held me to my knees. So I just lay there balled-up, knowing that my body would tell me when it was time to stand again.

Five minutes passed, maybe ten, as my body gained its strength. Then, as I rose to a kneel a searing abdominal pain reminded me of what I'd chosen to forget.

"OH NO!" I thought. "I remember now. My stomach's been filleted open, and my intestines are in the breeze!"

I didn't want to look. But I had to. Reluctantly, I looked down at my waistline, where, to my delight, the damage wasn't half as bad as I thought it was going to be.

There was a cut, and a pretty bad one too. But rather than seeing my intestines hanging out, I saw something quite different. My skin had been torn, in a jagged, whitish tear that looked like it had been pickled by the salt water. There was a sickening orange tint to the cut, but other than that, there were no intestines to be seen. There was just a long, jagged gash, and a blood soaked flap of bathing trunk, that had been torn loose when I plunged into the water.

I felt a bit light-headed as I stared at the cut. And as I pulled it open a bit, I could see that its puffy, jagged edges had a strange fatty look to them. There was a yellowish goo there, too, and as it seeped out of my skin, I realized that my mother was going to TOTALLY freak out.

Gathering my strength, I chuckled at the thought of what I was soon going to hear. "NO MORE SWIMMING OUT THERE FOR YOU!" she'd say. Then, as if I didn't already know it, she'd go on and on about how dangerous swimming was... ESPECIALLY by myself.

That thought amused me as I began to feel whole again, and as the wind blew I looked far down the beach toward the flags atop the cabanas.

The beach was wind-swept and empty. And of the few umbrellas that were there earlier in the morning, now only one of them remained. Fixing my eyes on the flags, I noticed there was something odd about the way they blew.

They were waving to me... waving for me to come home.

I stood bolt-upright when I realized what was happening. And as the flags beckoned frantically, a dark presence slid onto the beach, creeping up on me from behind.

"RUN, RUN!" The flags called out. "RUN FOR YOUR LIFE, LITTLE BOY!"

And I ran for my life, toward their welcome, waving arms, as a voice fell dead on the sand...

The Thumping Man

The work began a few weeks after winter was officially over. Long after the grass had poked its way through the snow, and long since my father had gone down to the filling-station to swap-out his snow tires.

I imagine that had we known we'd be moving across the country in just a few short months, none of the basement remodeling would ever have been done. But at the time we assumed we'd be living in our home forever, and the ambitious project that had been planned all year, now ran full-steam ahead.

Things were good back then, with my father enjoying great success at his new job, and Mom being pleased as punch over having her very own car for the first time in her life. We were all on the fast-track toward a lifestyle I couldn't yet imagine, but before the new reality of swimming pools and cocktail parties fell from heaven, we basked in the light of the moment, and the safety of our own little world.

The home we lived in was small, yet very nicely appointed. And thanks to my mother's keen sense of style, my parents had done a pretty good job of furnishing the place. "Danish-American," is what they called it. But to me, the home had a somewhat futuristic look to it, as if we'd all been transported into an episode of *The Twilight Zone*.

On weekend days, I'd watch in awe, as a group of workers transformed our basement into a newly remodeled work of art. For months my parents had planned the re-model, and now that construction was in full-swing, it began to look as if my father's underground watering hole would be ready by the beginning of summer.

He'd talked about it endlessly of course, nearly every day, as we waited-out the frost that had bent up the boards down at the lumber yard. For a while it seemed like the winter was never going to end, but now that spring had arrived, things were really beginning to come together. The new eight foot long wet bar had just been installed, and according to my father, once the water and electrical were hooked up, the job would be nearly complete.

I was happy for my father, although the concept of sitting on a bar stool half the night really didn't appeal to me. What excited me most about the project was the slick, new linoleum floor they'd just laid down. For now that they had, my toy cars were going to roll faster than any other kid's on the block.

Weeks had passed since the job began, and now that several phases of the multi-room project were complete, all that needed to be done was a bit of finish work, and a few electrical odds-and-ends. During the remodel all had gone well. Until a day when that all changed... With a scream that came from below. And the aftermath of that moment, which is something that changed my life forever.

It happened on a Sunday afternoon, soon after my father came home with a sack full of hero sandwiches and a half gallon of scotch. He'd been home barely a minute, when someone yelled "Lunch-time!" down the stairwell corridor. No sooner was the call heard, than one worker after another came clunking up the stairs, ready for lunch and a well-deserved shot of whiskey.

The kitchen was abuzz with energy as the sandwiches were handed out. Then, as the bottle of scotch made the rounds, the men began joking with one another, making everything feel so safe and secure, at least for the time being.

I sat on a tall kitchen stool, with a sandwich on my lap, and a bottle of cola between my knees. The room was filled with men, while sitting in the center of the group was my favorite uncle, who had led the project from the very beginning. They were a bunch of hard-working guys, most of whom were firefighters from the local fire-house. They were earning a few bucks on the side, and since my uncle was the local Fire Chief, that certainly wasn't a problem.

The sandwiches hit the spot, then, after everyone had eaten, one of the workers went downstairs to finish up some electrical work, while the rest stayed topside for another shot or two.

I felt like such a big boy, hanging out with a bunch of guys who were easily four times my age. Each and every one of them treated me like a man, joking with me as if I was one of their own. That meant a lot to me, as the off-duty firemen were heroes in my eyes, and to be considered one of their clan, was the greatest honor of all.

I was contemplating that when a shout bellowed up from the basement, followed by a wailing scream that stood my hair on end.

When the screaming began, my uncle sat bolt-upright in his chair, while my father jumped to his feet. They nearly pushed the kitchen table onto its side as they ran toward the basement stairwell, looking like they were in a race to see who'd get there first.

From where I was sitting, I couldn't tell what was happening, other than both men were crammed in the doorway. It would have been nice to have known what was going on, but from the look on my father's face, I could tell I was better off not knowing. He looked perplexed, almost scared in a way, and as he and my uncle faltered for a moment, I wondered for the first time, if the two really were invincible.

They listened a moment, then, as we heard a strange shuffling sound, the man cried out once again…

"GOD NO!" The man yelled. "GET AWAY FROM ME!"

That was all it took, for just a second later, both men bounded down the stairs three at a time.

As I listened through the thin kitchen wall, I could hear them thunder downward in their heavy work boots. As their foot-falls boomed, I felt for certain that at any moment I'd hear the sound of a slipped foot, and the corresponding "Thud" that always accompanies someone leaving a hairy chunk of scalp on one of the stair's metal edges.

The thought of that sickened me, especially because it could have happened to either of my two biggest heroes. But before any head-splitting could occur, the panicked worker rounded the stairwell corner, running head-on into my uncle at full gallop.

He was crazed, or at least that's what my father told me later on. I guess that accounts for why he slammed into my uncle, before scrambling up the stairs like a madman. No one knew what was wrong with him, nor did anyone have the slightest notion as to what he'd seen. We only knew that he was running for his life, as if he'd seen The Devil.

At least that's the way I saw things from my vantage-point on the stair's threshold, where I peeked between the legs of men who were easily twice my height.

We watched as the crazed man ran up the stairs, nearly bowling-over everyone that stood in his way. In theory, I should have been run over too, but because I was used to skirting runners at Home Plate, I dodged him as he bolted for the door, while babbling something about a monster.

My heart raced in a way I hadn't felt since the fateful day on the bay. I had no idea what was going on, and without any answers, I was growing more and more frightened by the minute. I needed some kind of reassurance, but now, as the others headed down below, I stood atop the stairwell all alone.

I yelled down to my father, desperately afraid that he'd been eaten by a monster. I called out over and over, hearing nothing but muffled voices and an errant shout here and there. Completely freaked out, all I could do was stand there with an ear to the cellar, waiting for someone to come-clean with what was going on. I could see shadows moving across the linoleum floor, and I heard a shout or two, but aside from that, there wasn't a tell-tale sign as to what had just happened.

A minute went by as I watched and waited, until just as I was becoming desperate, the first of the men made their way up the stairs. I waited anxiously as they plodded past, asking each of them what had happened. They wanted to tell me, but because I was just a small boy, I was told to ask my father about it, as they walked off in search of the crazed man.

After they passed, I looked into the stairwell, before calling down to my father again. "DADDY, DADDY!" I cried. "DADDY, I'M SCARED!"

I know he heard me, because no sooner did I say that, than both he and my uncle appeared at the base of the stairs. They paused a moment as my father pointed toward the boiler room. Then, after glancing back once more, they headed up the stairs with a markedly shaken appearance.

At my uncle's call, the workers regrouped in the kitchen, and once they had, the mood changed appreciably. Gone was the happy, summertime feeling. Now, in its place, was the pulse of fear, as each of the men faced the steep stairwell with a look of trepidation.

There were questions aplenty, yet as we stood there amid the ticking sound of my mother's rooster clock, it seemed like no one had any answers. I expected someone would go outside in search of the man who'd started all the ruckus. But instead of doing that, everyone just stood there, as they listened to the sounds of the basement.

They clustered together with an ear to the stairwell, yet for all their listening, all they could hear was the shuffling sound of their feet, and the ticking of the rooster-clock. A moment passed as they listened, then, as he turned his head in the strangest way, my uncle gestured sharply, telling everyone in the room to be very, very quiet.

No one moved a muscle as the thing stirred below. So quietly at first, that its presence was nearly indiscernible. It could have been dismissed as nothing at all, just a sound mixed in with all the others that need not be investigated. But my uncle knew to wait just a moment longer, until a strange thumping sound pierced the silence.

None of us said a word as the sound echoed up from below. We just cocked our heads and listened, as we tried to make sense of it all. At first I thought the thumping sound might have had a simple explanation, such as the pipes of the furnace bumping against the wall. But as we listened, there was something in the sound that wasn't quite right. Something eerie, that had nothing at all to do with warming pipes, especially during the spring-time.

This sound was altogether different. mainly because, as the thumping became louder, we began to sense something more. There was movement in the sound, along with a disquieting sense of purpose, as if something alive was stirring below.

Sensing movement, I remember thinking that things had definitely ratcheted up a notch. Especially now that all of us were pretty damn sure there really was something lurking down below. I watched as my father tip-toed toward the landing, then, as he took a long, cautious look around the corner, the tension grew so thick it made my hair stand on end.

"What is it?" one of the men whispered. "What the hell is it?"

My father didn't say a word, rather, he just stood there as the thumping sound grew louder and louder. As he turned his head to make sense of it all, he looked straight into my eyes, and as he did, I think that for the first time since the madness began, he realized that I was still in the room. At first he seemed to look right through me, then, as his eyes focused on mine, he pointed in the direction of the hallway, while mouthing the words "Go to your room."

I didn't want to leave, nor did I want to miss out on any of the action. But from the look in his eye, I knew it would suit me best to do what I'd been told. I hemmed and hawed a moment, mulling around the kitchen, until he gave me a look that sent me scurrying for cover.

My room was just down the hall, although both of us knew I wasn't going to stay there for long. Pacing back and forth in the bedroom hallway, my imagination ran wild, as I wondered what dwelled below. Consumed with curiosity, I slinked as close to the kitchen as I dared, listening for any clue as to what was going on. There were a few light whispers at first, until I heard my uncle's voice as he spoke to the men in the room.

"What the hell just happened?" he asked. "And what the hell is walking around down there?"

No one had an answer to either of those questions. Especially since the man who'd freaked-out had run off to God-knows-where. The only way we were going to get any straight answers was to find the guy and see what he had to say about it. But before anyone got around to that, there were a few loose-ends that needed to be tied up.

With my ear to the wall, I could hear someone shut the stairwell's doors, before throwing the bolt into the locked position. After the doors were shut, the men began to speak in a regular tone, and for the moment things seemed to have returned to normal. I heard my father say he was going to try to find the man who'd run from the house. Then, after he and the others headed out the door, I made my way into the kitchen, just a moment later.

As I stood there all alone, the bolt on the cellar doors was beginning to look a bit flimsy. I stared at the bolt as the rooster clock ticked, and as I did, the emptiness of the house began to close in all around me. "I'm all alone," I thought, "Alone in a house with a monster in the basement!"

That thought sent me running for the door, regardless of what my father had told me. And besides, he had his own problems to deal with, such as chasing down someone who appeared to have lost his mind. So I made my move, out of the house and onto the patio, where I felt quite a bit safer and much more in control.

Down the driveway, I could see that some of the workers had found the man. My uncle was among them, and from what I could see, he was attempting to calm the man down. As they spoke, I tried to hear what the man was saying, but he was too far away for me to make out anything coherent. What I could see was that he was still quite agitated, gesturing as if something had come rushing toward him. He flailed around at first, before making faces that were nothing short of horrifying. Seeing him do that was strange enough, but then, as he began hopping up and down, I began to wonder if he really had lost his mind.

A minute or so later, my uncle put his hand on the guy's shoulder, giving him a reassuring smile. The men mulled around a bit, until my father left the pack, heading in my direction. As he neared the porch steps, I half expected him to ask why I wasn't in my room. But he knew the answer to that, so, without stating the obvious, he put his arm around me, giving me a great-big shoulder-hug.

He looked at me a moment, as he wondered just what to say. Then, rather than make up a story about what *really* happened, he put his hand on my shoulder, while asking me if I was okay. I told him "Yes" in a way that was hardly believable, then, he smiled back, before glancing toward my uncle, who was headed back to the house.

Following his lead, all of the workers returned to the kitchen with the exception of the man who'd freaked-out. My father waited in the stairwell as the men gathered around, then, as they assembled in force, he threw open the bolt, pressing his knee against the lower door.

As he swung the top door open, a metallic hint of smoke filled the air. One that was strangely reminiscent of when a piece of bread burns deep within the toaster. My father smelled the smoke immediately, crinkling up his nose as the acrid smell wafted into the kitchen.

"Let's do it," he said, and with that, each of the men followed him down the stairs one by one. I didn't like the fact that they were going down there again, but given the nature of the thumping sound and the disturbing presence of smoke, I imagined there was enough cause for concern.

Several minutes passed, where I heard neither shouting, nor the sounds of a scuffle. That was a bit disappointing, as I'd hoped they'd drag up some crazed transient who'd been hiding under the stairwell all along. That wasn't the case, however, nor was there the slightest clue as to what had happened.

"Maybe the guy touched a live wire," I thought. "Or maybe he'd knocked back one beer too many during the lunch break." The live-wire theory made a lot of sense, especially in lieu of the phantom smoke that smelled of burned insulation. That sounded like a plausible explanation, so I hung onto that thought, with the hope that it would allow me enough solace to sleep the whole night through.

A few minutes passed, until one by one, all of the men came back up the stairs. Once they were topside my father locked the stairwell doors, double-checking the latch, just to be sure. He never told me what they were looking for, and as suspected, when I asked about the whole scenario, he mumbled some gibberish about the guy having had one drink too many.

That excuse seemed plausible, given that most of the guys had been drinking beer throughout the day. So, in the interest of my own mental health, I chose to believe my father's version of the story, until later on that night, when the mysterious thumping sound started all over again.

When it first began, I told myself it was the water pipes banging against the bottom of the house. Then, just as I was beginning to believe my own line of crap, the sound became much more animated, and I knew for certain that the monster in the basement was alive.

That thought scared the hell out of me, especially as I lay in my bed, while the thing moved beneath me. I could feel it move across the basement floor, and as it did, I wondered two things. The first being, "What the heck is this thing?" And second, "If it was scary enough to send a grown man running for his life, what was I going to do when it thumped its way into MY room?"

I didn't even want to think about what I'd do if that happened, so, focusing on the moment, I leaped out of bed, making a bee-line toward my parents room, where hopefully someone would believe there was a monster on the loose.

When I arrived at my parent's bedroom, I stood in the doorway a moment, watching them as they slept. Apprehensive about waking my father, I gently poked at him, until he woke with a start. "What's wrong?" he asked, as he stared at me. "What's wrong Sonny Boy?"

I told him everything about the strange hopping sound. Where I heard it, when I heard it, and worst of all, the way the thing sounded like it was alive. He listened with a look of concern, before putting on his slippers and robe. I followed him closely, as we walked softly down the hall that led to the kitchen alcove. Had I been less aware, I would have walked right into him, but as he stopped dead in his tracks halfway down the hall, I did too, just a half-step behind him.

We both heard the thump. Or at least we felt it as the sound surged up from below. Dad placed his hand on my shoulder as it thumped once more, holding me back a step, as he leaned toward the kitchen entrance. At that moment, I imagine I should have been back in my room, with my teddy and tiger, curled up under the no-monster covers. But it was too late for that, as the men of the house had some hunting to do.

We waited out the sound, hearing the thing move from left to right, as if it knew we were listening all the while. We moved right, and it moved left, countering us every step of the way. I felt teased by the thing, like was taunting us from below. But as my father cautiously opened the latch on the double-dutch doors, what was happening seemed like anything but a game.

With a finger to his lips, he swung the upper door open. Then, as he leaned forward, the thumping sound stopped on cue. I snugged up next to my father, peering over the lower door's edge as I stood on my tip-toes. We stood completely motionless, looking and listening for any indication of what the thing was. I felt for sure that my father was going to go down there, when suddenly, without warning, an acrid wisp of ozone shot toward us like an arrow.

My father smelled it first, quickly pulling back as if something was rushing up the stairs. He slammed the door shut, nearly trapping my fingers, before leaning his full body weight against both doors.

Turning toward me with a most disconcerting look, he asked, "Do you smell that? It smells like an electrical fire!"

I just nodded "Yes," being far more concerned with what he was holding back, than with what may have been on fire.

"I think it might be the linoleum adhesive," he said, as he leaned against the door. "I think it might be the glue that smells. But that thumping sound… That's just NOT right."

Not wanting to delve too deeply into the meaning of "Not right," I asked, "Do you hear anything, Dad? Do you hear anything?"

He said nothing, as he stood there with his arm against the door. Then, after a moment passed, he secured the latch on the door, double checking it one more time.

"Time to lock her up!" he exclaimed. "I think its just the pipes, and that damned glue."

I didn't want to disbelieve him, but as he shook the door's latch on the way to the kitchen, one hell of a chill ran down my spine.

"What about the fire?" I asked, feeling more confused than ever. "Aren't you going to check it out?"

"It's not a fire," he said. "It just smells like one. I don't know what it is. But I know it's not a fire."

How I ever fell asleep that night I'll never really know. Only that somehow sleep came, and I drifted off to a place where demons really were just a figment of my imagination. When I woke a new day was upon us, and luckily for me, I was headed off on a week's vacation at my grandparent's house. The trip couldn't have come at a better time, for both me and my sanity, which desperately needed some time away from things that go thump in the night.

The week went by in a blur, and due to all the fun I had, I'd pretty much put the strange thumping sound out of my mind. Besides, now that the week was over, I had jars full of caterpillars to bring home, plus a few dozen pollywogs that I'd caught down at the pond. We drove home without a care in the world, until my mother pulled into the driveway, where I caught sight of the small, folding windows that vented the basement from above.

"Ooooooooh," I thought. "The basement, the very place I've tried so hard to put out of my mind." I'd almost forgotten about it, but now, here it was, poking its head above deck, just to say hello, and give a shout-out just the same.

I hated our basement, and I hated knowing that a monster was on the loose. But here we were, back at home… And like it or not, I was going to have to live with it.

"Dad's home," I kept thinking. "He'll make things right. And he'll protect me from monsters, just like he always has."

That was a really great thought, and it was something I held near and dear as he read a bedtime story from my dinosaur book. I fell asleep quickly, awash in the glow of his protection and love, until around two o'clock in the morning, when my safe, happy haven was rocked by an event that altered my perception forever.

It was the middle of the night when I heard the first thump, and just like before, whatever hell lurked below was thumping away with reckless abandon. I could feel its movement as it hopped to and fro, with stabbing thumps that resonated with a strange metallic hiss.

Whatever it was, it wasn't human. That I intuitively knew. "But what of this earth hopped on a twisted steel spike?" I wondered. "And what then, if it isn't of this earth at all?"

That thought was incomprehensible, so, rather than dwell on it, I did my best to cope, while it moved about unmolested.

As it played its game of demonic hopscotch, I tried desperately to drown out the sound. I covered my head, clam-shelled my hands over my ears, and even put my head under my pillow. But no matter how hard I tried to muffle the sound, the damned thumping wouldn't let up. I pretended not to hear it for quite some time, until finally, when I'd had about all I could stand, I sat up in bed, determined to do something to preserve my sanity.

With a flick of a switch I turned on my bedside lamp, where immediately things didn't seem quite so scary. My goldfish stared at me with the "Who the heck just turned the light on" look, and my plastic dinosaurs smiled down from the shelf high above my desk. I looked up at the mobile above my bed, with its star and moon and silly little rocket ships. They moved in an arc, circling high above me, and for a moment I was transported far into space, where the Thumping Man didn't exist.

That thought was a wonderful one, until my dream-like trance was broken by a sharp, spiking *thump!*

Thump, thump, thump went its hideous foot, as it did its best to wake me from my dream. I still hadn't a clue as to what the thing was, but somehow I could sense its shape as it pulsed in the darkness. It moved back and forth, between the boiler room and my father's workshop. Then, as it paused a moment, I could tell it was near the stairwell, contemplating a short trip upstairs. That thought scared me to death, until, just as I thought I couldn't get any more frightened, I heard a loud scuffing sound somewhere near the kitchen.

"OH GOD NO!" I thought. "IT'S COME UP THE STAIRS!" That wasn't good, especially with my parents sound asleep, completely unaware that the monster was on the loose. I had to do something, and I had to do it fast. So, mustering all the courage I had, I slid slowly out of bed, before slinking down the hall toward my parent's bedroom door.

Sliding around the corner, I tip-toed up to my parent's bed, where my father was nowhere to be found. I expected to see him lying there, but instead, I saw rumpled bedsheets that had been hastily thrown aside. I knew he was in the house somewhere, but it wasn't like him to wander around after he'd gone to sleep. Seeing that he wasn't in the bathroom, I figured he might have gotten thirsty, and that the sound I'd heard may have been him getting a cold drink of water.

I should have been more cautious. Or perhaps I should have announced my presence as I wandered into the kitchen. But I was careless, and for that indiscretion, I rounded the corner, coming face-to-face with the barrel of my father's .38 Special.

"JESUS CHRIST!" He yelled, as he quickly lowered the gun. "DON'T EVER SNEAK UP ON ME LIKE THAT AGAIN!"

I just stood there in my cowboy pajamas, much too scared to do anything other than stare at that gun with the realization that something was very, very, wrong. Obviously shaken, he turned the gun in the direction of the stairwell, before saying in a faint whisper, "There's something down there. I don't know what it is, but there's DEFINITELY something down there."

That was the last thing I wanted to hear, because he always had all the answers, and whatever this thing was, it had spooked him enough to take up arms. I guess that's why he seemed so hesitant as he opened the upper stairwell door, stepping back a bit, just in case something decided to bound over the edge. I got right in behind him, holding onto his pajama pant as I hid behind his leg. "What are you gonna do Dad?" I asked. "Are you gonna go down there and get it?"

As scared as I was, I hoped that he was going to close the door and lock it for good. He could have done that, but as the ever-growing presence of demon-moss thickened the air, he leaned into the stairwell, before pulling on the chain that lit the overhead light.

The small lightbulb flickered to life, casting a sallow, yellowy glow against the dark wood paneling. Everything seemed lit with a haze, as the light did little more than accentuate the bluing on my father's snub-nosed revolver.

My father held the gun over the edge of the door, as if the stairwell was an arcade shooting gallery. I stepped a bit closer, until he held me back with his free hand, saying, "I don't know what it is Sonny Boy. I just don't know."

"Why does the thing stop thumping when we open the door?" I asked him. "If it really was the pipes, they wouldn't care what we did, which makes me think that the thing might actually be a monster!"

There really wasn't any answer to that, other than "Yes Son, it really is a monster, and for the time being, we'll just close this flimsy latch, in the hope that it doesn't kill us in our sleep!"

Of course he couldn't say that. Instead, as he closed and locked the door, he told me that all daddy's walk around at night checking out creepy sounds, and that if there really were daddy-eating monsters, there wouldn't be any daddy's left to eat.

I guess I believed him, especially after he promised that he'd have my uncle check and see why the pipes were banging around in the boiler room. That partially placated me for the moment, but I did still have my concerns, especially in regard to the movement we'd felt in the sound, and the strange acrid stench, that couldn't possibly have been the glue.

Two weeks passed, and over that time the thumping sound became ever more present. I'm sure my father was aware of all this, but in my mother's case, she was about as clueless as a pine cone. She slept while it hopped, sending vibrations through the floor that were intended to call-me-out. The thing was mocking me, teasing me, and daring me to will it up the stairs. I refused to give in, choosing instead to cover my head, as the sound gradually increased in both regularity, and the intensity of its purpose.

Curiously, despite my father's obvious recognition of the issue, he seemed satisfied with keeping the thing locked behind closed doors. I began to wonder if that was just the way things worked. If somehow, when things were a bit too scary to deal with, the best bet was to double lock the door, while hoping the thing wouldn't hop any closer. I suppose that might have worked for some people, but it didn't work for me, as I was growing more and more desperate by the minute. "At what point is someone going to do something about all of this?" I wondered. "And what's going to happen when I'm finally pushed over the edge?"

I didn't know where to turn, and in retrospect I believe it was foolish for me to ever think that my ultra-insensitive friends could have helped me out of my predicament. But I gave it a try anyway, spilling my guts to them about the Thumping Man, the incident in the basement, and everything else about the sordid nightmare that was taking over my life.

You'd think I would have gotten some support, or, at least, that my friends would have jumped at having the chance to investigate a real-live monster. But instead of lending an ear and a helping hand, they gathered up all of my fear, before rubbing it in real good, like salt in a fresh wound.

They started out with stories about portals to Hell, and how demons and imps had found their way into our basement. Then they began telling me that the thumping sound was actually the demons clawing the bottom of my bed. The whole thing was getting creepier by the minute, until one of my friends began to draw pictures of the thing, which pushed me straight to the edge.

The guy's name was Bruce, and he was about the worst friend a guy could possibly have. Bruce cared only about himself, and as far as being a friend, he came up short on all accounts. One day, as we all sat around talking about the strange sounds, he took out a box of crayons, and drew a rendition of what he thought the creature in the cellar may have looked like.

The monster he drew was creepy, so much so, that I hated him for drawing it. The thing stared at me from the paper, as if it was about to come alive. But what bothered me most of all, was that it looked exactly the way I imagined it had.

I remember how he started by drawing a picture of the furnace, with its stove-piped body, and four spindly legs. Then, after drawing the body, he fashioned what looked like hooves to the feet of the creature, along with yellow, glowing eyes that rounded-out his rendition of my worst possible nightmare. The thing bore a resemblance to a demonic, mechanical bull, and according to Bruce, the sounds that I was hearing, were its hooves, scraping and scratching along the boiler room floor.

Why I'd ever taken the time to mention any of this to my friends I'll never know. But now that I had, I was nearly driven to madness by the relentless goading of several nine year old boys. Maybe that's why I had no choice but to take a late night walk into the kitchen. A walk driven by madness, that took me straight to the brink of Hell.

The night started out like all the rest, with the covers over my head and the Thumping Man making his rounds. I knew my parents cared, but I was beginning to feel as if I alone was going to have to deal with the problem they'd sequestered behind closed doors. Of course, there was no doubt that if the thing came upstairs they'd jump to my aid, but as for my current psychological woes, there seemed to be no source of solace other than to take action.

I suppose that nowadays, I'd simply kick off the covers, walk on down the stairs, and stick my foot up its mossy, demon ass. But being that I was just a little boy, this was going to take a bit more doing.

Curled up in bed with one ear to the mattress, I could hear the thumping sound as it funneled-up from below. The thing was on the move, thumping around near the boiler room. It would hop a

56

few times, then shuffle in place before lying dormant for a while. I waited it out, listening intently. Then, as the thumping started up again, I sensed progressive movement, as it hopped from the boiler room, toward the large game-room area.

At first the thumping sounded like a small drum, with a strange, rhythmic pattern to its action. Then, as the sound sped up in its cycle, I sensed impatience in the rhythm, as the frenetic beat of its twisted foot tapped away like a crazed jack hammer. I hated it when it did that, and although I didn't yet know what the thing truly was, I knew it was yearning for someone to come on down and take a closer look.

As I listened to its spike pound against the cold, hard floor, it felt as if each unholy beat was taking the life out of me. Driven to near madness, I got out of bed, before tip-toeing toward the kitchen, where the thumping sound was the loudest. To my left was the kitchen table, where just weeks before we'd all eaten lunch without a care in the world. Behind it, in the corner, was a white, folding step-ladder that my mother used to access the pantry's upper cabinets. In the shadows, I could see the ladder leaning against the wall, while, just inches away, was the entrance to the basement stairwell.

With my back against the wall, I could see the flame of our stove's pilot light casting surreal shadows on the yellowed linoleum floor. The shadows seemed alive, as they reached out with spindly arms that clamored wildly across the floor. I smelled sulfur as they danced about, and could sense danger as they inched closer and closer. I wholly expected the shadows to drag me down to Hell. But for the moment they were content to dance around me, teasing and taunting, as if they knew what was about to happen.

I tentatively stepped toward the landing, pausing a moment to collect myself before doing what had to be done. A chill ran down my spine as I stepped into the alcove, standing face-to-face with the locked set of doors. They rattled a bit, in a sick sort of greeting, sent by something that stirred far below. I stared at the doors, and the large crack between them I'd never noticed before. The crack was much too wide for my liking. And as I stared into the inky void, I half expected to see a gnarled, pointed finger push its way through, feeling for the latch just inches away.

I stared at the crack, daring the finger to reach out for me, when a cold breeze crept up from below that made my shirtless torso crawl with goosebumps. The wicked breeze wrapped around me, as mossy, demon-scent wafted into the room. I knew without a doubt that I wasn't alone, and every sane bone in my body told me to run. But I couldn't do that, because tonight, no matter what, I was going to get an answer.

Driven by God-knows-what, I leaned forward, awash in the sickly-sweet smell of moss and flame. I stood fast as the breeze rushed around me, while running my finger along the door's gap as if on a dare. There was something near the edge that didn't look right. Something near the latch I'd never noticed before. I leaned forward to see what it was, and as I did, I gasped in horror.

The wood had been gouged away, as if it had been scratched and scored by something with a long, pointed fingernail.

"You HAVE been trying to claw your way out, haven't you?" I whispered to the thing. "You've been trying to get to us all along."

Ordinarily, I would have been completely freaked out by what I'd just found. But I needed answers. Even if the answers I sought conspired to consume me. Now, as the breeze blew with the sickly-sweet smell of moss and flame, I breathed it all in, feeling like I was ready.

"Do it, Do it, DO IT!" came a voice from inside my head. Then, as those words kept repeating themselves over and over, I unconsciously reached out, sliding the latch-bolt to one side.

"Open the door," said the voice. "Go on down and have yourself a look-see."

"DON'T DO IT!" I told myself. "DON'T DO IT!" But I had to, as there was now no other choice.

Reaching out with the hands of a madman, I swung the upper door open, as a surge of demon-air rolled overhead like fire in a hallway. "I'm doing the work of The Devil," I thought, "It's been The Devil down there all along."

I believed that to be true, as the breeze blew against me like I was standing on the edge of a cliff. I didn't think about it really, but there shouldn't have been any breeze at all, given that the basement was heavily insulated. That made no sense whatsoever, nor did the encroaching scent of moss and death, that was now stronger than ever.

Unconsciously, I reached up and pulled on the chain that lit the light bulb above. The dim light came on, illuminating the upper portion of the stairwell, while down below, the blackness pulsed and swelled like an unearthly bellows.

I stared into the darkness, where I could have sworn that something moved with intent. "Here I go," I whispered softly. Then, surely driven by madness, I began the dark descent, far down below.

I stepped down ever so quietly, with foot-falls that neither woke my parents, nor warned them of the eminent danger their child was in. Farther down I crept, not knowing what I'd find once I got there, or if I'd ever return. My ankles cracked with each tentative step, and as the dim light of the upper landing faded to twilight, I could barely see my hands in front of my face.

My senses reached into the darkness, as my vision gave way to the tactile. I moved slowly in the fading light, until the stairs gave way to the family room floor. How I ever made it that far without passing out from fear I'll never know. But now that I had, I needed to hit the lights fast, before something horrible grabbed hold of me.

As I reached for the light switches, all I could feel were the deep lines in the wood paneling. "Where are the switches?" I muttered in a scared tone. "Where did they go?"

It took a few seconds for the answer to hit home, and when it did, the senseless folly of what I was doing immediately came to light. "They moved all the switches!" I suddenly realized. "Everything's been changed in the remodel!" I'd made a terrible miscalculation, but none of that mattered anymore, as something reached out from the darkness, running a long fingernail down the length of my spine.

I spun around wildly as the hellish nail scratched a line in my skin, but all I could see were shifting shadows, hiding a step away from the twilight. Trying to scream, but somehow unable to, I stumbled backward, completely unaware that the thing was herding me deeper into the darkness. The air felt thick and cold as I back-pedaled against the wall, feeling for light switches that seemed to have disappeared. There was a crazed sense of desperation as I swept my arms against the wall, then, just as I was about to pass out from fright, the switches came within reach.

With the thing grinning over my shoulder, I flipped on the switches. And just like that... nothing happened.

Right then, it all came rushing back to me. The realization that some of the electrical work hadn't been finished yet, and because of that, the breaker was probably thrown. I was ready to run for my life, in the faint hope that if I did made it back alive, I'd never go down there again. But that wasn't going to happen, for just as I was about to bolt toward the light, something hideous made its presence known, with a loud, cracking, "THUMP!"

I froze in place as the sound rattled my soul, while the thing rushed to my blind side like a skilled predator. It was wickedly fast, and as it wrinkled its mouth with a hideous grin, it stared at me, like I was a foolish young lamb that had stumbled in front of a killer.

Knowing I'd made a fatal mistake, there was simply no time to react. The thing was upon me, and there was nothing I could do, other than face my darkest fear right before it consumed me.

Although I couldn't see it, I could sense that it was almost upon me. And just as I felt a tingle of proximity, a choking rush of ozone nearly overwhelmed me. My throat began to close as it hopped forward, and as its foot resonated with a loud "Cack, cack, cack," sound, I pressed my back against the wall.

There was nowhere to run, and besides, even if I could have, I'd probably have run face-first into the demonic "Boiler" thing that Bruce had cheerily illustrated. That would have been bad enough, but now, as I was pinned against the wall, I faced a more horrible menace, that lurked just out of view.

I tried to back away, but I was paralyzed by the affliction that overtakes us in that horrible moment of knowing. My legs were frozen in place, while the rest of my body wouldn't respond. So I just stared into the darkness, straining my eyes until they were nearly pulled from my skull. I could tell it was there, just a hop out of view, pulsing closer one moment and farther the next. The thing reeked like it had been burned, and as it pulsed up and down on its twisted spike, my throat began to close from a choking rush of ozone.

The burning stench of demon-fire rushed toward me, closing-off my wind-pipe as it drew nearer. I began to choke as it primed me for the kill. Then, as it inched closer, I felt the thing was about to consume me with fire.

Why it hadn't revealed itself, I'll never know. Other than it may have wanted to tease me to the point where I'd lose my mind. There was a perverse calculus to its movement, as it leaned into the twilight here and there. While it teased me with a taste of its form, just long enough to allow some of its smoldering scent to drift its way into my nose.

I guess you have to admire the way it caked-on the horror. Like it had baked a cake with an extra can of frosting. It caked it on thick, till all the frosting was gone. Then, after it put a cherry on top, the thing was ready to hop into view.

At first I saw a smoky shadow move in the darkness, before it hopped toward the base of the stairwell, where I saw its hideous form for the very first time.

The thing must have been born of The Devil, for it was freakish in ways I can't describe. All I could do was stare as it swayed back and forth in the nether-region between twilight and inky darkness. It looked so other-worldly, as if it was made of part solid and part gas. Then, as it moved closer to the light, its shape began to change, as it coalesced into something indescribable.

As its form solidified, all I wanted to do was scream. The thing looked like it had come straight out of a nightmare, frightening me so badly, that as I write about it today, I'm compelled to look over my shoulder. What business it had living in our basement I'll never know, but I do know that it had come straight out of Hell, and I have no doubt it was nothing less than a full-blown demon.

The thing's freakish shape was like nothing I'd ever seen. It looked like a demonic fence post, made of burned, rotted wood that was long and thin. It stood upon a tortured, wooden spike that was twisted like the root of a tree, while its skin had been horribly burned, in a fire that had nearly consumed it.

The demon hopped toward me, while its skin reeked of burned flesh and acrid ozone. It shared its smell with me, as if it wanted me to know what it was like to have been burned. It lingered a moment, just inches away, before it cloaked me in an electrical charge that smelled of burning teeth. I tried to look away, but I couldn't, for the burned thing's grip was much too powerful. It hopped closer and closer, savoring the horror with each terrible thump, and as it did, terror poured off me in waves.

"HELP ME DADDY, HELP ME!" flooded through my mind, as my throat began to close. "HELP ME!" But no matter how hard I tried to cry out, not as much as a whimper came from my mouth.

My time was up, and I fully expected it to consume me. But it did nothing of the sort, instead, it just stood there, as a high-pitched whining sound began to emanate from deep within its tortured body.

We faced one another, as the whining, whirring sound grew in both volume and frequency. It stood just inches from my body, where in the dim glow of the stairwell light, its burned wood skin seemed to shimmer with a nearly opalescent appearance. "Why hasn't it killed me yet?" I wondered, as it balanced on its tortured spike. "When is it going to pounce?"

I believe it read my mind, for as I thought those very words, the demon began hopping in place, somehow agitated by what I was thinking. Perhaps it was feeding on my discontent, savoring each hellish moment as it drove me to the brink of madness. I wasn't sure of anything, other than I'd been driven to the point where I couldn't stand it anymore. So I yelled out to the thing with my mind's-eye, telling it to get down to business… Or get the hell out of there.

The demon could have killed me, but instead, the hellish fencepost did something far, far worse. It leaned its burned self so close to me that my lungs burned with its fire. I choked on the rancid ozone, and as it began to snuff the life out of me, I begged the thing for death.

It heard me I think, but it didn't comply, perhaps because it had saved the most horrible trick for the end of the show. It moved closer, until I could taste its breath. Then, as it nuzzled as close as it could… It opened the burned lids of its bright yellow eyes.

That was it. That was REALLY it. It was all I could stand, and I couldn't stand any more.

Perhaps the horror had been caked-on just a bit too thick. Or perhaps whatever strength I'd summoned-up at the bottom of the oily bay finally came back to me. But for whichever reason it was,

I'd had enough, and now that I had, it was time for whatever power that dwelled inside of me to rise to the surface, and face off with this latest coming of death.

It started with a focus, a focus on the horror that transcended common sense. Putting me in a place where few have ever been. I looked deep into its glowing eyes, and as it stood there all rancid and burned, I began to feel a power build up inside of me that was nearly intoxicating.

I suppose the thing had done it to itself, for there was a limit to what a person could stand. Now that I'd been pushed to the brink, there were really only two choices. Stand there and die, or run for my life.

"YOU MUST BREAK FREE!" I screamed out to myself. "YOU MUST BREAK FREE BEFORE THIS THING KILLS YOU!"

Somehow I did, as if my mind had been overloaded, and my internal computer had re-booted itself. I chose not to think as I regained my senses, springing to life like I'd been shot from a cannon. Perhaps it was seeing what stirred deep in the creature's eyes that did it for me. Or maybe I'd had enough terror for one evening. But now that I'd regained the power of movement, I broke free of my paralysis, as I side-stepped toward the stairwell.

The demon hissed, while pounding in place like a scorned child. It did a pirouette, before rushing forward with frightening speed. I spun as it drew down on me, bolting toward the stairwell as quickly as I could, while one hop behind, the hellish thing took chase.

I was sure it was going to grab me, but until its hopping spike pinned my pajamas to the ground, it was my intent to move forward. I screamed as I ran, in a dream-like twilight that's hard to describe. Ahead was the stairwell, awash in diffuse light that wafted down from above. The stairs were a blur, their edges dulled by the twilight as I made my first foot-fall. I felt as if I might make it, I really did, until my bare foot slipped a step, sending me face-down with the full force of my body.

The shock of the fall stunned me, as did the fresh taste of blood that streamed into my mouth. I rolled to my back in the glistening twilight, while the demon looked down with a horrible grin. Its eyes burned with fire as it stared at me, while it hissed and thumped like a radiator that was about to blow…

I kicked my feet wildly as the thing drew closer, then, as it leaned into the stairwell, I wormed out from under it, as I began my desperate climb.

One, two, three steps I climbed, until I experienced a moment of tunnel-vision where the upper landing seemed a mile away. I clawed my way upward, but for some reason the top of the stairs faded farther into the distance. I imagine I might still be on the treadmill between Hell and Earth, had it not been for my father who appeared at the top of the stairs. He reached out for me, and in an instant, the spell was broken, as I flew into his arms.

As I crossed the threshold, he tossed me to the floor before throwing his entire weight against the stairwell doors. They shook violently as he held them in place, then, as the heavy bolt was thrown, he scooped me up with a bear hug, saying nothing, while saying everything, all at the same time.

I was nearly hysterical as I babbled about the demon and how it had almost killed me. There was no consoling me, and soon my cries brought my mother to the kitchen. When she arrived, I really don't know if she knew what to think, other than something had frightened me very badly, and it had been bad enough to rattle my father.

"GO TO THE BACK BEDROOM!" My father shouted. "YOU TWO GO TO THE BACK ROOM… AND STAY THERE… NOW!"

Neither of us liked the sound of that, nor did we like it when he picked up the gun that he'd pretended to hide a few moments earlier. I knew where he was going, and I knew what he intended to do. Although deep in my heart I felt the demon was much too powerful an adversary for even a man such as him.

My mother knew this too, so rather than listen to my father's stern order about where to go and what to do, she sat with me in the living room, as he made his way downstairs. The minutes dragged like hours as my mother held me tightly, then, just as I'd begun to give up hope, my father climbed back up the stairwell. He rounded the upper landing, placing the gun on top of the refrigerator, and as he did, I tore away from my mother, running straight into his arms.

"DID YOU SEE HIM? DID YOU SEE HIM?" I asked feverishly. But he just shook his head "No," while giving my mother a look that was anything but reassuring.

The doors to the basement were bolted shut with a heavy padlock that night. And those doors remained closed until we moved from the home three months later. My parents never spoke about The Thumping Man, nor did they act like it was something I needed to be fearful of. But I did notice changes in their behavior. Such as how neither of them ever went into the basement alone. And how, despite all the hype, there didn't seem to be much interest in going down to the wet-bar, especially at night.

For many years, that night in the cellar haunted my every step. And as you can imagine, I needed closure in regard to several aspects of what had happened. There were so many unanswered questions, and with no one willing to discuss any of them, it was beginning to look as if closure was something I'd never have.

Over time many things changed. My father became a top executive for an international corporation, and because of that, we moved thousands of miles from where the Thumping Man was last seen. Years passed, and lives changed, yet despite the fact that the demon hadn't been seen for years, I knew in my heart that there was unfinished business to attend to.

I needed to call the thing out. To see if it was still in the basement, and to see if I had what it took to send it straight back to Hell. So I patiently waited, for many years in fact, until a day when I was fully grown, and powerful enough to face the demon on even ground.

It all started with a business trip to Manhattan, one that took me close enough to my childhood home where my plans could become a reality. None of my co-workers had a clue about what I was planning. So, after feeding them a cock-and-bull story about meeting up with some long lost relatives, I hopped in my rental car, heading out on a mission that had no room for baggage.

Driving down the parkway just a tick ahead of rush hour, I felt a cold chill at the thought of what I was about to do. As I drove along, I imagined he knew I was coming, just the same way I knew he was waiting for me. I was ready for whatever came my way, and as far as I was concerned, the sooner we got things settled, the better.

As I neared my old neighborhood, I began to sense the feeling you get when you step back in time, and everything looks much smaller than you remember. After taking a nostalgic drive down streets I hadn't seen in decades, I pulled up curbside directly in front of our old home. Minutes passed as I sat there, fumbling with an old, dog-eared photo that I'd stowed away in my shirt pocket. I took a deep breath, before opening the car door as a flood of emotions swirled around me. On the home's front path was the square of concrete that my father and I had dipped our hands into decades ago, and in front of me was the narrow driveway, where we'd played catch a hundred times or more. The echoes of the past rushed all around me, and as memories unlocked one by one, I began to wonder if I really was doing the right thing.

I took a deep breath to center myself, then, as I looked around, I could see that most of the neighborhood had gone straight to Hell. It was sad really, with several homes looking like the current residents didn't give a damn about anything. Happily, I saw our old house still had the manicured, cared-for look my father had always strived for. That was nice to see, for ever since we'd moved, he'd always spoken of the place so fondly.

Taking it all in, I walked up the front path, before climbing the three red-brick steps that led to the front porch. In front of me was the same screen door that my father and I had installed over forty years ago. I ran my finger down its scrolled leaf pattern, unlocking memories that flowed like a fire hydrant. I was awash in feelings so unexpected, that I needed a moment to compose myself before ringing the doorbell.

I rang the bell several times, but to my chagrin, no one answered the door. "Damn," I muttered out loud, "I really hope someone's home." But no one answered, regardless of how many times I pushed the button.

Birds chirped in a nearby maple tree, and as their song echoed through the yard, I realized that my hopes of getting invited into the house had pretty much been dashed to the curb. I was crushed, having hoped so dearly that someone would have been home. "What am I going to do?" I thought. "With no one home, just how the heck am I going to enact Plan A?"

That was a plan I'd gone over many times during the drive from the city. I was going to knock on the door, and when they answered it, I was going to produce the photo that would surely be my ticket inside.

The picture was one I'd hand-picked for that very moment. It was a picture of me, back in 1964, sitting on the home's front porch with my G.I. Joe in my lap. That picture would have said it all to anyone who might have asked why I was there, as it proved unequivocally that I lived there as a child. Of course, I'd brought along other pictures just in case, some of the inside of the home, and some of the basement, taken just before the fateful remodeling job.

It would have liked the opportunity to pull out that dog-eared relic, and schmooze my way into the home. But that wasn't to be my fate on that spring day. So, assuming that no one was home, and knowing that nobody was around except a few birds in the trees, I figured it wouldn't hurt too much if I had myself a little look around.

Holding the photo in my hand, I figured I'd use it like a get-out-of-jail-free card if confronted by anyone. Confident that it would do the trick, I slunk my way into the side yard without being seen. Now that I'd moved away from the street-side of the house, I was pretty much out of sight as far as prying eyes were concerned. I felt safe enough to snoop around a bit, so I stayed carefully out of sight, as I began my trip down memory lane.

"Wow, everything's so small!" I thought, as I neared the garage. "And it's so old looking too."

Indeed most of it was, and as I stood there taking it all in, a rush of memories that had long lay dormant hit me like a wave. There were things that I'd forgotten, mixed with molded parts of the past that seemed a page from someone else's book. I was nearly giddy as I looked around the yard, until I spied something that hit such a nerve it stopped me dead in my tracks.

"Oh my God," I muttered, as the bent skeleton of my mother's clothes line came into view. "Oh my God…"

I stared at its rusted frame, while a memory rushed back that nearly brought me to my knees. I was warped back to a moment, many years ago, when my mother was tending the clothesline. The sheets blew in the wind, drawn to a point as if they'd been pulled by unseen hands. I sat in my fire engine with my feet on the push-pedals, watching the sheets snap and blow… "I want to go in now Mommy!" I cried. "Something's scaring me!" She looked at me a moment, with a clothes-pin in her mouth. When just then, the wind blew… And suddenly she was gone.

"Brrrrrr…" I thought, as my skin began to crawl. "The wind was warning us way back then, and we didn't even know it."

We hadn't known a lot of things I suppose. Not of the demon that had risen up beneath us, or its far-reaching grasp which was yet to be appreciated. The wind knew, as it always does, just as it had known of my fate that day on the beach many years ago.

I pondered that and more, as I stood in the backyard, where everything from the past seemed to have turned to rust.

"This is unreal," I muttered. "The ghosts are still here, just waiting to be awakened." I was lost in thought, nearly overwhelmed by it all, when something caught my eye that changed my mood appreciably.

There before me, in two shallow cut-outs, were the small, square windows that gave light to the boiler room. They were the windows to the basement, the very windows that provided light for whoever dared do a load of laundry in that demon infested cauldron. When I saw those windows, I froze in mid-step, until I realized something I hadn't considered before.

I was going to get a look downstairs after all. Even if it wasn't quite the look I'd originally hoped for.

Switching to Plan B, I walked up the stairs to the backyard landing, with the feeling you get when you're about to do something you shouldn't, yet for some reason you just can't help but do it. Sure, I was trespassing. But I did have the photo, right? So, knowing that I had a pseudo-excuse to be snooping around, I pushed my luck, kneeling down beside one of the small ground-level windows. The first one was closed tightly, so heavily covered with dust and grime, that as I tried to wipe it away, there was simply no hope of seeing through it. The second window was just a few feet away, and it appeared to be partially open, so, crawling on my hands and knees, I crept toward it for a little peek inside.

With my face just inches from the glass, I could see a portion of the basement that was hazily illuminated by the diffuse light. Squinting a bit, I saw that the old linoleum was still there, the exact same flooring that had been installed right before the demon was awakened. I was fascinated by the rush of both memories and emotion, and I moved even closer, taking the nostalgic look of a lifetime.

To my right was the workbench where we'd built our soap box derby racer. And just beyond that was the seating area, where my mother used to read to me as the damp clothes tumbled in the dryer. I was mesmerized by both a rush of memories, and the ever-present knowing that at any moment, the thing I feared most, could hop its way back into my life. Worming as closely as I could to the open window, I needed to know more. So I listened for anything living or dead that might still walk those cold, dark floors.

Half wanting to hear him, and half hoping he'd gone back to Hell, I lay there listening for anything reminiscent of a thump. I waited a long time, too long perhaps, until the voice of reason suggested I get up and run before the police arrived. The voice was right, I was stretching my calling card a bit thin. But I needed to listen just a little bit longer. So I did… And just a moment later, I heard a faint "Thump" far off in the distance.

When I first heard it, I thought it might have been the slamming door of a police car. But as I heard it thump once more, there was no doubt that something was stirring deep down in the darkness. I didn't know what to do… Not that there really was anything I could have done, other than lie there frozen in place, as the thing drew nearer.

I held my breath for fear of moving, as the thing I feared most inched closer to the boiler room. On the linoleum floor, I could see its pointed shadow growing longer, as it stirred in response to my scent. I could barely stand it, knowing he'd soon be upon me, but I couldn't pull away, or do anything other than wait and stare, as my heart beat wildly in my chest.

Thump, thump, thump, went my heart, as I lay on the concrete with my mouth bone-dry. It was coming, it really, truly was. Then, as shadow gave way to substance, the thing moved forward, before turning to look up at me.

Before me was a beast that never should have walked the earth. A freakish aberration of what God had once created.

It looked up at me from its hellish lair… And as it did, I gazed straight into the eyes… of a miniature poodle.

On my way back to the city, I stopped at a local deli for a hot pastrami sandwich and a potato knish. As the waitress took my order, she smiled, and for the first time since I'd left my associates back at the hotel, life seemed normal again.

I stared out the window as an endless precession of cars moved down the boulevard. They stopped all at once, their tail lights flashing like a strand of Christmas lights. "Life goes on," I thought. "Even without any answers at all."

I suppose that right then, I didn't know any more about the Thumping Man than I had for the past forty years. Other than that he couldn't possibly have been in that basement, not with the dinky, poodle-thing being alive and all.

"So where had he gone?" I wondered, as the tail lights twinkled in the distance. "Where could he have gone, on that charred spike of wood that he loved to hop on?"

"Don't think about it anymore," I told myself. "Don't think about him at all, lest you'll have nightmares, and think him back up, all over again."

That was good advice, words of wisdom that I held dear as I finished my meal, and said my goodbyes.

The evening air was crisp and cool, and as I walked back to my car I could see the city's lights, sparkling all around me. I unlocked the car's door, taking one last look around, before sitting down with the keys in my hand.

They jingled like a bell as I flipped them back and forth. And as they did, I pondered one last thing…

"Just how many hops would it take for him to get to California?" I wondered. "How many hops indeed?"

Audio Visual

I was a Cowboy. Or at least that's what my father told me, because we were moving all the way across the country, to the Wild, Wild, West. It was an exciting time for all of us, and much like it was back in the days of the Covered Wagon, there was just no telling, what we'd find around the bend.

Summer vacation was officially over, and it was the first day of a new school year. Ordinarily, I would have been bummed-out that the school season was upon us. But with new kids to meet, and new adventures to be had, I was looking forward to fifth grade being the best school year ever.

Not that I wasn't apprehensive, for heading off to an entirely new school, on the other side of the country did seem somewhat daunting. But I was ready, as ready as I was going to be, for the challenges ahead.

I finished the last bite of my breakfast just in time to see a group of neighborhood kids waving to me from the sidewalk. It was time to head off to school, and with a goodbye kiss from my mom, I bounded out the doorway, before running down the sidewalk to catch up with my friends. Settling into the pack, I walked along as we talked about many things. There was mention of football, baseball cards, and bullies down by the creek. Then, as our stride caught its rhythm, we joked with one another, as the sun beamed down from above.

After a quick half mile walk, we arrived at the school's gates where we said our "See-you-laters." I was new to the school, but having had the benefit of being shown where my classroom was during the open-house a few weeks earlier, I felt fairly confident that I could find my way around all by myself.

I walked beside a row of cookie-cutter bungalows, before my classroom loomed on the left. I paused a moment to take a deep breath, then, when I was ready, I tentatively stepped into the classroom. The room was packed with kids, and I half expected the piano music to stop as I stepped through the door. Yet as I did, not one of my new classmates took the time to notice that I was standing there. That was fine with me, better than fine in fact. So, with a little breathing-room, courtesy of the obligatory first-day chaos, I found a seat in the back that gave me a fairly decent view of the classroom.

Amid the ruckus of shouting kids and ringing bells, I scanned the room, where as expected, I didn't recognize a soul. Being the outsider was a new experience for me, and as I sat there sizing everyone up, I realized that if I was to have any measure of security, I'd need to make some friends as quickly as possible.

Soon we were introduced to our teacher, an attractive young woman, who wore a flowery cotton blouse, and a sensible brown skirt. After calming the class down with a tap on the chalkboard, she welcomed us to the new school year with a bright, welcoming smile. I listened as she went on about this and that, then, after going over the usual laundry-list of things we needed to know, she informed us that it was time to hand out "The Assignments."

I was like, "What the hell? I've been here barely ten minutes, and there's already an assignment?" That would have been really lame, but as the teacher continued, I learned that these assignments weren't of the usual variety. Rather, they were the type of assignments that denoted what type of "Job" we'd all have for the rest of the school year.

She explained that each of us was to occupy a very special position in the classroom, and that if we chose to accept the various assignments that would soon be put up for grabs, there would be perks down the line for each and every one of us. None of this was mandatory of course, but she explained that by being part of a team, it would make each and every one of us stronger as a whole.

I was up for that, so I hid behind the tall boy who was seated in front of me as the teacher dolled-out the assignments one by one. Some of the jobs sounded pretty cool, such as the "Safety Monitor," and the "Hall Monitor." While others, such as the dreaded "Vomit Monitor," definitely weren't as good.

Of course, that wasn't really what it was called. But to me, the thought of being the kid who shook sawdust over freshly spewed piles of vomit, didn't appeal to me at all. It was a terrible job to be sure. But seeing how infrequently you might actually be called into action, I guess that for some kids, it was worth a roll of the dice.

There was no way I was going to volunteer for that position, one that when put up for auction, didn't elicit a single raised hand. No one in their right mind wanted to do that, so, as the teacher scanned the room for someone who deserved the title above all others, I hid behind the guy in front of me, as that bullet whizzed by.

One by one, the assignments were handed out. Some of them put up for grabs, while others were dropped like a rock. Naturally, some kids jumped at the chance to do certain things, practically begging for the job. I could have jumped on one just like all the rest. But instead, I watched and waited . . . Biding my time until just the right one came along.

"Eraser Monitor," "Trash Monitor," "Light Monitor," all got snapped up, one by one. Gobbled up by the greedy who didn't have the good sense to wait just a little bit longer.

Perhaps I was numbed into complacency by the process itself, or maybe I'd simply zoned-out for the moment. But for whatever reason it was, when the much-coveted "Ball-Monitor" position was put up for grabs, I was completely asleep at the wheel.

Missing out on that one by at least three raised hands, I told myself, "No more screw-ups. When the next good one comes along, you're gonna jump all over it no matter what!"

I was ready, for what I didn't know... Then, as if she'd purposely saved the very best job for last, out of my teacher's mouth came the sweetest words of all.

"Audio-Visual Monitor."

When I heard those words, I sat up at attention like I'd been struck by lightning. Thrusting my hand up so high that it nearly hit the ceiling, I yelled "I'LL TAKE IT, I'LL TAKE IT!" before anyone else had a chance to react.

I looked around, certain that someone would challenge my right to the throne. But no one did. Not one person at all. And then, just like that, I was the chosen one.

It seemed too good to be true. I was officially going to be one of the school's movie projectionists for the entire fifth grade year. I felt like I'd just received a gift from God, tantamount to being elected President of The United States. Only this was a hell of a lot better.

Stunned, I tried to wrestle with the scope of what had just happened. Minutes earlier I was just a boy who couldn't tell you where the bathrooms were. But now, by some fickle twist of fate, I'd been chosen to perform the coolest job in the entire world.

Everything about this was so wonderful. And everything seemed so right. Except for one tiny detail…

I didn't have a clue about how to run a movie projector.

But that little detail wasn't really important, was it? I mean, it was only the first day of school… So what could possibly go wrong?

Putting aside thoughts of failure and embarrassment, I cued-in on just how cool it was going to be as I traveled from classroom to classroom, showing movies to kids who were totally envious of my job.

After all, it was the coolest job in the world, for back when I was a kid, there were few things better than seeing a movie during class-time, and no job better than being the guy who made it all happen. I was going to be that guy. The guy who transported us all to a far-away world where books didn't exist, and for the time being, homework didn't either.

I loved the days when we'd watch films in class. And each time I noticed a gray film canister lying on the teacher's desk, I'd train an ear to the hallway, listening for the sound of the audio visual cart as it rolled noisily down the hall.

Ever since I could remember, I'd envied the guys who ran those projectors, thinking they must have been the coolest guys in the world. Maybe it was the way they strolled into the classroom like a gunslinger that caught my eye. Or maybe it was the way they effortlessly looped the film around the projector's rollers that was so damn cool. I wasn't sure which was cooler. I only knew that they were at the top of their game, and I couldn't wait to become one of them.

But I was made to wait, for several days, until the magical morning when my teacher called me up to her desk. "Here's a note for you," she said, as she handed me a small, folded envelope. "It's from The Custodian."

I mumbled "Thank you," at first not having a clue as to what the note was all about. Then, as the light came on in my head, I suddenly realized what she'd just handed me.

"Is this from The Camera Guy?" I asked. "Am I going to get to show movies now?"

"Yes you are!" She said with a smile. "Now make sure you read the note so that you don't miss your appointment!"

"Thank you!" I nearly shouted, with a huge smile on my face. "Thank you VERY much!"

Heading back to my desk, I was so stoked I could hardly contain myself. My time in the sun had finally come. Now, all I had to do was open the envelope without tearing the note inside.

I held the envelope up to the light, before tearing it open on the side where the paper looked the thinnest. I blew a puff of air into the envelope, and just a second later, a pencil-written note fell onto my desk.

"Meet me in room 305 at eleven o'clock," the note said. "Ask for Bill."

Excited beyond description, I wriggled in my seat as an hour and a half crept by. The clock seemed to tick backward at times, then, as it struck the eleventh hour, my teacher gave me the nod of approval.

I was off like a shot, heading down the long, outdoor corridor that led to uncharted territory. Along the way there were a great many classrooms, most of them filled with students just like mine was. I walked the rows, seeing class after class go by, until I reached the edge of the northernmost buildings, where the rooms took on a more utilitarian look.

Here, I found rows of classrooms that seemed to have been abandoned. Rooms where tables and chairs had been stacked upon one another, as if the rooms were being used as large storage sheds.

As I searched for room 305, not only did I notice that the far-away buildings looked and felt different, but I also noticed that the individual room's numbers didn't exactly follow the most logical progression. One said this, and another said that, all of it adding up to my feeling completely lost.

I slowed my pace to make sense of it all, while I looked for a sign that I was heading in the right direction. I tried my best to find the place, but with one building being numbered in the two hundreds, and the next one in the fours, the 300 building was nowhere to be found.

I was becoming desperate, partly because I was ten minutes late, and mostly because the far away halls of no-man's-land, were beginning to give me the creeps.

As I shrugged off a chill, I thought, "Oh man, my only chance to make a good first impression, and here I am, completely lost. These guys are NEVER going to trust me with a projector."

That thought was disheartening to say the least. Then, just as I'd pretty much lost all hope, I saw a man in a uniform waving to me from far down the corridor.

He was a tall man, and an old man by my young standards, who was wearing a dark gray button-up shirt, and dark blue work pants. The man approached quickly, and as he came closer, he held out his hand in a token of friendship. "You must be Lee!" he said, as I shook his hand. "My name is Bill!"

Looking up at him, I could see warmth in Bill's eyes that was quite uncommon. He smiled a broad smile, then, after we exchanged pleasantries, Bill turned in the direction he'd come from, saying, "Come on, son, let's get to work!"

Bill walked fast for an old guy, and as he barreled along, I did my best to keep up with him. As we headed for the camera room he told me that he was in charge of the entire Audio Visual Department, and that while I was going to be operating film projectors on school property, he would be my mentor.

We walked down the hall at nearly a gallop, and as we did, I couldn't help but notice the giant ring of keys that jangled loudly on Bill's hip. The key-ring was enormous, holding more keys in one place than I'd ever seen in my lifetime. I marveled at how many keys he had on that ring, and as Bill led the way with a hopping hitch in his stride, those keys rang out like a patio full of wind chimes.

Bill told me that not only was he in charge of the entire Audio-Visual Department, but he was also in charge of the entire custodial staff as well. He told me that his real title was "School Engineer," and even though they didn't call on him to fix things that often, whenever something did need "Fixin'" he was definitely the man to call.

I thought that the title of "Engineer" was a really cool one, and I believed him of course. But it seemed odd that he was an engineer, given that an engineer was the man who ran a train, while wearing one of those blue and white striped hats. It all seemed strange to me. But then again, there was once a time when an elderly woman mentioned that she worked on the hospital's auxiliary, and I assumed she was a diesel mechanic.

Soon we arrived at the end of the school where the Main Custodian's Office was located. The place was tucked way back in the far-end of the building, pretty much as far away from the classrooms as possible. Bill told me that he and the other custodians liked it that way, because being far away from the school's office, meant they were rarely bothered by anyone.

I glanced at the header above Bill's office, noticing that we were now in the 300 section. Here, at the end of the school's rusting fence line, the buildings had a much more industrial look to them. They looked sad in a way, and for whatever reason it was, they seemed to have been forgotten.

Things looked that way all along the 300 building's shadowy corridor. And as Bill showed me around a bit, I noticed that many of the empty classrooms seemed to have a stagnant haziness to them.

Something about those forgotten rooms didn't sit right with me. The air inside felt heavy, and depending upon the way you looked at them, the rooms seemed to sparkle, in a way that didn't make any sense at all.

Naturally, I was curious about the far end of the school. But before I had a chance to inquire about the eerily abandoned rooms, Bill stopped beside a classroom door that had a large metal plate bolted to it, then, after reaching down for the key-ring on his belt loop, he pulled them from his hip on a zip-chain retractor. I was amazed at how many keys he'd fit on that one silver ring, and although I hadn't made the acquaintance of many custodians before, I was pretty sure that with a ring full of keys that big, Bill had to have been The King of Custodians.

As I marveled at the size of the key ring, I was amazed at how Bill seemed to know exactly what each one of the keys was for. I watched as his calloused fingers flipped through the keys one by one, until finally, the proper one fell into his grasp. He fumbled with the door's lock, and as he did, I looked up to where a faded, black and white placard read, "Audio-Visual."

"Welcome to your new office!" Bill said, as he pushed the door open. "Step on in, and get yourself acquainted!"

I did just that. And as I did, a ghost appeared before me -- the ghost of a classroom anyway. For as the door swung through air you could cut with a knife, I stared at a museum of the forgotten. Part chaos, and part frozen history, the interior of room 305 looked like someone had taken things from a by-gone era and plowed them to the side of the room.

At the far end of the room were some desks, stacked atop one another like a strange, abstract sculpture. Beside the desk-pile were some chairs, which were so tightly crammed together they looked like the kindling of a bonfire.

As I followed Bill through the room, I saw an assortment of yellowed, dog-eared maps that looked like they were about to turn to dust. While to the rear, I could see a row of pale-green chalkboards, which were covered in writing that must have been there for decades.

At the rear of the room were two golden-based flag stands propped-up beside one another. Each was topped with an American Eagle, while two golden-tasseled flags hung below. The flags bore forty-eight stars each, and as I stood near them, I felt a wave of sadness, as their time-worn, ragged ends reached down in muted glory.

The room felt like a tomb, yet for all its creepiness, Bill didn't seem to care that the lights weren't on. He obviously knew where everything was, and as he fussed around beside a row of projector carts, I walked over to a sturdy, wooden rack that held a number of large, aluminum film canisters.

As I fixed my gaze on the canisters, Bill said, "That's The Big Rack! It holds all of the longer films that run over sixty minutes."
"You'll need to remember that!" Bill said, "Because if you ever need to show a long film, The Big Rack is where you'll find it!"

I took it all in as best I could. Then, after he poked around in a storage box, Bill turned on what lights still worked, before showing me where everything was. It was all fascinating I suppose, but as Bill went on about this and that, what I really wanted to know about was the row of old-school movie projectors, that were lined up like fighter planes on the deck of a carrier.

Walking over to the carts, I picked up the worn out pig-tail of a projector's power cord. It was coated with cloth, a faded, gray cloth that smelled of old men and rotting asbestos. The cord felt like it was going to melt in my hand, and I stuffed it beneath the projector, before the whole thing fell to ashes.

"Feels old, doesn't it?" Bill said, as I took a step back. "You don't have to be afraid of it though; it's just a machine."

"There's a lot of old stuff in here," Bill went on to say. "I suppose it's sort of a resting place, where things can take a breather."

"Besides," he said, "the stuff in here is good for training, but it's a bit too old for front-line use." He then went on to explain that room 305 was a catch-all of sorts, a place where they stored the older, more "experienced" projectors, that were just perfect for training new guys like me. "These projectors can practically run themselves," Bill said. "In fact, in many ways, I'm sure they can."

I wasn't quite sure what he meant by that, but with so many things to learn, there really wasn't time to dwell on any of it for too long. After showing me around the room, Bill spent the next hour familiarizing me with the projectors, along with many other facets of the trade. Time flew by as if it was carried on the wind, then, after my first training session was over, I said goodbye to Bill, before heading down the long hallway, in the direction of the real world.

The next few weeks were a blur, with Bill teaching me the equivalent of Film-Projector 101. He taught me everything there was to know about the projectors, including how to create the infamous "Slack-Loop," that kept the film from going "slap, slap, slap," like it always does in a bad horror movie.

There was a lot to learn, but with Bill as my mentor, it was only a few short weeks until I was ready to fly. Sure, there were a few disasters along the way, like the time the reels of the projector stopped turning, and I burned a hole in the film, or when one of the projectors flew off the cart when I took a turn too sharply. But that was all to be expected I suppose. And since nobody ever gave me any grief about it, as far as I was concerned, everything was moving along just fine.

Soon enough, I'd graduated from trainee to full-blown fighter pilot, and before I knew it I was heading out to classrooms with my own projector in tow. It felt great to be the Audio Visual Guy, and as I walked the halls with my head held high, I felt for the first time, that I'd really become something special.

It was a magical time in my life. Partly because I had some real responsibility for a change, and mostly because I felt like I was part of something "bigger." Because of my position, I got to meet a lot of new people, and I also got to know nearly everyone in the school. Knowing most of the kids was a real asset, but of all the characters that came into my life, it was the grandfatherly, old custodians I found most endearing, because they always took the time to talk a while, and most of all, they treated me like a full-grown man.

Those old guys were a hell of a lot of fun. Friendly and affable, each and every one of them always had time for a wave, and time for a smile. Even as they pushed their mop-carts down the hall, none of them ever seemed to be in the least bit of a rush. And best of all, they loved to sit and chat a while, as they stretched out the years till retirement.

There was Clyde, the kindly, black gentleman who always forgot to lock the door to the Audio Visual Room. And Mike, a guy who knew a whole lot about projectors, but cared more about the L.A. Dodgers than anything else. Then of course there was Bill, who was truly The King of Custodians, as well as the over-all kingpin of the rag-tag group of old-timers.

Bill felt like family, and he was responsible for teaching me things I remember to this day. He used to tell me that the people we'd see on those old reels of film had been kept alive somehow. Immortalized on cellulose, and reincarnated every time someone cared enough to give the film a spin. Whenever he told me that he would get a far-away look in his eyes, and I often wondered if there was someone on one of those old reels of film that he once knew.

I imagine Bill would have told me if I'd have asked, but in a cool sort of way, he didn't tell me everything. For there was magic in those halls, and Bill knew to keep it closely guarded . . . at least until the end of his watch, which, in retrospect, wasn't too far off.

It was a day like any other, where I'd been sent to retrieve a loop of film for one of the sixth grade classes. Since the film I was looking for was on a large reel, Bill had sent me to room 305 to retrieve it from the Big Rack. It was a simple task really, but not one I was especially thrilled with, because every time I walked into that dusty room, I just couldn't shake the feeling that I was being watched. That was creepy enough. But now that I'd heard whispers in there a time or two, every time I entered the room, all I wanted to do was run.

Yeah, I'd done that a time or two. But this time was going to be different. This time I promised myself there would be no more running out the door like a bird in a coo-coo clock. This time, I was going to walk in there like John Wayne, and secure the film canister like the real man that I was.

Puffed up like a turkey, I walked down the hall toward room 305, where I found the door unlocked and open. "Maybe Bill left it that way," I thought. "Or perhaps it was one of the other custodians who'd left the door open." It didn't matter who'd done it, for I simply figured the open door was just an oversight. Taking a deep breath, I stepped into the room, flipping on lights that flickered with a gaseous, yellow glow. I stood there for a moment, not half as brave as I hoped I'd be, while the projectors stared at me, like steel gargoyles that were ready to pounce.

I'd made it through the doorway. Now all I had to do was walk across the room and secure the film in question. So I shuffled my feet a bit, as I worked up a sack of courage, before bolting across the room, toward the old wooden rack.

As I ran, I prayed that the film would be among the first of the cans on the rack. That would have been really nice, for after reading the label, I could have been out of there in a heartbeat. Of course, as fate would have it, when I arrived at the Big Rack, none of the reels were in any kind of order, and the film I was looking for seemed to be long gone.

I squinted as I read the fine print on the canisters, but none of them bore the name I was looking for. One by one, I pushed the canisters aside, growing more and more frustrated as I shuffled through the lot. I was completely caught up in my own little world, which probably accounts for why I was oblivious to the fact that just a few yards away, stood a white-haired man in a custodian's uniform.

He could obviously tell I was frightened, and he didn't want to scare me any further. So, very softly, he cleared his throat, before speaking in a tone that sounded apologetic.

"What are you lookin' for, son?" he asked.

I heard his voice, plain as day. And as I did, I froze like a deer in the headlights. He chuckled when he saw my reaction. Then, as he stepped out from behind a projector, the man smiled in a way that seemed to light up the entire room.

"Sorry to scare you!" He said. "My name's Clyde."

I didn't answer at first, probably because my hair was still standing on end. Then, as my senses returned, I smiled back, completely relieved that I wasn't the only person in the room.

"Bill's gonna need that reel," Clyde said. "Would you like me to help you find it?"

Still shaking a bit, I said, "No thank you, sir. I'll find it here in a second."

Clyde knew that I was full of crap, and he also knew that if I was lucky the reel would fall from the sky and hit me in the head. So, in his fatherly manner, he gave me just a little hint, while allowing me to act like I knew what I was doing.

"Did you look on top?" Clyde asked. "Sometimes the other boys stick them on top."

Knowing he was probably right, I looked up, to where several large canisters were stacked on an out of the way shelf. I reached for the canister that was balanced on top, and with a tilt to the lights, I saw it was the exact one I'd been searching for all along.

"Thank you, sir," I said, as I tucked the canister under my arm. "Thank you very much!" Then, with a glance over my shoulder, I waved goodbye to my new acquaintance, who just chuckled as I walked out the door.

A couple of months passed, and late one winter afternoon, I was making my way past the ball check-out room without much of anything on my mind. I'd just played a game of pick-up baseball on the after-school playground, and now that it was over, I figured I'd take a stroll through the upper halls, just to see if any of my custodian friends were still around.

As I walked down the 300 corridor, I heard Bill call out from down the row a-ways. "Hey!" he said, as he hurried my way. "I'm glad you're still here. Would you mind helping me rustle-up an item or two before closing time?"

He apologized for asking so late in the day, saying he wouldn't have bothered me, if it wasn't for the fact that he needed to get home before his wife's meat loaf turned into a brick. I couldn't let that happen to a friend, especially since I'd choked down my own mother's meat loaf a time or two. So, I told him I'd gladly help out, especially with something that important on the line.

It was late in the day, and now, close to the dinner hour, the narrow halls had taken on an ominous appearance. I needed to get home soon, certainly by the time the street lights came on. So, I acted fast, asking Bill exactly what he needed, so I could get a move on.

Bill grabbed a projector cart from the room he'd just been in. Then, after scribbling on a dog-eared piece of paper, he handed me a list of the things he needed. Before I could read what he'd scribed on the note, Bill said, "Toss those items on the cart, then roll em' down to the bike racks when you've got em' all. Okay?"

With a quick nod, I was off and running. Until Bill called out, stopping me dead in my tracks.

"Get four empty canisters too!" He yelled down the hall. "The large ones, from 305. The door's unlocked."

"Great. Just Great," I mumbled. "Room 305, the VERY last place I wanted to be.

Going into that room was creepy enough, but now that it was nearly dark, the concept seemed even creepier. But Bill was my buddy, and he'd asked me to do him a favor. Besides, as Clyde had shown me, being scared of that room was silly for the most part. Especially since the only things that were lurking there were the ghosts of the past.

So I pushed the cart as quickly as I could, toward the 300 building, which just happened to have the darkest corridor of all.

Moving fast, my goal was simple. I was going to grab the

empty canisters, rustle up a couple of things, and get outta' Dodge. That was it, plain and simple. I'd grab the cans, grab some stuff, and run like hell… before anything had a chance to creep up on me.

When I arrived at room 305, the first thing I noticed was that the room's door was ajar. Bill had mentioned that it was unlocked, so, without as much as a second thought, I reached inside, and flipped on the light switches.

Half of them came on. Maybe. At least those that didn't look like their ballasts were about to burst into flames. I looked up as the lights flickered, watching the dull fluorescent gas flash with life. As I shuffled into the room, I scanned left and right, hoping there might be a few empty canisters tucked beneath the projector carts. It would have been a real time saver if that was the case. But in keeping with how almost everything in room 305 seemed to have the uncanny ability to disappear into thin-air, all I could see were a few small canisters, none of which were what I was looking for.

Figuring I'd grab the other items first, I found them quickly, before securing them on the cart's lower shelf. As I glanced out the door, I could see the veil of darkness creeping closer. There was still a bit of daylight left, but with each passing second it was fast fading. I was starting to get scared. Really scared. For not only was the veil closing in, but there was a sense that someone else was in the room… along with a strange whispering voice that was just out of range.

As I bristled from the sound of the phantom voice, my instincts were screaming for me to run away. But running wasn't an option, nor was letting Bill down, especially on meatloaf night. So I gathered up some guts, before walking purposefully toward the Big Rack, where I hoped to find the elusive canisters.

I was about half way to the dusty shelves, when the feeling hit me again… that old, familiar feeling, that I needed to run like hell.

"What is it?" I thought, as my skin tried to crawl off my body. "What is it about this room that sets me off this way?" Sure, there was the creepy old equipment, and the smell of rotting asbestos in the air. But something else just wasn't right. Something palpable and eerie, that superseded all reason.

I stood completely still, as the air seemed to come alive… Then, as my hair began to bristle, I quickly spun around, coming face-to-face with what had come upon me.

It was Clyde standing by the open door, awash in amber, flickering light.

"You scared the heck out of me!" I nearly yelled, as he stood there in his gray overalls. "Man, you really scared me."

Clyde smiled, before looking down at my hands, which were shaking about as much as Bill's usually did.

"What are you scared of, son?" Clyde asked. "What are you always so scared of?"

Not knowing what to say, I stood there feeling like the little boy that I was. Then, I just shrugged my shoulders, saying "I dunno. I'm just scared of ghosts and stuff."

Clyde looked at me with understanding eyes. Then, in his typical, grandfatherly style, he pointed at the projectors, saying, "Son, this room's full of ghosts. And you know what? None of them are ever going to hurt you."

"Besides," Clyde said, "you have nothing to be afraid of, 'specially not YOU."

I stood there staring at him, not knowing what he meant, nor knowing what I was supposed to say.

"I guess next time I won't act like such a chicken," I told him. "It's just that sometimes I give myself the creeps."

"I give myself the creeps sometimes too!" Clyde said with a laugh. "I suppose we all do."

Clyde mulled around as I gathered up a few things. Then, just before he headed out the door, he asked me something I'll never forget.

"Don't you know who you are?" He asked. "Don't you realize you're different?"

I looked at him, feeling like an idiot for not knowing what he was talking about. While realizing in a strange, intuitive way, that it would all make sense someday.

So I just stood there as Clyde waved goodbye, before he stepped out the door, into the night.

Time seemed to stand still, as I pondered the significance of what Clyde had just said. Looking around the room, I realized that the old machines probably weren't going to turn into gargoyles after all. They were simply ghosts, things that no longer had anywhere to go. "You're not really scary, are you?" I said to the machines. "You just want to be remembered and cared for once in a while."

One of them seemed to be smiling as its empty film reel began to look more and more like a happy-face. And as I stood there, Clyde's words slowly began to make sense.

How long I stood there pondering Clyde's cryptic question I'll never really know. But as reality came rushing back to me, I realized that if I dilly-dallied any longer, the streetlights would come on, and my mother would be in a total panic.

With a stroke of luck, I found four empty canisters on a shelf by the flags. They seemed to have materialized out of nowhere, but I didn't care, as long as they were the same size that Bill had asked for. After loading up the cart, I was out of there like a shot, with the cart's casters sounding like they were going to fly off the rollers. Down the hall I flew, riding the cart like a sleigh, until I hit the playground blacktop, where the casters smoothed out to a hum.

Seeing Bill just ahead, I skidded my feet on the ground, slowing the cart until I rolled up beside him. He smiled a broad smile, ruffling up my hair with his hand, before thanking me for my help. I walked beside Bill as he rolled the cart into a small storage shed. Then, after he closed the shed's doors, he told me to get my bike so that he could lock up the playground before heading home.

Bill took a long last look across the yard, just in case any other kids were still out there. Then, satisfied that the yard was clear, he reached down with shaky hands, grabbing the key-ring on his belt. He fumbled with the ring as he flipped through the keys. Then, as he found the right one, Bill opened the gate's padlock, before threading it through a heavy length of chain.

Watching him do this, I looked at him with a quizzical stare.

"What is it, son?" Bill asked. "What is it?"

"It's Clyde," I said to him. "Aren't we going to wait for Clyde?"

Bill stared at me with a look on his face that made no sense at all.

I asked again. "If we lock up the gate, how is Clyde going to get out?"

He didn't answer. Rather, Bill just stared at me with his mouth wide open.

I began to think he'd had a stroke, until his expression changed markedly, as he asked in almost a cry, "WHERE DID YOU SEE HIM?" He asked. "WHERE?"

"In 305," I told him. "He's always in there."

"GO HOME NOW, SON!" Bill said loudly, as he back-stepped into the playground. "EVERYTHING IS OKAY… JUST GO HOME!"

So I did just that, racing off into the night, as Bill hobbled toward the old Audio Visual Room.

No one knew who Clyde really was except for Bill who disclosed to me, just prior to his passing, that he'd known the gentle, old man, and that it was a rare gift that I'd made his acquaintance.

I find it ironic that a ghost gave me the strength to face my fears. And how the very thing I feared the most had lit the way when the night was at its darkest.

Many times since, I've looked around, hoping to see Clyde in the shadows. But now, with maturity, I've grown to realize that his time has come and gone.

I learned a lot from those guys back then, about how to face my fears, and what it took to conquer them. And most of all, I learned the importance of taking the time to teach someone something they'll always remember.

Sadly, all of the old timers are gone. They've gone off with their wives perhaps. Or maybe they're with Clyde, somewhere in time where there's still a projector or two that need fixing, maybe even one that needs just the right set of hands -- hands that know exactly how to thread the film, so that the slack-loop doesn't go clackity, clack, clack, clack…

And that's the way it ought to be. Because someday, when I grow old, maybe I'll be the man with trembling hands and a huge set of keys. And maybe, with God's blessing, I'll be the one who shows a curious young boy the ways of the world.

I'd like that very much. For if I'm lucky enough to be that man… in the eyes of a small child, I might just be…

The King Of Custodians.

Shoshone Avenue

Moving to Southern California was the best thing that ever happened to me, and now that we'd been living there for a couple of years I was really beginning to feel as if my life had caught its stride. I was doing things I'd never done before, and thanks to a great group of friends, there seemed no end to the adventures we could have. There were tree-houses and lizards, and fish down by the creek, all there in the sunlight of a place that I called home.

Our lives had changed dramatically over the last two years, and as my family embraced a more casual lifestyle, I felt like the opportunity to live a little was finally within our reach.

My father's ascension up the corporate ladder had been nearly meteoric, and due to the windfall of what seemed to fall from heaven, for the first time in a long while I was beginning to feel whole again.

Gone were the thoughts of the concrete jungle, as were the nagging reminders of a thing that went thump in the night. I'd had time to sort it all out, and now that my life was fully on-track, there was no time to look back… no time at all.

It was a beautiful summer's eve, the kind of night where the frogs were croaking, and you could smell the burgers cooking from two houses away. I had my whole life in front of me as I sat Indian-style on our avocado colored corner-group, and from my perspective, things couldn't have been more promising. It was the biggest night in television history. A night of such immense proportion, that all things before or after, have simply paled by comparison.

No, it wasn't the moon landing, nor was it a re-hashed viewing of the Kennedy assassination. This was MUCH bigger than that. A moment so stupendously significant, it was quite possibly the biggest television moment of all time…

It was the world television premier of The Brady Bunch's Hawaiian Vacation.

As I sat there, I couldn't believe that show time was just an hour away. Just sixty short minutes until Marsha wore her bikini, which to me, was heaven on earth.

I could hardly wait for the show to begin, but just because it wasn't going to start for nearly an hour didn't mean I wasn't good-to-go. I was dialed-in, with a bowl of candied popcorn on my lap, and a can of cocktail peanuts on the bright orange end table beside me. This was all just an appetizer of course, something to get me started while the frozen pizzas heated up in the oven. So I just kicked back and relaxed while waiting patiently for the kitchen's bell timer to signal that dinner was hot and ready.

It was a night filled with promise, especially because both my parents and grandparents were heading out to a cocktail party, which assured at least a few hours of blissful alone-time. Of course I wasn't going to be totally alone, for lyiing on the far end of the couch was my basset hound, Spunky, a beast who enjoyed candied popcorn every bit as much as I did.

We were ready for the long haul with a fridge full of junk food and a couple of quarts of cherry soda. Mom and Dad had set us up right, and now that they'd tacked an emergency phone number to the kitchen cork-board, it was time for them to head out and join the party.

After both my parents and grandparents gave me a lecture about "not burning the house down," they bid me adieu before heading out toward the garage. A few minutes later the garage door closed with a thud, and I leaned back with my feet on an ottoman as I settled in for a night to remember.

I was a latch-key kid, and I wouldn't have had it any other way. I loved it when the elders went out for the evening, because it gave me an unsupervised run of the house, which favorably increased the chance that I might find some of my father's Playboy magazines by accident, on purpose.

There was always a chance that might happen, but for the moment, I was content with matters at hand, such as the television show, and the huge bowl of popcorn on my lap. I stuffed my face with the candy-coated goodness while the dog raised an eyebrow as if to say, "Dude, you're killing me!" Maybe I was. I mean, the stuff was that good. So I threw him a hand-full of the sticky goodness as we lay there like book-ends, crunching away blissfully.

The hour before the show breezed by quickly, and during that time the hound and I made short work of at least three mini-pizzas. Soon the show came on, delivering the goods in a way that only seventies television could. Then, during the commercial between when Bobby found the cursed idol and Greg wiped out on his surfboard, I headed back to the kitchen to pop a couple more pizzas into the oven.

I moved quickly, not wanting to miss a second of the show. Then, after loading the pizzas into the oven, I grabbed a couple of chocolate chip cookies from the teddy bear cookie jar before heading straight back to the family room.

We sat on the couch for hours, watching the show, as well as a late night police drama or two. The dog and I were both in a daze, half asleep in our junk-food coma when suddenly, and without warning, all hell broke loose...

It began with a loud crash, followed by a series of grinding vibrations that nearly shook me to the floor. At first I thought it was an earthquake, but then, as the shaking stopped, and a thumping sound echoed in the distance, I leapt to my feet, sending the bowl of popcorn flying half way across the room.

The dog flew too, launched off the couch with fear and surprise. He landed on the carpet with a heavy flop, then, with a move most un-hound-like, he bounded to his feet with surprising agility

With a look on his face that only a dog could give, Spunky appeared to say "WHAT THE HELL?" as we stared at one another. We stood there silently, neither of us moving a muscle, until we had some idea of what we were dealing with. A few seconds passed, then, as the sound echoed to silence, I craned my neck around the doorway to see if anyone or anything was coming down the hall.

The hallway was empty, and from my vantage point I couldn't see anything that shed light on what had just happened. I knew it hadn't been an earthquake, but other than that, I supposed it could have been anything. Fearing my worst nightmare had thumped its way across the country, I looked down at my silly dog, thinking, "There's just no way he's going to be able to take on something like The Thumping Man. There's just no way!" I was dead-right about that, yet as small a dog as he might have been, his protective nature gave me some measure of solace.

The dog joined me at the doorway, where we looked left, right, and left again. The hallway was clear on both ends, so we crept forward ever-so-slowly as we made our way toward the kitchen area.

When we arrived I peered into the pantry alcove where everything seemed to be in its proper place. The dog's food bowl was centered on a green and yellow place-mat while freshly laundered bath towels were neatly stacked atop the clothes dryer. As I moved stealthily across the kitchen floor, I tried to be as quiet as possible, but the dog had other ideas, noisily crunching away at some kibble from the bottom of his bowl.

"That's just great," I thought. "Some hunting dog he is. We're just seconds into the hunt and he's already got food on his mind!"

That suited him just fine, but in my case, I knew I didn't have the luxury of that kind of complacency, especially since it sounded like the roof had come down, and a sound that ferocious couldn't possibly have come from anything good.

Taking a deep breath, I moved through the kitchen, toward the master wing's hallway. On the way, I paused in the entry foyer, in the hope of hearing something that would clue me in as to where the noise had come from. I listened, but there wasn't anything to be heard other than a strange clicking sound at the far end of the house. It sounded like something had broken loose, almost as if a snapped clothesline was blowing in the wind. I didn't like that sound at all, fearing the worst, until proven otherwise.

I could have bailed out the front door, but that would have made too much sense. Besides, for all I knew, the thing that made the sound could have been hiding just outside the door. Knowing that, I felt there was no option other than to follow the clicking sound, where, hopefully, it might shed some light on what had just happened.

With the hound close behind, I tip-toed into the living room, where I could hear the clicking sound much more clearly. It tapped away in a completely random pattern, with a few clicks here, and a click or two there, none of which made any sense at all.

It didn't sound like a monster, but having run from my share of them, I wasn't about to take any chances. I listened to the sound for a moment, then, after moving past the fireplace, I slipped into the dining room, where I ducked behind a heavy Spanish-style table.

Whatever this thing was, it was tapping away like crazy. And although I knew it wasn't The Thumping Man, it gave me the creeps none-the-less. This was something different altogether. Something with movement that made no sense… other than it had no earthly business being in my home.

I moved slowly, doing my best to remain hidden behind the long wooden table. The going was good, and soon I reached the far end of the dining room where I had a good view of the large, rectangular rec-room.

At room's end was our wet-bar, while next to that was a door that led to my father's home office. I walked into the rec-room with my back to the wall, while across from me was a wall of plate glass windows, that looked out onto the pool deck

The sliding windows were at least seven feet tall, and combined, they spanned at least thirty feet in width. They were covered with floor-to-ceiling drapes, which when closed, spanned the entire width of the rec-room wall. Ordinarily, the drapes were pulled to one side, allowing a panoramic view of the pool-deck and tropical plant forest. But since I was home alone, they'd been drawn closed by my father just prior to them heading out for the evening.

And that's how he'd left them. With the latches locked and the drapes pulled closed, in such a way they couldn't possibly have come open. But now, everything seemed so wrong, because, for some unexplained reason, the drapes were blowing in the wind… and as they did, my skin began to crawl.

As I tried to make sense of it all, I knew for certain my father had locked the slider. There was no question of that, given he had thrown the latch, just before he fetched me a snack table from the office closet. The house had been locked up tight, and I knew that for sure. "So how could the sliding door be open?" I wondered.

"And who on earth could have unlocked it with the latches being on the inside?"

"Maybe something smashed through the window," I thought. "Maybe it was an errant baseball, or something else that had flown into the yard."

The baseball idea was comforting, except that it would have taken a thousand baseballs to make the kind of sound we'd heard. And as far as I knew, none of my friends were out playing baseball in the middle of the night.

Once again, things just weren't adding up, and for all I knew, the wreckage of Air Force One might have been sticking out of our pool. But I wasn't going to have any answers until I drew the drapes aside. So, despite my monster-filled reservations, I decided it was time to have a look behind the veil.

As the drapery beckoned, the clicking sound grew louder, which was a curious side-bar to the intoxicating blend of what-if's that gripped me at that moment. I took a deep breath before cautiously sweeping the drapes aside, revealing something I never expected.

Something had torn one of the large glass sliders from its tracks, then, in some inexplicable way, it had hurled the window against a wall nearly twenty feet away. The door had been torn clean out of the runners, while beside it lay the remains of its companion screen, somehow twisted by hands that couldn't possibly have been human.

The drapes blew in the warm summer breeze, and as they did, a tension cord with a metal spring adjuster, slapped against the wall with a tell-tale clicking sound.

"What the heck did this?" I wondered. "What on Earth could do something like this?"

I pondered that, as the clicking sound of the tattered cord echoed through the rec-room. None of it made any sense. None of it at all... until something crossed my mind that gave me quite a chill.

"What if the thing that caused the damage was still in the house?" I wondered. "And what if it was hiding somewhere planning its next attack?"

A wave of nausea crept over me as the reality of the situation came to bear. "The thing might be in the house somewhere!" I thought. "Maybe in a room I haven't searched yet!"

That thought was enough to make my skin crawl, and it was more than enough to prompt me into action. Stunned by the implications of what might be, I flipped on the pool and patio lights before jumping onto the pool deck. A few seconds passed before the pool lit up, then, as the tropical jungle of plants and palms glowed with colored light, a familiar calm settled over me.

As I looked around, I glanced toward the corner of the yard, where my friends and I had engineered a "secret passageway" through the slatted, wooden fence. If necessary, I could have run to that corner, where it was just a diving leap into the neighbor's yard. That thought was comforting, especially because two of my best friends lived next door, and if need be, they would have helped me out in a heartbeat.

With my escape route intact, I watched the hound sniff the ground as he zig-zagged across the patio. He was on to something, but from the way he was walking in circles, I wondered if he was going to find it. Curiously, he seemed unable to track whoever it was that had been there, which was odd as hell, given that no one had ever been able to get away from his all-knowing nose, especially when we played hide and seek.

"This is weird," I thought. "Perhaps the person who did this doesn't have a scent. Or even worse, maybe it's some kind of monster!"

But monsters did have scents, and I knew that if the damage had been caused by the likes of The Thumping Man, my dog would have been onto his acrid trail in a heartbeat. That thought was comforting, as was the notion that thumping three thousand miles, wasn't a practical option.

The dog nudged up against my leg, and right then I realized it was probably best to re-rack the slider and shore things up as best I could. It wasn't easy, as the thick glass door weighed nearly twice as much as I did. But since it was partially propped up by the rec-room wall, I managed to drag it back to the tracks without killing myself.

As I mopped up the carnage, there were a couple of moments where I was sure the window was going to fall over and smash into a million pieces. But by propping it up against the back of a couch,

I was able to gain enough leverage to re-track the slider in its original position. Once the frame was in the groove, I ran the window the full length of the track, as a deep *thump, thump, thump* sound echoed from the track runners. It was the same sound I'd heard earlier, and recognizing it for what it was, I immediately dismissed the notion that The Thumping Man might be around.

With the window back on track, I locked the slider-latch with a host of questions on my mind, such as, "Who or what did this?" And, more importantly, "What if they were still in the house?"

I didn't want to think about the latter, while preferring to believe the neighborhood kids may have been playing tricks on me. That scenario made the most sense, so, I locked the doors, and drew the drapes, just in time to hear a loud, crunching sound in the bedroom hallway.

The sound scared the hell out of me, because it wasn't the boys, and it wasn't the wind… and whatever the thing was, it was locked inside along with me.

Needing to get outside fast, I cautiously stepped toward the sliding door as the crunching sound moved closer. Whatever this thing was, it was stealthy, and as I fumbled with the latch of the slider, I began to feel a scream well-up in my throat.

Click, click, click, went its monstrous feet. Then, as I was nearly panicked to the brink, the beast rounded the corner, rushing toward me as fast as it could.

It was Spunky, my trusty hound, running toward me with a wagging tail, and candied popcorn stuck to his whiskers.

I had to laugh, for while I was off searching for monsters, he'd given up the hunt, in favor of eating the popcorn that was scattered all over the floor. I guess I should have known that he was up to something, especially since he'd been way too quiet for far too long. But I did have other things on my mind, all of which weighed heavily as I brushed the remaining popcorn from his face.

As funny as it was, the dog-noise thing had given me quite a scare. Maybe that was good, for now that I'd been shocked out of my complacency, I realized there would be no solace, until I'd searched the entire house, room by room.

Putting together a search-plan, I took stock of everything I'd need in order to do a thorough sweep of the home. At the top of the list was getting a cold drink, which I remedied by mouthing the bottle of cherry soda in the refrigerator. Then, after grabbing a flashlight and my father's Army bayonet from the kitchen's utility cupboard, I was pretty-much ready for the hunt. Pretty-much, that is, for now, all I needed to do was get my hands on two crucial items that would tip the balance of power in my favor.

Ordinarily, getting hold of those two things would have been easy. But on this night, that wasn't the case. Because the things I needed most were locked away in my father's home office, the very same place where the intruder might be hiding.

I didn't relish the thought of entering the office wing, as it offered a labyrinth of hiding places that were ripe for the taking. And it was dark in there too, giving a distinct advantage to anyone who might be lurking in the shadows. Going in there alone was a bit of a risk, but the reward loomed large. So much so, I felt it was worth the gamble.

With the hound close behind, I walked toward the office-entry, before softly pressing my ear to the door. There wasn't a sound to be heard inside the office hallway, except for the ever-present hum of the air conditioning system. I was relieved that I hadn't heard anyone rustling around. So, being reasonably sure there wasn't anyone in the hallway, I drew the bayonet from its sheath, before slowly opening the door.

The entry corridor was dark, so dark that I could barely see the outline of the couch in the library area. I flipped on the lights, fully prepared to run, but to my delight there wasn't a person to be seen. "Main hallway's a go," I whispered to the dog. "Now all we have to do is clear the bathroom area."

The bathroom was my biggest concern, because it was the darkest room of all, and the perfect place for something large to lurk. I needed to light up the room, but with the light switches being in the bathroom itself, that wasn't going to easy.

I was a bit freaked out, but as I stood there listening, I couldn't hear a tick or smudge of sound anywhere near the bathroom corridor. There was no palpable sense that anyone was hiding nearby, so, with much trepidation, I reached around the doorjamb, with the bayonet close to my side.

The light switches came within reach, and as I flipped them on the room lit brightly, thanks to a row of recessed lights that my father had recently installed. I moved slowly toward the door . . . Then, after peeking around the corner, I saw that things looked as normal as they'd ever been.

The bathroom area was clear, except for a couple of beach towels and a faded pair of skin-diver fins that my father kept near the pool door. I was relieved that there wasn't anyone hiding in the bathroom, and now that the last hurdle had been cleared, I had a better than good chance of getting my hands on exactly what I needed.

To my right was the office library, where bookcases full of mystery novels stood floor to ceiling high. The room was partially lit by the light of the bathroom corridor, and from what I could see the coast appeared to be clear. There didn't seem to be anyone hiding anywhere in the office, so, taking a necessary chance, I sprinted toward the closet at the far end of the room.

I reached the doors within seconds, before fumbling with a key that was hidden nearby. It took a moment to find the key-slot, but then, as the key found its mark, a half turn is all it took, before the double doors swung wide open.

Before me was pure salvation, a masterful blend of hardwood and steel that, for all intents and purposes, leveled the playing field. They were simple guns really, yet to me they were two of the most beautiful things in the world. One was my father's .177 caliber pellet gun, and the other was my trusty Daisy Red Ryder, a rifle that could dish out a hailstorm of BB's as fast as anyone could pull a trigger.

Grabbing the smaller rifle, I rattled it up and down, hearing the familiar swish of a hundred BB's or more. Pressing the red safety button until it disappeared into the stock, I cocked the lever once before bringing the weapon to bear...

It felt good to hold the gun in my hands, and with a twisted, wicked smile I now knew that I'd become the hunter. Sure, it was just a BB gun, but with the looped repeater handle, I could fire off rounds so fast, she was practically full-auto. I didn't care who or what had torn off the sliding doors. If they got in my way, they'd be mercilessly peppered with lead, until steam came out of the barrel.

Now that I was properly armed it was time to bring the rain. As

101

I filled the breach of the heavier gun with the larger .177 pellets, I began to feel that not only did I have the ability to defend myself, but I now had the firepower to go on the offensive. With my back to the wall I loaded the gun, carefully feeding her pellets one by one. Then, once she had fifty or so in her belly, I closed the breach, standing there like The Rifleman.

For the first time since the fireworks began, I finally felt secure. With the guns fully loaded, I grabbed a roll of duct-tape from the closet's shelf, before tearing off a piece at least two feet long. With the larger rifle between my knees, I fixed the bayonet to the barrel's end, taping it down tight, with multiple wraps around the handle.

Now the gun had gone from adequate to damn near wicked. It was just what I needed, the perfect tool to root out a monster that might be lurking beneath the hundred and one dresses in my mother's bedroom closet.

With both guns drawn, and the hound by my side, I was ready to begin the hunt. Perhaps it wasn't the smartest thing to do, but with two loaded guns, and a fresh bowl of popcorn, I felt like I had things pretty much under control.

I searched room by room, sending the dog in first, as I covered his back with both barrels. We moved slowly, being extra careful not to walk into a trap. Then, as each room was cleared, I locked the door upon exiting, so I could cross that room off the list. Not a closet or bedside was left unchecked, until ultimately, all that was left to do was shake-down my parent's bedroom.

Before entering the master suite, I realized something I hadn't considered before. There were two separate entrances to that wing of the house, and because of that we had a bit of a problem. For while we searched one end of the wing, there was always the chance that something could sneak out the other door and circle around behind us. There was no way I was going to let that happen, so I locked the door to the bathroom corridor, ensuring there was only one way in, and no way out.

With the second entrance secured, we made our way into the master suite, knowing full well it was the very last place where something could be hiding. As I slinked along like a commando, I realized the dog probably thought I'd completely lost my mind.

During the hunt, he had given me a strange look or two. But despite his wondering if I'd snapped my cap, he stood-fast, as I kicked the bed-skirts, and poked the closets with the bayonet-tipped rifle. He even waited patiently as I poked the rows of dresses in my mother's walk-in closet. A place where he'd never been allowed, for fear that he'd hair-up her mink stole, or the thing in the corner that looked like a bathing suit, with a thousand shiny sequins hanging from it.

We searched everywhere. In every conceivable hiding place, until I was reasonably assured there wasn't a monster among us. There had been a scare or two along the way, especially in regard to my grandmother's wig head, but over-all, everything went down pretty smoothly. I remember feeling disappointed that I didn't get to pop off at least a round or two. But I figured it would be best if there weren't any incriminating holes in the wall that need not be there.

After checking each room twice, we returned to the family room, and the comfort of the corner-group. It was getting late, and although I didn't expect my parents' home until the wee hours of the morning, there was still a good chance my grandparents would get a ride home early. Awaiting their arrival, I sat cross-legged, with both gun barrels trained on the hallway just in case anything happened to pop its head around the corner.

Now that the dust had settled, two lingering questions swirled through my head. The first being, "What the hell really happened?" And the second was, "Is it going to happen again?"

I didn't want to dwell on either point too long, especially since it seemed as if the sliding door had been torn open from the inside of the home.

"What if this thing has the ability to move through walls?" I wondered. "And what if it can come into the house any time it wants to?"

Those thoughts were most disquieting. Especially the thoughts I was having about it wanting to do us harm. I didn't even want to consider that, so, doing my best to put it out of my mind, I shrugged off my fears as best I could while vacuuming up the last of the spilled popcorn.

After doing my best to straighten things up, I watched some TV with an ear trained to the garage door. I figured that once the door began to open, I'd run to the office, re-rack the rifles, and pretend the whole "guns" part of the evening hadn't really happened. Sure, I was going to tell my father about the incident, but I wasn't going to mention it to my mother or grandmother, for fear that my grandmother would spend the next year swinging a dead chicken over her head.

Time went by, and as it did, the whole "slider" incident seem more and more surreal. I was shaken, but having the television on made me feel a lot less alone. "Everything's going to be alright," I told myself, as I listened to the laughs of a television audience. "Everything's going to be just fine."

My mind wandered, and as it did, I began to feel like everything that had happened may have had a rational explanation. "Dad will figure it out," I thought. "He always has all the answers."

That thought brought me consolation, and a surprising sense of serenity. Right up until the moment… when the door was torn open again.

I screamed as the shock-wave passed through the home. And as the tearing sound of chaos resonated through the walls, I cowered in the corner with both rifles aimed at the doorway. This time around, the crashing sounds were much more intense. There was a pulsation I hadn't felt earlier, and unlike last time, there was an ominous feeling in the wave, as if something large was approaching.

Frightened beyond description, I screamed, "WHO ARE YOU?" as loud as I could. But all I heard in reply was the sound of destruction. I could have run straight for the door, but needing to know what this thing was, I moved down the hall with the Red Ryder in my hands. The hound followed close behind, and from the way his ears were folded back I assumed he was more interested in getting the hell out of Dodge than he was at identifying our assailant.

As the dog ran for cover, I stepped into the dining-room where the sound was louder than ever. Something terrible was in my midst, yet for all the horror, I wasn't going to rest until I'd seen the thing with my own eyes. So I gathered up some courage, as I walked toward the rec-room, where I laid eyes on the beast for the very first time.

From across the room I could see everything so clearly... the way the monster pulsed like a candle, and how it tore at the glass doors as if they were the wrapper of a demonic Christmas present.

What it was I can't fully describe, only that it looked like energy charged cellophane that was pulsing in the wind. It had form, I suppose, in a nondescript way, and as it tore a door from its tracks, I could have sworn I saw hands, gripping the door's perimeter.

I was stunned by both the sight of the monster and its implications. The thing was completely comprised of energy, phasing in and out as its form changed with the wind. I stared at the thing, half out of fear and half out of wonder, before it slammed the door down in a final act of destruction.

It looked at me, I suppose, as there was a cessation to its chaos as it turned to face me. For whatever reason it was, the thing seemed content to end its destructive tirade. And now, as it shimmered in the cobalt glow of the swimming pool, there was a beauty to its form that's hard to describe. The thing pulsed with the light of a thousand stars, then, just as quickly as it had appeared, the beast began to dematerialize, straight into thin air.

As it disappeared, I stood motionless, trying to feel where it had gone. At first I couldn't sense a thing, until suddenly, I was enveloped by a cloud of ozone that harkened back to The Thumping Man.

I half expected he'd appear in all of his grinning horror. But as I spun around, there was nothing there at all... save for the sharp smell of ozone and a high-pitched hum that I'd long since heard.

"Something's here," I thought. "It's here in the house, and it's waiting."

That thought was scary enough, but knowing it was looking right at me was a notion most terrifying. I listened for the slightest sign that something was there, but all I could sense was presence without form. It was so very close as it hid behind the veil. Then, as it moved forward, the thing slid past in a cloud of charged particles that were ready to ignite.

The thing was gone, and I guess I could have run, only there wasn't anywhere to run to, nor was there anywhere to hide. Now there was only silence, and a light summer breeze that luffed the drapery like a shortened main-sail.

I walked toward the broken sliders, where I could see that this time around, the thing had done a hell of a lot of damage. The safety glass was intact, although from the look of the runners and window screens, there would be no way of keeping this from the elders. So I did my best to minimize the carnage, before I drew the drapes closed, in hope that the play was finally over.

After doing my best to straighten up the mess, I called out to the dog, who'd been hiding under my bed since he'd first seen the monster. I called him only once, and within seconds he skidded around the corner, before running into my waiting arms. It was comforting to feel his touch, and I hugged that silly dog for all he was worth.

Now that the monster was gone, I stood there with the strangest feeling. I felt like I'd been violated somehow. As if our family home was no longer a safe haven from the things that hid in the shadows. That notion was very disturbing. But regardless of how it made me feel, I was dead-set on quelling the notion that my new home was no longer a safe place to be.

After a few minutes, I re-racked the guns and returned to the family room. Just as I was about to sit down, I heard a hum, as the garage door began to open. I was ecstatic, and before either of my parents had the chance to exit the garage, I ran outside to greet them, nearly tackling my father in the process.

"Whoa, Big Guy!" he said with a smile. "How was YOUR night?"

I told him it was fine, but from the look in my eyes he knew that was far from the truth.

"Dad, there's something I've got to show you," I told him, "only without Mom around."

He looked at me with knowing eyes before asking me straight away, "Did you do something you shouldn't have?" I shook my head, "No," before telling him it wasn't so much something I'd done, as it was something that I'd SEEN."

When he heard me say that he got a look on his face I didn't much like. Then, he said, "Hold that thought!" as he told me to say goodnight to my grandparents before meeting him in his office.

A few minutes passed before I headed to the office where he

was leaning back in his executive chair. He was about to speak, but before he could say a word, I asked, "Dad, do you remember the thing in the basement? ... Do you?"

He gave me the strangest look, before saying, "I'm not quite sure what you're talking about. What thing in the basement?"

There was silence, because he and I both knew damn well what I was talking about. We stared at one another, as he leaned back with a poker face. Then, without burdening me further with any more bullcrap, he simply said, "Show me."

We walked toward the rec-room where the drapes pulsed as if they were breathing. I pointed toward the slider, but before I could show him what had been done, my father moved me aside as if he was protecting me from something. He listened for a moment, then, after sweeping the drapes to one side, he looked outside, to where the twisted screens now lay.

He walked onto the patio, before dropping to a knee beside a broken screen door. Running his fingers across its tortured, twisted frame, he looked up at the displaced slider before asking in nearly a whisper, "The thing from the basement, you say... What do you mean by The Thing from The Basement?"

"You know EXACTLY what I mean! I told him. "You know exactly what I'm talking about."

He stood up, looking quite concerned as he ran his hand along the slider.

"It wasn't THAT." He told me eye-to-eye. "There's NO WAY it could have been that!"

I wanted to tell him he was wrong. But before I had the chance, my father hugged me with the kind of hug that only fathers give. I hugged him back, wanting desperately to believe him. And I tried as best I could, as he told me that everything was going to be just fine.

We didn't talk about it anymore that night. Not as I brushed my teeth, or when he tucked me into bed a few minutes later. He told me a silly story, then, after my father turned on my night light, he paused in the doorway before saying one last thing.

"Don't tell your mother about any of this," he said. "Whatever you do... DON'T tell your mother."

The Fire Dog

Have you ever read an old Grimoire or ancient Druidic text? If you have, it's no doubt you've noticed these books contain images depicting many things unsavory and not of this earth. There are dancing imps, and demons aplenty, all lurking about on a tortured landscape where no man would ever dare to tread.

These are the illustrations of the underworld, images born of men's minds that have been brought to life through imagination, creativity, and political necessity. Created to manipulate and control the fearful, these images emblazoned unforgettable icons into the minds of the masses, giving substance to their fears in an unprecedented manner.

History, of course, tells us that many of these illustrations were the fodder of the church, images created by artists compelled to keep the masses faithful, and the plates filled with coins. It all makes perfect sense in a business sort of way. Establishing checks and balances among men and women who might otherwise think for themselves. But let's look beyond the manipulation and fear mongering for a moment, to ponder something truly frightening.

What if some of the things drawn in those hellish illustrations were actually real? And what if even one creature depicted in those musty old books had ever really walked the earth?

Have you ever considered how frightening that would be?

Well guess what? It's time to be frightened. For some of the hellish creatures so artfully depicted in those ancient wood-cuts have walked the earth. And I know that for a fact. Because I've seen them with my own two eyes.

Revisiting the memory of what happened long ago has been quite a soul-searching experience, because what transpired back then still echoes to this day. And the thing we released that cold Fall's eve, still scratches at the door from time to time.

I was thirteen years old, and like so many others of my generation, I didn't feel like I fit in anywhere, or with anyone. Far from a boy, yet not nearly a man, I had desires that reached well beyond my ability to realize them. Because of this, I found myself intensely frustrated by the limbo that had taken over my life. Everything I strived for seemed a step out of reach, while the things I could do felt hopelessly steeped in mediocrity.

It's because of my pent-up frustration that I chose to dabble in a thing or two that weren't necessarily in my best interest. I should have been more careful, but with the amount of angst that was churning within me, there was no containing my need to run free.

Driven by the frustration we all shared, my friends and I resorted to pulling off some pretty risky stunts back then. Some were tame, by our standards at least, while others were anything but... often placing us in the cross-hairs of one hell of a lot of trouble.

There was the wind-swept night when we rolled giant, car-sized tumbleweeds into a busy traffic intersection, nearly setting off a multi-car pile-up. Then there was the time we decided to jump our bicycles off the roof, into the deep end of my friend's swimming pool, which was good for at least a broken bone or two.

I suppose if there hadn't been a finite amount of tumbleweeds in the field, or a limit to how many bones we were willing to break, we'd never have transitioned to the next level of darkness. But for reasons most unexpected, we were soon driven into the shadows, where, over time, the darkness we unleashed grew into a monster. One that some say, nearly got away from us.

You'd think it would have been drugs or alcohol that took us to the edge. But it wasn't anything of the sort. Rather, it was something you'd never suspect that led us to the gates of Hell . . .

A harmless little book.

Not that it was the book's fault all its own. Nor was it the fault of the person or persons who wrote it. Rather, if to place the blame properly, it was the fault of my friend's brother, who never should have allowed us to get our hands on the thing in the first place.

The book was a Grimoire, or book of shadows, a very old text filled with chants, spells, and incantations that should never, EVER have been allowed in the hands of a child, let alone the hands of reckless adolescents such as ourselves. It was a very old book, and

111

for all intents and purposes it should have been kept safe and secure in a collector's private library, or atop an altar where it could be watched over carefully.

It's strange how after all these years I remember the book so well. Everything from the way the paper felt in my hands, to how the thick, black binder smelled of moss and time. There was an undeniable power in that book, and to hold it in your hands, was to feel like you'd lost all control.

From the first moment I touched it I sensed it was evil, and I knew I'd be much better off if I never opened its cover. I should have put it down and run for my life. But there was something within those molded pages that wouldn't let me go... something living, that latched onto my soul.

When I first saw the book it was in the hands of my friend, Mike, who told me that he'd borrowed it from his older brother. I didn't have any reason to disbelieve him, but as time went by, I knew with certainty that Mike's brother would never let a book of such magical power fall into Mike's dark hands.

Mike handed it to me like he was handing me the TV Guide. As if he had zero reverence for its contents, and even less concern for its capabilities. Placing my hand upon it, I could feel dark energy pulsing inside, almost as if I'd just shaken the hand of someone I didn't want to know. Opening its heavily bound, partially torn cover, I was mesmerized by what I saw. They were the images of Hell. Pictures meticulously drawn in classical wood-cut style, beside spells and incantations designed to bring to life that which had no business walking upon the Earth.

There were dancing imps, and demons on tip-toe, who lurked about behind wind-blown drapes. Along with those creatures were others in their company, for whom imagination played heavily in their creation. I turned the pages one by one, drawn in by the horror and opulence of it all. Until suddenly, I saw something that made me shudder... something that stared right back at me.

It was The Thumping Man. Standing on its hideous, hopping point with its scorched wooden body and the eyes of The Devil. I stared at the thing as it stared back at me, and in that skin-crawling moment something became glaringly clear.

The Thumping Man had been real.

I looked at Mike with what must have been a look of horror, because in a rare gesture of humanity, he knelt down beside me, asking what was wrong. I turned the book toward him, pointing to the image of the horror that I'd long hoped hadn't been real.

Mike stared at the page, while weirdly mumbling to himself as he read the accompanying text over and over. I waited for him to say something, but he just stood there with a furled brow, leafing through book's pages while making a strange humming sound.

"Mike," I asked. "What do you think it is?"

He began to say something, then stopped, as if he was still trying to make sense of it all. Then, as his facial expression changed from a look of concern, to a weird kind of sneer, he blurted out, "It's some kind of DEMON!"

"IT'S A DEMON! IT'S A DEMON! It says so right here!" Mike exclaimed.

"IT'S AN OLD-WORLD DEMON!"

I really didn't know what to think, for the implications of what Mike had just said were almost too much to bear. "What the hell?" I thought. "Are demons really real? And if that was the case, what business did one of them have living in the shadows of my basement?"

I didn't like any of this. And now that The Thumping Man had hopped back into my life via an illustration in the scariest book ever, the creep-factor of the whole thing ratcheted-up to the Stratosphere.

Looking at Mike, I hoped he was going to say something that would at least partially allay my fears. For after all, he did know a thing or two about things such as The Thumping Man. So I just stared at him, waiting for him to say something, which I hoped and prayed would sound at least partially sane.

But that wasn't to be the case. Because after Mike stood there a moment, gazing at the image of The Thumping Man, he came up with an idea so hideous I couldn't believe it had actually crossed his mind.

"Let's conjure the thing up!" Mike proclaimed. "I want to see the thing for myself!"

I was like, "WHAT THE HELL ARE YOU SUGGESTING, YOU IDIOT?"

Then, nearly consumed with anger over his irreverence for my feelings, I told him in my sternest voice, "DAMMIT MIKE, DON'T YOU EVER MENTION SUCH A THING AGAIN!"

He looked at me with the look he always had on his face just before he was about to piss somebody off. Then, in typical Mike fashion, he goaded me further as I turned to walk out the door.

"Maybe I'll conjure him up myself and send him over to YOUR HOUSE!" he said, as I exited the door. "MAYBE HE'LL BE IN YOUR ROOM WHILE YOU SLEEP!"

I flipped him the bird, as I stormed through the garage. Yelling, "GO SCREW YOURSELF!" over my shoulder.

At that moment I was so pissed off I nearly saw red. Wanting nothing more than to forget about the madness, I side-stepped the tree roots that had buckled up through the sidewalk. "What the hell just happened back there?" I thought. "And what was that strange book really all about?"

I didn't have answers to either of those questions, nor did I have a clue as to where any of this was heading. None of it made any sense, but I did know intuitively that whatever road it was we were destined to travel, somehow, in some way, we'd be passing way too close to the flame.

Heading down that road was inevitable. But before anyone would be traveling anywhere, I'd have to eat some dinner. Scurrying down the twisted, leaf-strewn sidewalk, I passed beneath an old maple tree whose remaining leaves twitched like bats in the autumn wind. I sped up as the bat-wings rustled, before crossing the street to where I could see my grandmother through the kitchen's front window. She was fussing with something in the oven, and as I paused by the side door to kick some mud off my shoes, the comforting sound of silverware on dishes filled the air.

That evening came and went, as did the next few days as well. By the time a week or two had passed I'd begun to feel as if the whole episode in Mike's room had really been just a dream. Because of that, I soon put the thought of demons and witches far into the back of my mind, where such things are given the chance to simply fade away.

And that's what would have happened. Had the phone not rang one afternoon, disrupting the serenity that was beginning to overtake my overly active mind.

It was such an ordinary day, a day like so many others where I found myself sitting on the family room couch watching re-runs of some seventies police drama. I was lost in the fog of mindless car chases, when far off in the kitchen, our telephone began to ring. I hurried toward the phone, then, after saying "Hello," I waited for a reply. A moment passed, but rather than hearing a voice, all I could hear was an eerie humming sound, that made me want to hang up the phone that very second.

The sound made my skin crawl, yet for some unexplained reason I couldn't help but listen to it. Hoping to hear something familiar through the din of static, I stood motionless, listening for the slightest indication that there was a living person on the other end. The hum pulsed to static, drawn long and thin through miles of twisted wire. At first there was nothing but buzz, until a moment later, when a strange, mewling voice began to break through.

The voice was so faint it seemed to be coming from a different dimension. "Speak up please," I asked the strange caller. "I can't hear what you're saying."

I was about to hang up, when after a long, uncomfortable pause, I heard a low, but recognizable voice on the end of the line.

It was Mike. And he sounded very, very strange.

"There's something I need to show you," he said. "And you need to come alone."

Pausing a moment to reflect upon his request, I felt strangely entranced by Mike's invitation. It was creepy as hell, that's for sure. Yet hidden within his nearly breathless request, was something that said much more. I knew not to go, but I also knew that if I turned him down, fifty years later, I'd still regret my decision.

As if I was a moth being drawn to a flame, I said, "Okay," before softly hanging up the receiver. What madness lay in store for me I really didn't know. I only knew that if I ever wanted to break free of the monotony my life had become, it was moments like this that would show me the way.

Walking to my room, I readied myself for whatever awaited me. Not knowing what Mike had up his sleeve, there really wasn't anything I could have done to prepare myself for the unknown. Yet strangely enough, I felt that I needed to do something before heading off to his house. So I stood in front of the bathroom mirror and stared... straight into the eyes of an adolescent who was about to step WAY too close to the edge.

With a nod to my grandfather, I yelled out, "I'll be home in time for dinner," as I headed onto the patio courtyard. To my left was my trusty Schwinn Stingray, with its banana seat and boxed handle bars, poised and ready for action. Grabbing it by the bars, I rolled it out the side gate and onto the front pathway. First looking left, and then right, I stood on the pedals, pumping vigorously down the pathway. The bike was fast, and within seconds I flew off the curb with a wild bunny-hop. It felt good to be in the wind, and as I rode my way toward God-knows-what, I pushed back the thoughts of the hellish book, and whatever it was that called to me from within its molded, rotting pages.

Arriving at Mike's house, I dipped the Stingray hard to my left, rounding the twin trees at the corner of his property. With a wild fishtail I skidded into the driveway, where I could see two other bicycles lying on their sides. Recognizing both of the bikes, I surmised that Mike had invited some of the other boys from the neighborhood to his little "mystery meeting." This gave me some measure of solace, because as of late, Mike's weird behavior was starting to give me the creeps.

I tossed my bike beside the others, before heading through the garage toward the kitchen entry. Walking in unannounced, I couldn't see anyone in the kitchen or living room, so I called out down the hall to see if anyone was home. At first there was no answer. But then, a moment later, I heard a voice ring out, saying, "We're in here!"

At the sound of the voice I headed down the dimly lit hall that led to Mike's room. On nearly every wall were black-light posters, some of Jimi Hendrix, and others of various "Acid-rock" bands that were popular back in the seventies. I thought it was cool as hell that Mike's dad let him decorate the place that way, and the fact that the hallway light had a black-light bulb in it, really pushed things over the top.

I wished my house could have been cool like that, but with my grandparents living in the guest room, a full-sized poster of Black Sabbath's *Master of Reality*, somehow didn't seem appropriate.

Nearing Mike's doorway, I heard a booming laugh which told me one of the neighborhood's biggest smart-asses was already there. His name was Vance, and because of his propensity to say things that really pissed me off, I'd force-fed him a mouthful of mud a time or two. He was a pretty annoying guy, but because I'd promised to be a kinder-gentler person in recent months, I hadn't had to beat him too bloody in quite a while. That had been good for neighborhood relations, along with the fact that he and I were actually enjoying each other's company as of late. So, preparing myself for an evening of sarcasm and dim-wit, I rounded the corner, readying myself for what was to come.

Entering the room, I was greeted by two hellos. One from Vance, who sat in Mike's red, oversized bean bag chair. And the other from Todd, another friend of ours who's metal-flake blue Stingray was in the pile of bikes out back.

Mike was there too, facing the wall with his back to the room. He didn't say anything at first. Then, a moment after I greeted the other two boys, he mumbled his best hello, while carefully placing the needle of his turntable on one of his brand new records. Once the LP was cued up, Mike turned around slowly, before ceremonially welcoming us to what he coined "A Gathering."

We all sat on one chair or another as Mike filled us in on what he'd planned for the evening. He spoke softly, in a nearly hypnotic tone, and as he did I noticed that my friends were listening to him like he was some kind of prophet. From the look of things, there was no question that the other two guys were on board with the recent occult goings on which seemed to be the latest cold-weather trend. They didn't seem surprised by any of it, and as Mike went on about spells and incantations, I realized right then that they'd most likely been to one of Mike's gatherings in the recent past.

It was a bit unnerving that Mike had become the Master of Ceremonies, but despite the feeling that a child had gotten hold of his father's gun, there was a certain charismatic charm to him that made me feel somewhat safe, despite the relative danger of recent events.

Mike went on about this and that, and as he did, we watched him set up what was beginning to look like a ceremonial altar. First he produced a dark lavender tapestry that he snapped in the air like an unholy tablecloth. Then he held the cloth before us like a magician, before draping it lengthwise over a gnarled wooden table.

Mike looked down upon his creation for a moment, then, after making sure everything was just right, he lit a match, before slowly running his fingers through the flame.

Mesmerized by it all, I watched the flame flicker as it slowly slid around his fingertips. I half expected him to do the lick-your-fingers-and-pinch-out-the-match trick, but, to my surprise, he spared us the theatrics, lighting the remainder of a half-melted candle, which he placed on the table before us.

Flickering at first, the flame soon grew taller, until it burned with an odd twist of black smoke that rose from its pointed end. I was entranced by the flame as it danced before me, with a heart of sulfur yellow, beneath a crest of crimson red.

Mike sat behind the low-slung table, before placing his continually bare feet lotus-style atop each leg. He turned in place, reaching behind him to where he'd stowed something prior to our arrival. Once he had hold of it, he paused for a moment, before turning to face us with the Grimoire in his hands.

Placing the book atop the make-shift altar, Mike began to run his fingers through the candle's flame. I didn't like where any of this was headed, but before I could voice my concerns about the book and what Mike had suggested days earlier, he looked at me as he played with the fire, saying, "Don't worry Lee. We're not going to do THAT."

I was somewhat relieved by his comment, but also a bit creeped-out, for as Mike spoke to me, the flame that should have been burning his fingers, was dancing around them as if he had entranced the fire itself. I stared in disbelief as he danced with the flame, then, I gasped, as he ran his wrists and forearms through the fire. There was something very wrong going on, and I knew it. Mike should have been burned without question. But instead, for some freakish reason, the flame simply danced around him.

What I was seeing was much more than just the simple matter of Mike quickly passing his hands through the fire. He could have done that I suppose, but in this case what I was seeing had nothing to do with theatrics. For as I watched the flame cozy-up next to his skin, in some otherworldly way, it seemed as if the fire had "chosen" not to burn him.

What I was seeing was weird, and what I was seeing was wrong, because as far as I knew, fire wasn't EVER supposed to think.

As Mike continued his freakish communion with the candle, I was troubled by his irreverence to the fire, but was awed by his command over the flame. We would all learn in due time that it wasn't so much a command he had over the fire, but rather a lack of respect that we were seeing. And as you can imagine, when someone loses respect for the fire, it has a nasty way of reminding that person who's really in control.

But that lesson would have to wait for now. For in the moment, as the flame danced on Mike's fingertips like an imp on a pin cushion, I felt for the first time that Mike must surely have been in league with The Devil. And in retrospect, I'm certain that he was.

As we watched the freakish fire-dance, the sun began to set. And as the room became darker and darker, the flickering flame moved about, casting crazed shadows on the wall that danced in unnatural ways.

I watched the shadowy arms feel their way around the room, as Mike lit several more candles that he'd retrieved from a large wooden box. In this box were many things that Mike claimed to have been given by his older brother Frank. According to Mike, his brother was quite the sorcerer himself, and as we were told, he'd passed down a thing or two to Mike along the way.

I wasn't sold on the concept that Frank had been as careless with his magical box as Mike had suggested. But since Mike did have possession of the box, and its entire contents, who was I to argue about how he got his hands on it. Additionally, Mike told us that since Frank had moved in with his long-time girlfriend, he had given Mike permission to use all of the things that he'd left in his room, at least until he came home to claim them.

That of course, wasn't the entire truth, at least not the part about Mike having permission to rifle through Frank's belongings. Sure, Frank had moved in with his girlfriend somewhere in town. But if he had known anything about what Mike was really up to, Mike would have gotten the ass kicking of his life. Especially because

Frank had given him strict orders not to mess with anything in his room… especially the things in the old wooden box.

But there we were. With the box lid open, and the darkest, most dangerous book ever, in the hands of a teenage boy, who didn't have reverence for the flame.

Squirming a bit, I sat cross legged, waiting to see what Mike had up his sleeve. Naturally, the little voice in my head was telling me to get out while I still could, but I imagined it wouldn't be acceptable to excuse myself right in the middle of some kind of ritual. And besides, as creepy as the book with the torn cover was, my adrenaline was firing on all cylinders… and I liked it.

Mike proceeded with the gathering, opening the Grimoire with a devilish grin. Looking down at the page, he took a deep breath, probably for affect, before slowly turning the book around so that we could see the words printed atop the page's header.

I squinted as he held the book before us, leaning into the glow of the candles, until I could faintly read the words "To summon forth a Demon."

"Ooooooh-kay," I thought. "This is not good. NOT a good idea at all."

Mike of course, didn't agree, and as the three of us looked at him while trying to decide if he was serious, I asked him the question we all had on our minds.

"Mike," I asked, "ARE YOU OUT OF YOUR GOD-DAMNED MIND?"

He said nothing. Instead, he just looked at me, with flames flickering in his eyes.

Mike waited a moment, then, after another dramatic pause, he went on to pontificate about how he knew everything there was to know about this kind of thing, and how much fun it would be to scare up something wretched, in all of its hideousness. He promised he'd be able to get rid of it of course, and banish it right back to where it came from just as soon as things got out of hand. But as much as I felt Mike had somewhat of a handle on this sort of thing, deep down inside, I knew that he was completely full of crap.

I was like, "Dude, this thing will eat you alive! And if it does get loose, there's NO WAY you'll be able to control it!"

Mike dismissed my interjection as ramblings, then went on to say that he felt this was something he needed to do, and that after he'd done it, his actions would serve notice to the underworld that "Mike The Sorcerer" had finally arrived.

I told him sternly, "Mike, you can scare up anything you want to, but leave me out of this, okay? I've had enough demons lurking around for one lifetime, and since there isn't a basement at my house, I can't stomach the thought of him grinning at me from my half opened closet!"

My friends looked at me like I was completely over reacting. "Dude," Todd said, "It's just something fun for us to do. Mellow out."

I took the deep breath, before asking very slowly, "Alright Mike, what are you proposing here?" Once again he said nothing, as he toyed with the flame as if it was his new, best friend. I was about to speak up, when he asked rhetorically, "Is everybody in?"

Mike stood up, turning off the record that had been providing the soundtrack to the rapidly darkening gathering. Then, he slowly sat down, explaining what he'd planned, and how he was going to do it. He went on about how there was only one word printed on the Grimoire's page, and how that singular word be the crucial link in summoning forth a demon that was anxiously awaiting its release. As he continued, I imagined a hellish waiting room filled with demons, awaiting their call on the overhead intercom. This made me wonder and ask, "Mike, are there several types of demons that are just hanging around, waiting for the call? And if so, just what kind of demon are we going to be calling forth here?"

None of us knew the answer to that question, especially Mike. So, instead of answering me, he just pointed to a picture on the page he'd previously chosen, saying "I guess that one."

The three of us leaned forward in order to see the demon that Mike had chosen as our companion for the evening. There, in the candlelight, the image looked so small, almost as if it was nothing more than an errant smudge of charcoal on the paper. It was a harmless looking image I suppose. Of an old man standing next to a horse-drawn wagon filled with straw. The man was dressed like a peasant, while at his feet, sat a small, furry dog.

We all agreed that the drawing didn't look too bad, and if the worst thing to happen was a horse showed up in the room, we could all live with that. I chimed in with the fact that Mike's room was already a pig-sty, then, after we all chuckled a moment, Mike asked if we were ready to call the demon forth.

As he began, I could hear that familiar voice saying, "Get the hell out NOW!" But for some reason I chose to act like an idiot, pushing the voice aside, in exchange for a quick rush, and a lifetime of trouble.

So I sat there… as Mike began, saying,

"There's only one word in the spell, and it has six letters.

You read it once as it is written.
Then you read it again, omitting the last letter.
Then again, omitting the last two.
Then again, omitting the last three.

Until you are left with just one letter.

The letter O."

It seemed so easy. It seemed so simple. And it seemed so very, very wrong.

So we did it. Just the way we shouldn't have.

"All-together now," Mike said, like a deranged orchestra conductor. "All together now."

Vance was like, "Wait! Make sure we have the word right!" He had a good point, as we didn't want to be conjuring up anything from one of the book's other pages. Realizing that, we studied the strange word a moment longer, until slowly, in unison, we all began to chant.

Like Gregorian Monks, we chanted long and slow, to be sure we got the word right. Electricity filled the air, then, after five chant cycles, we finished with the letter *O*, before looking sheepishly around the room.

There were shadows dancing about, cast by a flame that burned brighter than ever. They swayed to and fro, wildly at times, but for some odd reason none of us seemed to notice.

"Let's do it again," Mike said. "I don't see a demon, so let's do it again!"

That's where we definitely should have stopped, and written the whole thing off to a good-old session of Bloody Mary. But Mike was hell-bent upon raising a demon. And since nothing had happened yet, and it didn't seem like anything would, we all chanted again, until we'd completed three separate chant sequences in all.

As I looked around the room, I let out a deep sigh of relief at the thought that we may have actually dodged the demonic bullet from Hell. Seeing that nothing had happened, I began to relax, and I actually started to believe that I'd be sleeping that night without a pillow over my head. That was a nice thought. One that I would have loved to have seen come true. But as luck would have it, there wouldn't be any sleeping that particular night, because what we had called upon moments earlier was well on its way toward making our acquaintance.

Maybe he needed to freshen-up a bit before making an appearance. Or maybe he needed to polish his hooves. But regardless of what held him up for a moment, all we had to do was wait a few seconds for the elevator from Hell to arrive.

One, two, three seconds passed, as we sat cross-legged in the dimly lit room. No one said a word as we stared at the book, each of us expecting something, while none of us knew exactly what it was to be.

During all of this, Mike was trying his hardest to keep his best game-face on. But even he knew that his credibility was going to take a huge hit, unless something extremely creepy happened, very, very soon.

Luckily for Mike, tarnished credibility wasn't something he was going to have to worry about that particular evening. In fact, after the fires were put out, and Hell had found a cozy new home on Earth, Mike's credibility was the last thing any of us would be concerning ourselves with, for we were on the cusp of our last moment of innocence, a moment that burned away with a sense of friction in the air.

There was an acrid smell, reminiscent of when a tire burns in the wheel-well. It may have been the fabric of time wrinkling. Or maybe it was the sense that something was pushing through the membrane that lies between where we are, and where other things dwell. None of us was quite sure what was really happening, only that we sensed something in the air, just a second before the elevator arrived, and You-Know-Who joined the party.

He came up from below, and as the elevator doors opened, I could almost hear him say, "First Floor, Women's Hosiery, Intimate Apparel... and FOOLISH TEENAGE BOYS!"

Well, maybe he didn't come up quite that way. But he sure did come. And for the record, I smelled him first, just a second before he burst through the wall.

It was a hellish creature, shadowy and slim, and it sprang from the wall like it had been shot from a cannon. It leaped like a gazelle, bounding into the room on spindly legs that came straight from the pages of Dante's Inferno. The thing was comprised of pure shadow, a living wisp of smoke that bounded deer-like through the room. We gazed in horror as it zig-zagged back and forth, then, as it stood on its rear legs, it hopped up and down in a freakish dance.

I was frozen in fear as the thing twisted before us, half covering my eyes, yet unable to look away. It stood there a moment, with trails of smoke twisting from its skin, then, it bounded toward us, grinning wildly with glowing, yellow eyes.

The thing approached on its spindly legs, coming so close we were nearly trampled by its hooves. The demon shimmered as it leaned over us, before it leaped over the table, knocking both the Grimoire and the candles to the floor.

Mike scrambled to his knees as the candles rolled onto his bedroom's thick, shag carpeting. He tried to pick them up, but within seconds several small fires erupted as the flames quickly found their mark.

I imagine the demon must have been laughing as we desperately tried to snuff out the flames. And it certainly must have taken pleasure in knowing the home was likely to become an inferno. I suppose it very well would have, had Mike not been the quickest fat kid I'd ever seen. He moved wickedly fast, blotting out fire after fire with just the palms of his hands. Then, as he busted a move that might even have impressed the demon, he picked up his bean bag chair, snuffing-out the flames like it was a giant fire blotter.

With the fire suitably contained, we found ourselves in total darkness, except for the hundreds of glowing embers that were burning deep within the carpet. The demon-thing screeched, as it jumped around the room, and as it did, I rolled up in a ball, choking on the smell of burned nylon, and the rot of moss that had come up from below.

As I lay on the smoldering carpet, I heard one of the others yelling for someone to open the door. For a moment it sounded like someone was going to do just that. But then, just as I heard movement to my left, there was a loud crash that sounded like someone had walked through a plate glass window.

When I heard the crash, I rolled up like a pill bug, as several things flew around the room. There was yelling, and screaming, and a weird buzzing sound, just a moment before something large fell to the ground beside me.

Whatever had fallen, it was big. And I had no doubt that it was someone's freshly dead corpse. I was frozen in place, afraid to stretch out my legs for fear of kicking whoever it was that lay dead beside me. I felt we were doomed, until the lights came on, when I saw Mike standing on a badly bloodied foot, beside a shattered, glass-topped coffee table.

Vance lay beside me in a heap, babbling to himself with crazed, wild eyes, while Todd just sat on the floor, as if he'd been knocked on his ass by a semi-truck. The demon-thing seemed to have disappeared. Now, as I looked around the room with squinted eyes, all I could see was stagnant smoke, and a strange stillness that felt most unsettling. We just stared at one another, mostly out of disbelief, until Mike chimed-in, as loudly as possible…

"AREN'T YOU GUYS GOING TO HELP ME?" He yelled, "I'M BLEEDING TO DEATH HERE!"

As usual, Mike was being a tad overly dramatic. But seeing that the shattered tabletop had filleted his foot wide-open, we had no choice but to spring into action. Needing to find something that would work as a make-shift bandage, I looked around the room, but all I could find within reach was a basket of soiled laundry, and a few grass stained socks.

I paused a moment to assess the situation. The demon had run off into the house, most likely sometime between the onset of the fires and Mike's unfortunate table smashing incident. Where it was I hadn't a clue, other than that it was no longer in the room, and no longer on my radar. For all I knew, it could have been hiding just around the corner, so that it could pull another "Sudden-Demon" moment the second we walked out there. I'd had enough of those for one evening, so, choosing to blot the thing out of my mind for a moment, I decided to concentrate on helping Mike, rather than focus on something I wished would go away.

As I searched for some kind of bandage material, I reluctantly stuck my head out the doorway, before looking both ways down the hall. To my left was the kitchen, and to my right was the hallway bathroom, which seemed the most logical place to find something sterile. I was about to head straight there, when common sense reminded me that there was little or no chance of finding a clean bandage in a bathroom filled with Mike's dog-eared porno mags.

"Bad idea," I thought. "Better go to the kitchen."

I was right; the kitchen was the place to go. Only that the pesky demon had made venturing in that direction a very risky proposition. I didn't want to leave the room, except that the puddle of blood beneath Mike's foot was growing, and he was starting to get a look on his face that was quite disconcerting.

Taking a deep breath, I crept toward the kitchen, while flipping on every light switch within reach. The lights came on, and to my delight, there wasn't a demon to be seen. Moving fast, I grabbed a clean dish towel, soaking it with water from the kitchen sink. Once it was wet, I grabbed another towel, before sprinting back to Mike's bedroom. When I returned, Mike was sitting cross-legged on his bean bag chair amid the smoldering ruins of his once pristine room. He'd pressed a wadded-up t-shirt against the wound, and as I approached, he lifted the bloody shirt from his foot, poking his finger against a large flap of skin that was hanging from his instep.

I handed him the towel, while Mike put on his best I-didn't-have-anything-to-do-with-it face. Ordinarily I would have allowed him to continue deluding himself and everyone around him. But this time, I looked him dead in the eye, telling him exactly the way it was.

"Mike," I said, "YOU'RE A GOD-DAMNED IDIOT!"

I believe Mike was just about to admit that he was in way over his head, when across the room, Vance looked up from his flopped heap, saying, "Do you guys think that was real? Do you think that really happened?"

"NOOOO... It wasn't real," I told him. "And now that you've believed that one, let me tell you about how I just rolled my eyes back and saw my BRAIN!"

I was like, "OF COURSE IT WAS REAL, YOU IDIOT! And now that it's loose, I'm sure it's going to visit you, just as soon as you're tucked in for the night!"

Vance hoped I was kidding, as did the rest of the guys in the room. But despite my attempt at sarcasm, all four of us knew deep down inside there may have been truth to my words.

Nobody said a word as it all sank in. Then, as we all realized there was nothing more we could do about the situation, Mike's little gathering had officially come to an end.

Saying my goodbyes, I walked across the living room with a world-class case of the creeps. Mike would live, that I knew. So, heading out the garage-side door, I quickly walked to my bike which was just a few yards away.

Night-time had never been darker. And I think that in many ways, the shadows seemed darker still. I fumbled through the bikes until my hands found my own, then, after mounting the Stingray as quickly as I could, I pedaled like a madman, with the burning feel of demon eyes on my back.

I arrived home within minutes, where dinner came and went without the slightest mention of what had just happened. That was all for the better, given that "I went over to Mike's, and we summoned up a demon," wouldn't have been the best topic of conversation during dinner. So I pretended that nothing had happened, while I picked at my food, lost in thought over the events of the evening, and their possible repercussions down the line.

"Where did the demon go?" I wondered. And more importantly... "When will it be back?"

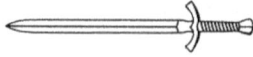

After dinner, I returned to my room with one hell of a load on my mind. The thought of something hellish running amuck was quite unsettling, as was the notion that the demon might leer at me while I slept. I didn't want that thing staring at me from a dark corner of my room, nor did I want to see its pointed fingers curled around the crack of my partially opened closet. So, I turned on every light in my room, before cramming the upper edge of my desk chair against the closet's knobs, just to be on the safe-side.

How I slept that night I'll never know. But somehow I did, and soon enough the routine of normal life filtered its way back into my reality. Time passed, and although I knew the demon was out there somewhere, I did my best to put it, and the memory of that evening, far into the back of my mind.

One night, a couple of weeks after the demon ran free, my father asked if I wouldn't mind taking the dog out for his evening constitutional. I said "Sure," figuring that I could also take the trash out to the cans on the very same run.

I shook the dog's leash up and down, then, after he was suitably worked-up, I clipped onto his collar before heading out the door. With the trash bag in tow, we headed through a courtyard, walking over a row of stepping stones that bypassed the garage. The dog led the way, leading me to a coach-lamp that my father had installed the previous summer. He lifted his leg, peeing all over the thing, before looking up with the "Where to now?" look.

I said "Come-on boy," as we walked from the light toward the large barn-like doors at the entrance to the side yard. After setting the trash bag down, I swung the doors open as their hinges creaked loudly. The side yard was long and narrow, its air pulsing with a mossy chill that harkened back to The Thumping Man. I paused a moment before stepping through the threshold, immediately taken aback by how dark it was that evening. It was unusually dark. So much so, that as the hound and I shuffled toward the garbage cans, not a single one of them could be seen.

It wasn't the kind of night where you wanted to be alone, nor was it the kind of night where either of us had any business poking around in the dark. With that in mind, I figured that rather than drag the dog up and down the street, I'd simply un-clip his leash so he could run off and do his thing in the adjacent side yard.

I felt my way down the taut, chain leash until my fingers found the clip on his collar. With a snap the dog was loose, running far into the yard with his dog-tags jingling. He had business to take care of, and as he did what dogs do, I shuffled toward the trashcans, doing my best not to trip and kill myself.

Something was amiss. Something other than the dark, and the cold, and the feeling that we'd walked into a trap. There was a murky wetness in the air. The kind of wetness you feel when you're changing a tire on a lonely road, while something large rustles in the bushes.

A touch of panic rose up as I felt my way through the darkness while hoping like hell that I didn't bump into something with deer-feet, or a twisted spike that defied all reason.

Soon enough, I stumbled into a trash can, nearly knocking it over in the process. After feeling around for the handle, I tossed in the trash bag, before slamming the lid closed with a loud, metallic *clang!*

The job was done. Now all I had to do was find the dog and get the hell out of Dodge. He had to be nearby, but I couldn't tell where. All I knew was that he'd run off to do his duty, somewhere in the expanse of the backyard.

As I listened for the jingling sound of his collar, I hoped he hadn't wandered too far away. Yet as much as I wanted to believe that, the sense that I was alone became undeniable. He certainly wasn't in the dog-run, nor was he anywhere nearby. So I called out to him... But despite my call, all I could hear was the wind.

Since he wasn't in the dog-run, I figured he may have run off into the garden, or the small grove of fruit trees beside the southern fence-line. I called out over and over, until just as I was beginning to feel a surge of panic rise up, I heard a familiar jingle, just around the corner.

"That's him!" I thought. "The silly beast has probably been drinking out of the pool again!"

With a sigh of relief, I walked in the direction of the jingling sound. The yard was every bit as dark as the dog run was, yet as I approached the far end of the home, I began to see a strange, orange glow coming from the pool patio area. It was an unnatural looking light, one that faded from crimson red, to yellowish orange as it phased from one color to the next. I paused a moment as the fiery glow rose and fell, until a shadow moved within the flame that nearly made my skin crawl.

There was something within the light that seemed very wrong. Something within its core that told me to run and never look back. But I couldn't do that, for my dog was somewhere in the yard, and I no choice but to save him.

So I crept toward the corner of the house. And when I peered around the bend, nothing on Earth could have prepared me for what I saw…

Before me stood my dog with his tail out and chest forward, facing an adversary that simply should not have been. It was another dog, of medium height and build. It looked very much like any other dog you'd see walking in the park, except for one tiny detail…

It was on fire.

I was horrified by what I saw, for the creature must surely have come straight out of Hell. It was definitely a dog of some kind, but that's where the resemblance ended. This thing was alive with fire, aglow with flames that wicked from its body as if it was a living torch. The creature stared at me as it tilted its head from side to side, and as it did, the flames on its back seemed to grow in intensity.

Everything about that moment defied logic, yet for all the horror, one thing became crystal clear. The dog hadn't been lit on fire… It was *made* of fire. And as its glowing eyes looked into my soul, I knew it was time to run.

Reacting on instinct, I grabbed my dog's collar, in an attempt to pull him backward. I pulled as hard as I could, but the muscular dog stood his ground. He was ready to fight, to what end I don't know, showing his teeth to the demon as if he was ready to lock horns. I cried out as I pulled, begging the dog to run for his life before we were both consumed with fire. He stood fast for a moment, then, as the Fire-Dog cocked its head to one side, something flashed across its flaming eyes that made my blood run cold.

My dog had seen it too, for in that moment, whatever he'd seen in the creature's eyes seemed to have re-wired his instincts. Suddenly his whole demeanor changed, as he quickly spun in place, nearly knocking me over as he bolted toward the vegetable garden.

We ran for our lives, tearing through the garden as the Fire Dog took chase. It was close. So close, that as we ran, its flaming fur back-lit the yard and everything around it. I could feel the demon's heat as we rounded the fruit trees, then, as the beast was nearly upon me, it skidded to a stop, as if it had come across some type of unnatural border.

I haven't a clue why it stopped, nor do I know what kept it from coming any closer. I only know that as we ran for our lives, the demon paced back and forth with a frighteningly uneasy gait.

As we ran, I paused by the fence-line to look at the beast once more. The Fire Dog stared at me, turning its head from side to side as flames danced on its fur. In many ways it was just a dog, standing there with a look on its face that could have meant many things.

"What is this thing?" I thought, as the glow from its fur-fire illuminated the garden. "What is it, and why does it look so familiar?"

A second passed, then two, as I stood there ready to run . . . When suddenly, I was overcome with a rush of realization that was nearly overwhelming.

"HOLY CRAP!" I thought. "I know where I've seen it... IT'S THE DOG FROM THE GRIMOIRE!"

That it was. It was the very same dog -- the dog that was sitting quietly by his master's side, partially hidden by the shadow of the horse-drawn cart.

"What the hell is HE doing here," I thought. "And why is he consumed in flames?"

"BECAUSE IT'S A DEMON!" Mike's voice said. "IT'S AN OLD WORLD DEMON!"

And with that, I ran... as if The Devil was chasing me.

It's been nearly forty years since I saw the Fire Dog. And

although I haven't seen him since, I have seen his image in print several times over. Being both frightened and fascinated by what I saw that night, I was eager to find out more about him. But knowing that it's not a good idea to stir up things long laid to rest, I cautiously researched his origin, while being careful not to tread too close to the flame where, according to some, he still resides.

The search began decades after my initial encounter, a great many years which had brought both insight and knowledge to my quest. To begin my search for the truth, I researched the possibility that there may have been another copy of the old Grimoire somewhere in the world.

With the help of a close friend, I searched tirelessly, throughout a covert network, above and below ground. No stone was unturned, until finally, after searching world-wide, we secured a copy of the book from a collector overseas.

We waited patiently for the book to arrive, and when it finally did, she and I poured over it as if it was the only book in the world. As we turned the pages, images of the past burned brightly once again, affecting me in such a way that I needed to sit down, before continuing any further.

Each page snapped with a stiff report as I peeled them back. Yet for all my breathless anticipation, the images I so desperately needed to see, seemed to have been washed away with time. There were spells and incantations on every page, mixed in with woodcut images and the like. But for all my gasping and toe-curling, neither the demon-chant, nor the demons themselves appeared.

With a trembling hand, I brushed the pages aside, until only the cover remained. The demons were gone, as was the spell we'd chanted that fall evening. I felt like we'd been cheated somehow… until we looked at one another, as something became glaringly obvious.

The book had been stripped of its teeth, cleansed of any and all ways that might allow a person to unleash the kind of thing that ran wild that day. Gone was the image of The Thumping Man, as was the likeness of the old man and the straw-cart, with the obedient dog by his side.

I was incensed at the thought that someone would selectively abbreviate the works of others simply to allay their own fears. But sadly, as I soon learned, that is often the case. Doing a bit of research, I discovered that over the years, several publishing houses had taken it upon themselves to censor certain books that had been deemed "Unsavory" or, even more-so, "Dangerous." We learned that the book we sought had fallen into that criteria, and that the Grimoire I speak of is notoriously feared by many in the literary world, so much, in fact, that all runs of the book post-dating the 1950s, have had all the dark magic removed from within.

Doing further research, we learned that the Grimoire Mike had in his possession was one of only a few in existence, and that it was quite possible the book dated back two hundred years or more. Moreover, I learned that editions such as Mike's, which contained the rare wood-cut images, may even have been translated directly from Druidic script.

Learning of this, we became more eager than ever to get our hands on an older copy of the book. My friend and I explored nearly every avenue, but as one lead after another dried up, we began to fear there might not have been an accessible copy left on earth. We'd nearly given up hope when, out of the blue, an international contact discovered a copy in Northern Ireland.

You can imagine our excitement upon hearing the news, as the book was finally within our grasp. Wasting no time, we secured plans for the book's delivery, having it shipped immediately, using a confirmed, respected carrier.

I waited nearly two weeks for its delivery, but sadly, as I was later told, it was last seen being loaded onto an airplane headed for Florida.

So ends the story of The Grimoire, a book that, for the time-being, simply doesn't want to be found. And what of the demon who leaped from the wall that dark evening? Well, let's just say he's still around, although he treads more carefully in my presence now that my power has matured.

And The Fire Dog... what of he?

Well, as it turns out, he's quite an interesting creature. Look him up if you'd like. He's in many books of shadows, for it seems that, according to ancient folklore, when spells have been cast on the first moonless night of fall... often times, a fiery dog is seen.

The Devil Fish

The big day had finally arrived. And now, as I watched the men from the port-authority load our fishing gear into the cargo hold of our seaplane, I began to feel the butterflies in my stomach that always preceded an incredible adventure.

Dad winked at me as the last of our gear was loaded up, then, after each of the watertight doors were fastened down, he nodded, as it was time to saddle-up.

After stepping onto the small entry ladder, I crammed through the narrow doorway as I entered my old friend. She was a Grumman Goose, one of the most beautiful aircraft ever built. And as I made my way toward the co-pilot's seat, she reached out and touched me in the most ethereal way.

I plopped down on the hard steel seat, atop a leathery pad that slid back and forth. The seat was cold, and I donned my down jacket before leaning against the backrest.

"Let's get going, and warm her up!" I yelled over my shoulder. "I'm freezing to death up here!"

Maybe I wasn't dying, but it sure was cold. So I donned a set of headphones, in the hope they'd work like earmuffs, until the morning sun filled the cockpit.

They worked a bit, until the starboard engine started, sending a freezing blast of air through the cockpit's side window. I closed the window as quickly as I could, before tightening my seat belt as the airplane's engines throttled-up. "We're off on another adventure!" I yelled out, as The Goose rolled down the tarmac. "We're gonna have fun!"

My father tapped me on the shoulder, before handing me a pair of sunglasses. They were the same kind of glasses he wore, and as I put them on, I felt like the biggest boy in the world.

"We're off, Sonny Boy," Dad said. "We're going to have all sorts of fun!"

He was right; we were going to have a good time. Then, as a flurry of air-traffic lingo came over the radio, he put his finger to his lips, as we were cleared for flight on that beautiful summer morning.

The Goose rolled into the water, before heading West, under the Vincent Thomas Bridge. Once we'd cleared the bridge, it was time to fly, and with our nose to the wind, we blasted skyward, out and over The Los Angeles Harbor's shipping channel.

The take-off was exhilarating, so much so, that I dug my nails into the leather seat cushion. I nearly held my breath as we cleared the breakwater, then, as we flew over the Pacific, I looked into the water, searching for signs of the giant fish that swam in the channel back then. Most of these fish were sharks, grown to such gigantic proportions that you'd have thought you were flying over a full grown whale.

I remember vividly, how we were skimming above the swells, when my father spotted something large breaking the surface roughly a quarter mile away. From our vantage point in the sky, the jet-black object looked like a giant dorsal fin, or maybe even the conning tower of a submarine that had just surfaced.

As the twin-engine seaplane quickly narrowed the gap, the mysterious object began to slip beneath the sea's glassy surface. In order to get a better look at it, we sharply rose to altitude, before dipping a wing, for a spiral look-down at what had just sounded.

As we tipped our wing, I looked down through the open side window. The early morning water was flat and clear, and as we spiraled above the object's last known position, something amazing caught my eye, just below the surface.

It was a shark. A fish so large I'd never seen anything like it. Nearly thirty feet long, and two yards wide, it glided through the water like a small submarine. As I tried to identify the species, I thought it might have been a giant basking shark. But then, as I saw its chiseled, pointed snout, I knew for sure that it was all predator. We were in awe of the fish as it swam below us, then, after circling the beast a minute or so, the shark sounded deeply, to where it was no longer visible.

"Guess she sounded," I said to my father. "The thing's gone so deep, I can't see it anymore." He nodded in agreement, before we headed westward, toward the crude landing facility at Catalina Island's Southern end.

The Goose was fast, and within minutes we had a clear view of the island. Buzzing the rocky coast, we headed north toward the rough-cut breakwater at land's bitter end. As I looked into the water, I could see huge kelp forests shimmering just below the surface. There were countless fish in those forests, and I was eager to catch as many as I could, just as soon as we got settled in.

After throttling-up to increase speed, we nosed toward the sea on our final approach. That part of the flight always scared me, and I closed my eyes just before we hit the water. There was a giant *splosh* as we slammed the water's surface, then, as we slowed to cruising speed, water sheeted from the windshield as if we'd just flown through a car wash.

As we motored toward the east-end boat ramp, I could see our driver waving to us from the cliff-side service road. We motored toward the boat ramp, then, after dropping the landing gear, the Goose rolled up the gravel launch ramp with a thunderous roar, and a hell of a lot of prop-pitch. Once level, we taxied onto the small, circular round-a-bout, before doing a tail-spin that oriented the airplane seaward again. After shut-down, we piled out of the Goose, transferring our bags to an old Town-and Country station wagon that was our ride into town.

Once our gear was loaded up, we drove down the craggy service road that snaked along the island's Eastern shore. It was a short drive, and within minutes we'd arrived at the turn-around that marked the end of the road. Back then, as it is today, gasoline powered vehicles weren't allowed in the city of Avalon. Because of that, unless you had a bicycle or golf cart, once you got to the turn-around, you had no choice but to hoof it to your destination.

Luckily for us, my father had made prior arrangements, and as soon as we parked in the turn-around, our driver loaded the bags onto a rolling luggage cart. Dad tipped the driver as I poked around the breakwater, then, with a loud whistle, he motioned for me to get a move on. I ran to his side, pushing the cart down the road just a few feet ahead of him.

We moved along, while everything we'd stacked so neatly did its best to fly off the cart. Bump, bump... *clang!* went the cart's metal wheels, and as I tried my best to keep it all together, my favorite tackle box flopped onto the ground.

"Dammit!" I yelled, as the box cart-wheeled end-over-end. "Now all my sinkers and hooks are gonna be all mixed up!"

"Relax Sonny Boy!" my father said with a smile. "Nothing bad ever happens when you're on vacation. And we've got several long days to sort the gear out!" He was right, so, rather than getting all uptight about a few mixed up hooks, I re-stacked the box between a couple of large suitcases.

We rolled down Main Street, past one tourist trap after another. There were several boutiques and art galleries, followed by a noisy waterfront bar with a row of fake palm trees set up out front. It was all so delightfully kitsch, and as we passed one oddity after another, I took it all in like a kid at the circus.

There were trinkets of all kinds being hawked on the boardwalk, all of them back-set with the striking view of Avalon Harbor. We passed the vendors one by one, until my feet hurt so badly that I relinquished control of the luggage cart. Before long, we rolled past the large, green fishing pier that's been an Avalon landmark for nearly a century. "It sure is green!" my father said with a laugh, "Leprosy Green!"

He was right, the paint was kind of ugly, but aside from that, I thought the fishing pier was a thing of beauty. It was the center of my universe, a place where things had happened that I'll never forget, and a place where, even to this day, I often long to be.

Just past the entrance to the pier, was the small, seaside hotel that we always stayed in. After a quick check in, and the obligatory talking-to from my dad, I was ready to see if anything interesting had happened on the island since my last visit a couple of months ago.

Sensing my excitement, my father greased me with five dollar's-worth of spending money, before heading off to find himself a good Bloody Mary. As we walked through the hotel lobby, we agreed to meet up at the room no later than three o'clock, which would give us plenty of time to freshen up before his business associates arrived on the afternoon ferry.

I was eagerly anticipating the arrival of the boat, because not only were his associates arriving, but their kids were as well, which always made for a fun time on the company sponsored getaways.

The boat wasn't due for hours, so I figured I'd kick around the wharf a while, in order to get the scoop on what had been going on since my last visit to the island.

I headed for the pier, knowing it was the best place to begin my recon. The weekend crowd was thick, and I ducked and dodged my share of tourists as I walked along the green, slatted planks. With nothing to do, I just roamed around, until the sight of something wondrous stopped me dead in my tracks. It was a fish, a gigantic blue marlin, hoisted up by its tail for all the world to see.

The fish was huge, perhaps three hundred pounds, and as I watched a crane-boom lift it high above the crowd, I couldn't help but feel its life had just been wasted. It was sad the way it hung from the gallows, and I couldn't help but think that after a few trophy photos, it would be cut down and left to rot in the mid-day sun. The thought of that end for such a regal beast just didn't sit right with me. And it left a bad taste in my mouth that I still have to this day.

I moved on, walking past a gawking crowd of tourists that looked like they'd never seen a fish before. The crowd thinned a bit, and soon I spied a row of commercial vessels that had made-fast to the pier's bitter-end. On board these boats were "Real" fishermen. Men who'd earned their furrowed brows from years of scanning the horizon for diving birds and boiling bait fish. There wasn't a landlubber among them, and knowing these guys were the real-deal, I figured they'd be the best source of information regarding where and when to catch myself something fishy.

The first boat I came across had a couple of men working on it, but neither of them looked like they were in the mood for talking. They looked way too salty for me to even hazard a query, so I passed them by, hoping to find someone to talk to who looked a bit more approachable.

I walked along the pier, past the tall ropes and rigging, until I came upon a boat that was occupied by just one crewman. I stood near the boat, figuring that after mulling around a while, I'd ask the guy a question just to break the ice.

It seemed like a good idea, but before I had the opportunity to inquire about the fishing, the man called out to me, asking if I could do him a favor.

"Hey little buddy, can you toss me that rope?" He asked with a smile. "The one right there!"

"Sure!" I said, as I picked it up. "Happy to be of service!"

After giving the rope a hearty toss, I watched the man loop it around a port-side cleat. He seemed pleasant enough, so I asked him, "How's it going?" And to my delight, I discovered he was more than willing to talk a while.

"My name's Larry," he said, as he fussed with a latch on the boat's transom door. "I'm the owner of this boat, and the ship's Captain too. Although sometimes I wish I had someone else to run her, so I could get a day off once in a while!"

I nodded as if I could actually relate, then, after we chatted for a while, I graduated from standing at the dock's edge, to sitting on the boat's port gunnel.

We talked about this and that, and as we did, Larry mentioned the tourists, and the yachts, and the general mayhem Summer-season was all about. I asked him about a lot of things, from the kind of fish he caught, to who made the best hamburger on the island. He was a really pleasant guy, but when I got around to asking how the fishing had been, he gave me an answer that made my hair stand on end.

"The fishing hasn't been good as of late," Larry said. "Because of The Devil Fish!"

I was like, "THE WHAT? The WHAT kind of fish?"

"The Devil Fish," He said. "Haven't you heard of it?"

"No," I told him. I'd never heard of The Devil Fish. But now that I had, there was no way I was going to leave the dock without learning all there was to know about him.

I could see by the look in Larry's eye that he realized he'd captured my interest. So, being the nice guy that he was, he sat down beside me, doing his best to tell a story that sounded almost unbelievable.

As he began, I interrupted him for just a moment, asking one thing for clarification.

"Are you talking about a Manta Ray?" I asked. "That kind of devil fish?"

"Nope," Larry said, "Not this one. He's called The Devil Fish because he glows like fire… just like The Devil!"

I was like, "HUH? Glowing like the Devil… is this for real?"

141

But then, as he told me the story, it began to make sense, in a weird sort of way.

It was the story of a monster. So wild a yarn, that I thought Larry might have been handing me a total line of crap. But as I listened to him speak, there was a thread of honesty in his voice that began to win me over. Besides, what did he have to gain by telling me such a story in the first place? So I decided to believe him unless the facts proved otherwise, which was a good move in this case, because later on that summer, I would learn with certainty, that The Devil Fish was as real as any beast on earth.

As I listened to the greatest fish story I'd ever heard, I learned that The Devil Fish made its first public appearance sometime during February of that year. No one knows where it came from, and no one knows where it went. But for a three-year period in the early 1970's, The Devil Fish terrorized many a person on the waters surrounding Catalina Island.

The understanding was that the beast made its debut late one night in the waters adjacent to the West end of the island. A place where the offshore banks rise up, and the food source is strong. Perhaps it was the abundance of bait fish that attracted the beast to the area. Or maybe it was the large schools of squid that frequented the banks in the wintertime. We'll never really know, but for whichever reason it was he showed up that evening, he made an entrance that's nothing short of legendary.

It was during a routine bait-net recovery that the creature was first sighted, and in his typical Devil Fish style, his entrance was a real show-stopper. According to Larry, a large off-shore trawler had been dragging a giant bait net in the hope of capturing a large amount of sardines. The night had begun like any other, with the boat moving slowly, and the net filling up at a rate that was predictable. Everything was going as planned, until deep down below, something latched onto the net, straining the ship's cable-boom to the breaking point.

Something huge had been caught in the net, but with the net suspended hundreds of feet down in the water column, there was no way of knowing exactly what it had snagged onto. With the net fully laden, and the cable spool whining under the strain of the load, the crew began the arduous task of winding over a thousand feet of cable back onto the boat's main-spool. Nearly a half hour passed as the trawler's net drew nearer, and as the anticipation rose, the crew stood deck-side waiting for the first glimpse of the bounty below.

As they stood in the glow of the crane-boom's light, the crew listened as the boom-arm creaked and groaned. It had never sounded like that before, and they knew from experience that they'd captured something gigantic. Surely it must have been a huge scoop of bait, for aside from a whale or a giant shark, there was nothing else down there large enough to fill the net. Nor was there anything large enough to make the cable spool smoke and whine in such a manner.

That's what you'd have thought, had the winch operator not felt a strange pulsation in the boom-arm that was most disconcerting. It was as if something was pulling against the ten-ton strain of the motor, with an enormous broom-like tail.

Feeling the creaking pulse in the over-loaded boom, the winch operator slowed the pull, and as he did, the boom-arm bent down so violently it nearly tore the through-bolts from the transom. This had never happened before, and as the load was pulled downward time and time again, the captain feathered the engines to relieve some pressure, before there was a catastrophic equipment failure.

In theory that was a good idea . . . To bleed-off some headway in the hope of lightening the load. But on that Winter night, the net-load was anything but normal, and the loss of momentum created just enough slack to give something huge a bit of elbow-room.

For a moment everything returned to normal. The boom regained its shape, and the winch motor quelled its screaming wail. "Resume normal operations!" the Captain called out to the boom operator. "She's all free'd up!"

Nobody really believed that… not one man on deck. But the Captain was the Captain, and on his ship, his word was the law. So, they re-started the pull, slowly at first, with the winch motor only, until the engines engaged, and the slack was pulled from the line.

Maybe the thing didn't like that. Or maybe it had grown tired of being dragged around. For according to Larry, just a second after the slack pulled from the cable, whatever it was they'd hooked into, began to buck the hundred ton ship as if they'd hooked into a whale.

That was a scary moment for the crew, because cutting the net loose wasn't an option, and pulling the load to the surface seemed dicier still.

"It's probably a huge load of squid!" The captain yelled. "There could be hundreds of them in the net… really big ones!"

Playing his hunch, the captain engaged the screws, as the boat's forward motion evened-out the pull. It worked for a moment, and after a minute or two, whatever it was they'd snared, began to move in sync with the smooth pull of the trawler.

"We're going to pull it up underway!" The captain said over the comm. "It's probably more squid than we've ever seen before!"

The winch-drum moaned as the net approached the surface, and as it did, every hand on deck stared down into the water, hoping for a glimpse of what was surely the catch of the year. At first there was only black water… Swirling like an eddy behind the powerful twin screws. When suddenly, there was a flash of light down below, that made no earthly sense whatsoever.

"Cut the lights!" the winch operator yelled. "There's something HUGE in the water!"

It took a moment for the halogen lights to dim. Then, as the red-hot filaments faded to black, the crew stared into the depths as their blood began to run cold.

Something terrifying was down there, a beast twice the boat's width that glowed like fire. The thing beneath them had the horns of The Devil, and as they gazed down in horror . . . It beat its monstrous wings.

As Larry continued the story, I began to get a major case of the creeps. "Could there really be things down there that glowed like that?" I wondered. "And, if there were, could they really grow that big?" It hardly seemed possible, but I listened none-the-less, as Larry went on with even stranger tales of recent run-ins with the hellish thing from the deep.

According to Larry, The Devil Fish had recently migrated from the West-end of the island, to the warmer waters just outside Avalon harbor. That wasn't good, for now that he was a local, sightings of the creature were beginning to surface with alarming regularity.

Larry told me that most of the run-ins involved people who were ferrying themselves between their buoyed motor yachts and the mainland. I thought that was comical in a way, because many of those stuffed shirts had no business being out on the water to begin with. And if The Devil Fish gave them a scare or two, it was all the better in my book.

But that wasn't the only problem. For apparently, the creature's strange attraction to light had become such an issue, that it was wreaking havoc on commercial fishermen who relied on deck-mounted lights to ply their trade.

That was a bummer, because the same lights that attracted fish and squid to the fisherman's nets, was also attracting The Devil Fish to the fishing boats. Larry told me that as long as "He" was swimming around, it was becoming harder and harder to find men willing to work the "Haunted" waters. That was bad enough, but then, as Larry told me that The Devil Fish was scaring all the other fish away, he began to get a far-away look in his eyes.

I listened intensely as Larry told me one Devil Fish story after another. Some involving incidents with private boats, while others involved commercial outfitters such as he. I listened to every word he said. Then, when I was sure that I knew as much as I could about the gigantic horned devil, I decided to do what any sensible person would . . .

I was going to try to catch it.

After thanking Larry for all his wisdom, I headed down the pier with my imagination running on high. "Could I really catch something that big?" I wondered. "And if I could, just how was I going to wrestle the thing back to the dock?"

I wasn't sure how I was going to do it, but as I pondered the logistics of such madness, a notion suddenly struck me that made things seem a bit more plausible. "Maybe the beast wasn't really as big as the stories made him out to be," I thought, "for he might have been big... but certainly not THAT big."

So, with that rationalization running through my mind, I actually began to believe that catching The Devil Fish was a good idea. Now all I had to do was convince someone else to accompany me on my wild adventure. And with a bit of luck, we might both become REALLY famous.

Of course, I never had the intention of actually boating the beast. For as far as I was concerned, simply getting it close enough to the boat for a photo-op was good enough for me. With that in mind, I figured that all we'd have to do was hook the monster, and let luck do the rest. After all, The Devil Fish couldn't possibly be as big as people said it was, and with any luck, we might even be able to tow it back to the dock with our boat.

The plan was set. Now all I needed to do was to find a partner in crime that was up to the task. There were many kids to choose from of course, especially with the rest of our group scheduled to arrive on the ferry later that afternoon. My recruitment options were numerous, but with some of the other kids being a bit "Soft," I was going to have to find a hardy soul, if my plan was to have any chance of succeeding.

After all, this was the business of wrangling monsters. And when doing so, softness will get you killed quicker than quick. The last thing I needed was to have some babbling nimrod yelling for his mommy when things got tough. I'd be better off alone than to allow that to happen, so, I decided to keep my plans to myself until the right person came along.

A couple of hours passed before I met my father back at our hotel room. After "spiffing-up" a bit, we headed to the pier where the Island Ferry had just arrived. I watched a deckhand work the lines, then, at the ring of a bell, tourists began spilling onto the dock like ants on a snow-cone.

I watched as the masses stumbled onto the dock. Many of them looking like they'd been sea sick for days. A woman with a huge sunflower on her dress began hurling over the side of the pier, gathering more bait-fish in one place than I'd ever seen before.

"Land-lubbers," I thought, as another woman spewed over the side, "land-lubbers who won't stand a chance out on the open sea."

My assessment was dead-on. Especially judging by the way many of them looked. There were brown sandals with socks, and an outrageously fat woman whose feet looked like eggplants. I glanced down as she walked by, and I could have sworn that there were corn-chips where her toenails should have been.

We stood beside a lamppost as the masses spilled from the ship, until I finally began to see some familiar faces in the crowd. We said our hellos, then, after I was introduced to few people I'd never met before, we all headed down the pier toward the downtown strip.

Among the crowd were many kids that I'd known for years. Summer friends I suppose, who followed their parents from one adventure to another much the same way that I did. It was good to see the summer crowd, and as we walked along the bright green pier, I began to feel magic in the air.

Walking back to our hotel, I scanned the crowd while my father chit-chatted with his associates. Most of the men I knew, as well as their wives and children too. We'd been to several resorts together over the years, and due to the social nature of my father's business, we were all part of a pretty tight clique.

It was a great group of kids for the most part, and over the years we'd chased a dragon or two. I knew who I liked, and I knew who I didn't. And I also knew just who was willing to take things to the extreme.

Having shared history with nearly all the other kids, it was easy enough to begin the sorting process. Some of the kids may have been up to the task, while others were a tad too introverted. I had all that night and the next day too, before I needed to figure things out. So I just walked along with the crowd, listening to several of the kids complain about how hot the sun was.

"Wow," I thought, "What a bunch of wimps! Haven't any of them ever been out in the sun before?" You'd have thought not, from the way most of them were acting. But then, just as I was beginning to think there wasn't a soul among them that was up to the task of wrangling The Devil Fish, I caught sight of a boy I'd never seen before.

He was a boy I didn't recognize. And I assumed he was the son of one of the men I'd recently been introduced to. There was something different about this guy. Something that distinguished him from the others in a way that was almost laughable. He looked a lot more rugged than the other kids did. And I could tell by the way he carried himself that he had a flair for adventure.

He seemed a likely candidate for the First-Mate position. Now all I had to do was get to know the guy, in short enough time to put my plan into action. I was wondering just how to do that, when I learned that he and his parents were staying at the same hotel we were. Using that as my intro, I walked up to the boy and introduced myself while our fathers chatted a while. He was really cool, and as our dads went on about this and that, he and I got caught up remarkably fast.

His name was Steve, and as we talked it seemed uncanny how much the two of us had in common. He was a fisherman just like I was, and from what I understood he was a darn good one too. There was no question that he was the best choice for a first-mate. Now all I had to do was mention my hair-ball plan, and see what he thought about it.

Reaching the hotel, I told Steve I'd catch up with him at the meet-and-greet-dinner. There would be plenty of time to tell him about The Devil Fish later on that evening. So, after we said our goodbyes, I headed back to our room in preparation for the big dinner party later on that evening.

Back in the room, I hopped in the shower for a quick rinse off before dinner. As the water ran, I stared at the fish designs on the shower tiles, wondering if The Devil Fish looked like any of them. There was a Hammerhead shark just a few tiles away from a Mermaid. Then, on another wall was a Marlin, with a happier look on his face than the one I'd seen strung up on the dock.

"No Devil Fish," I thought, "maybe because they'd need a bigger tile!"

As the water ran down my back, I thought about what Larry had told me earlier. "How big could this thing be?" I wondered. "And if we really do hook into it, do we stand a snowball's chance in Hell of actually bringing the thing to the boat?"

Those were two points we'd have plenty of time to ponder. But before any pondering could be done, there was one small detail that needed to be addressed, namely... What were we going to do about a boat?

"I'll figure that out later." I thought. "Where there's a will there's a way. And there's GOT to be a way."

So that was the plan. I was going to fly by the seat of my pants, and with any luck, we'd come back alive, with a monster in tow.

For starters, I figured I'd ask Steve if he wanted to go fishing later on that evening. Then, after we fished a while, I planned upon bringing up the whole Devil Fish thing.

I was going to butter him up with talk of fame and fortune, and how we were going to be recognized as the famous "Devil Fish Hunters." But before I had the opportunity to do that, things got a hell of a lot easier. That's because just as I was wondering about how to sell the whole monster-fishing trip to someone I barely knew, one of the kids at the dinner table mentioned The Devil Fish, and how scared he was about going in the water.

The kid was freaked-out, and as we listened to a story about a child-eating monster with flames coming out of its nose, even some of the adults at the table took notice. That's because it sounded like the story might have had a slight ring of truth to it. And the more he embellished it, the more frightening it became.

He went on about how late one night, a woman had been knocked from her boat by one of the creature's wings. Then, as she screamed for help, the beast came up beneath her, swallowing her whole.

Steve's eyes lit up as he listened to the story, and as I watched him swallow the bait, I knew for certain that he'd join me in my quest. "The day after tomorrow will be the day," I thought. "We'll load up the boat we don't have yet, and head out onto the high seas!"

Later on that night, long after Steve had become intrigued by the dinner-time story, I sat beside him outside the ice cream parlor, ready to spring my plan. As I saw it, we'd take one of the small skiffs that I was going to talk my father into renting. Then, after sneaking past prying eyes, we'd head out at first light, in pursuit of the prize.

Of course, there would be a few logistical glitches to work our way around, such as the boat-thing, for example. But those issues could be handled on-the-fly, and I really didn't see any reason to worry about them.

Going for broke, I told Steve all about my plan. At first I didn't know what he was going to say, but then, as I fluffed-up the story as best as I could, he was all-in before I'd even finished my proposal.

"That sounds AWESOME!" Steve said. "It's just the kind of thing I've always wanted to do!"

I was totally stoked, and quite happy that I'd made a friend who wasn't afraid to live a little. Now all we had to do was rustle-up some gear, before spending the entire next day, preparing for our adventure.

As I headed back to our room, I had one hell of a case of butterflies in my stomach. I stared at the ceiling for hours, planning my strategy, and making sure I had all the bases covered.

We'd need a boat of course... and lots and lots of bait. Then, we'd need at least two REALLY big hooks, and some bailing wire to make leaders from. The rest of the stuff would be easy to find, just a length of rope and a pail or two. I knew that most of the stuff we needed was in the junk pile behind the old Avalon Ballroom. So, except for a sturdy boat rod that we could easily rent at the tackle shop, all we needed to do was scrounge around the island, for a thing or two here and there.

The way I saw it, we'd be pretty much ready for anything, especially if The Devil Fish really wasn't that big. Now all I had to do was wait for the big day to arrive. So I closed my eyes and drifted off to sleep, amid the thoughts of bending rods, screaming reels, and something huge breaking the surface.

The next day was a blur, as we rustled up everything we'd need for the hunt. We found some heavy wire in a boat yard near the Ballroom, and thanks to my looking under a tarp or two, we soon found two giant-sized hooks that were nearly the size of my hand.

Now that we'd managed to scare up nearly everything on our list; all that needed to be done was for me to talk my father into renting a skiff for an extra day. He was reluctant at first, but seeing how we'd planned on renting one later in the week, he figured an extra day's rental wasn't going to hurt anyone. And besides, I promised him that if I did use it, I wouldn't leave sight of the harbor.

Now we were ready. Fully geared-up for anything that came our way. Everything had been set to plan. So, after doing a final gear-check, we spent the rest of the day pretending we had no plans at all, just in case one of the other kids got a little bit nosey.

That night, as Steve and I fished for Pile perch along the breakwater's rocks, I looked toward the moonlit harbor, wondering if The Devil Fish was nearby. "He's out there somewhere," I said to

Steve. "He's feeding in the moonlight, with his woman-eating mouth!"

"Do you really think he's that big?" Steve asked. "Do you think he might swallow us whole?"

"Nah!" I told him. "He hasn't really eaten anybody. That guy who told the story was a total dork!"

"Dork, dork, dork, DORK!" I said loudly, as I fanned my hands like a seal. "That guy was a total DORK!"

We laughed aloud, then, as Steve set the hook on a nice sized pile perch, he said to me, "Maybe after tomorrow's adventure, we'll be sitting here with a picture of him… if we come back alive!"

I smiled as he reeled in the fish, saying, "We've got no choice… We need to return the rental rod!"

Five A.M. came quickly, and as my alarm went off, I jumped out of bed like a jack in the box. I was ready to go within minutes, being sure to grab the lunch I'd packed, and a couple of cans of soda. As I set my fishing gear by the door, my father said, "Good Luck Sonny Boy! I hope you catch something big!" I told him I'd try, then, as he rolled to his side, he was out like a light.

I shut the room's door before tip-toeing down the dew-soaked stairs. Steve was waiting at the stair's landing, dressed for battle, in a pumpkin orange down jacket and gray hoodie sweatshirt. Taking stock of our gear, it appeared that we were ready, and on that foggy Southern California morning, I could feel success within our reach.

We walked toward the fishing pier, where a group of men were clustered around the bait-receiver. They were waiting to board one of the charter boats, and we waited for them to load-up before entering the bait shop.

The shop was small, and it only took a minute to scoop up what we needed. I stacked a pile of sinkers onto the counter, along with a box of frozen squid. The bait-shop guy knew that we were up to something, but being an islander, he'd definitely been in our shoes. "Ya goin' rock-codding?" He asked. "If you are, you'd best anchor-up off the East end."

"Yeah, my dad's taking us," I said. "That's pretty much the plan."

That worked for him, so, after giving him our room number, I checked-out a sturdy boat-rod with the biggest reel I'd ever seen.

Steve and I walked down the pier, before transiting to a finger dock where I'd tied up the skiff the night before. We placed our gear on the dew soaked dock boards, then, I steadied the craft as Steve climbed on board.

It was a capable little boat, but I knew in my heart that a sixteen foot skiff was probably a bit small for what we intended to do. But as I'd promised my father the night before, all we were going to do was fish near the harbor's entrance. And no matter what, we weren't going to venture offshore.

Believing my own line of crap, I checked our gear twice, making sure we hadn't forgotten anything. In the boat were the heavy wire leaders we'd made the day before, along with a couple of medium duty rods that my father and I had brought along on the seaplane.

After loading the boat with the day's supplies, we were as ready as two boys could have been. I hopped on board, quickly starting the motor, then, as Steven shuffled forward, he settled in amid-ships on the skiff's front thwart. We untied fore and aft, before sliding past the bait shack like a greased muskrat.

Once we cleared the pier, we burbled through the marina, past several rows of yachts that were attached to overnight mooring balls. As we passed the larger boats, I made sure to keep the skiff's motor chugging along quietly, so I wouldn't raise the ire of the yacht's sleeping owners. "So far so good," I thought. "Nobody's seen us, and nobody will."

After nearly stalling the motor a couple of times, we reached the farthest mooring buoy, where I throttled-her-up, pushing the skiff onto plane. We motored South, toward the area where the monster was last seen. Steve sat mid-thwart, dead-center in the front of the boat, and with the nose held down by his weight, we slid along the morning glass with surprisingly good speed. I'd been warned by my father not to stray from land, and because I pretty much always listened to him, that was definitely my intention.

We sped along, rising and falling with the swells, while the skiff's bow cut through the patchy fog that hung like curtains on the water. The water hissed as we slid along, and soon the harbor was a couple of miles behind us. I slowed the boat as I scanned the water's surface, then, after just a minute or two, I found what I was looking for.

It was a seagull, bobbing on the surface like a kid's rubber ducky. I slowed the boat, circling the gull, while I looked for signs of other birds in the area. At first there was nothing but fog, but then, just as I was wondering if I'd chosen the right place, a gull flew out of the soup, smacking the water's surface with a loud wallop.

The bird crashed head-first into the water, and as it did, a school of bait-fish scattered across the surface like raindrops on a puddle. We watched as the gull disappeared beneath the surface, then, with a splash, the bird surfaced with a large anchovy in his mouth.

Throwing the motor in neutral, I held completely still as I scanned the water around us. "Wait just a second," I could hear my father say, "Wait just a second for it to happen."

Heeding the voice in my head, I motioned for Steve to stay quiet, as I watched the glassy water with a trained eye. Nearly a minute passed as we stood dead still, until something began to form, that rippled the water's surface.

It first began as a swirl, then, within seconds, a flash of color broke into a boil that churned the sea around us.

"They're Bonita!" Steve yelled, as a school of mid-sized tuna tore into the bait-fish. "They're everywhere!"

He was right, they were everywhere, and there was no time to waste. Upon seeing the frenzy, Steve grabbed one of the lighter fishing rods, quickly tossing a chunk of squid straight into the center of the boil.

His line went slack for a moment, until seconds later, when his reel began to sing with the sound of a sizzling drag.

"FISH ON!" he yelled, as the tuna took the line. "It feels like a pretty big one!"

I was stoked, for not only had we found the perfect place to catch some monster baits, but things were going a lot better than I'd expected. Now that we were into the tuna, we'd be bringing some seriously bloody bait into the boat, which exponentially improved our chances of catching the beast we were searching for.

Following Steve's lead, I tossed a bait into the water, and before I knew it, I was hooked up as well. It was a full-blown fishing melee, and within ten minutes, we'd boated several of the small tuna. It had been a whole lot of fun working the school, but as I brought the last fish to the boat, I knew there was work to be done.

After stuffing the fish in a gunney sack, I reached over the gunnel with a large, plastic bucket, letting some sea water spill in. Once it was half full, I horsed it into the boat, before placing it in the deep-set notch near the bow's front triangle.

Steve held the gunny sack while I wrestled a tuna from the mix. The thing kicked like crazy, but after I cracked it on the head with the anchor a time or two it became much more agreeable. I pulled out my fillet knife, and before the tuna could voice any concerns over what I was about to do, its head rolled to the floor, where it had an unobstructed view of the sky.

One by one I hacked off their heads, and as expected, the damn things bled like crazy. They thrashed like they were possessed, one of them splattering Steve with a stream of arterial blood that must have shot five feet into the air. I couldn't believe how blood-soaked he'd become, and as he sat there with blood all over his face, I couldn't help but laugh my ass off.

"Dude, you aren't supposed to BE the bait!" I told him. "You'd better wash that stuff off before the sharks smell you!"

Steve did his best to rub off the blood with a very fishy towel, and as he did, I placed the headless tuna bodies stump-down in the pail-full of water.

The water turned bright red, as the twitching fish carcasses looked for their heads. "The chum's looking good," Steve said, as he leaned over the bloody bucket. "It's really starting to thicken up!"

Steve smiled as he sat there in his blood-splattered jacket, looking as if he'd just survived a zombie apocalypse. He looked so content as he poked at a fish tail in the bucket. And in that moment, I knew I'd made the right choice in bringing him along.

I grabbed myself a soda, and as the headless fish thrashed in the bucket, Steve and I discussed the game-plan. We both agreed that we needed to present a bait on the edge of the deep-water shelf, where hopefully, if it drifted down just right, we might just entice a monster. That was the best bet by far. So I started the boat and motored seaward, toward the blue-green water of the offshore shelf.

Soon we were cruising on plane, with the small boat rising and falling on the soft swells of the Catalina Channel. It was a beautiful morning, and as the fog slowly burned away, I leaned back, as warm, radiant sunlight beamed down on my face.

The skiff motored along, and as it did, neither of us said a word. There would be plenty to talk about later on that day. And even if things didn't go as planned, we knew we'd still have a story to tell.

Thinking back on it all, we really hadn't planned much of anything, other than deciding to chase The Devil Fish as we would any other top chain predator. The idea was simple. We were going to place ourselves in the richest part of the food chain where we'd offer-up the bloodiest bait possible, in the hope of tantalizing the beast with a feast it couldn't resist.

The plan was right on track, now all we had to do was wait just a little bit longer, until the sun rose high enough that we could see color in the water. That was important, because once we saw where the green water met the blue, we'd know exactly where the current-break was.

And that's where we were going to find him. Where light gave way to the dark, and something monstrous could hide, before revealing itself to its prey.

As we cruised along, the fish tails looked like giant stalks of celery sticking out of the world's biggest Bloody Mary. The tuna-baits looked great, and I couldn't wait to send one of them down to the murky depths.

We motored toward deeper waters, where I began to look for just the right place to stop. There was still a bit of patchy fog here and there, but as we rounded the island's end, the sun broke through, lighting up the water in several vibrant colors. Slowing the skiff, I circled a promising area, where the blue-green halocline formed a curtain-like wall in the water. The conditions were excellent, so much so, there was no sense in traveling any further.

I killed the motor, watching the shoreline to see if we were caught up in any kind of current. To my delight there was little or no drift, a factor that placed a cherry on top of an already glorious morning.

Now that we'd arrived, Steve helped me rig the boat rod by running line from the 9/0 Senator reel through a sequence of roller guides. Once the rod was rigged, I took the line's end in my hand, tying on the biggest barrel swivel that I'd ever seen.

We were almost ready for action. Now all we had to do was hook one of the wire leaders to the swivel, and slap on a bloody tuna carcass. So, without further ado, I grabbed one of the leaders, before giving the wire a twist with my trusty, rusty pliers.

"Are you ready, Dude?" I asked Steve. "Are you ready to catch a monster?"

Steve nodded an affirmative, "Yes," as he grabbed one of the tunas by the tail. Blood dripped everywhere as he held the fish up high, while the sun shone brightly on its iridescent skin, making it appear almost magical.

He handed it to me, just before I drove the tip of a giant hook clean through the Bonita's meaty tail. It sunk in just right, and as the hook's tip tore into flesh, I could feel its point scrape along the tuna's bony spine just the way I wanted it to.

With the bait hooked and ready, I swung it over the skiff's port gunnel, where it's sunk down very slowly. As the bloody bait fell from sight, I slowly let out some line so that it could drift naturally. A few minutes passed, and judging by how much line was left on the reel, I could tell that the tuna-torso was down at least two hundred feet or more. That depth was about right, so, I threw the reel's drag brake closed, before leaning back against the skiff's port gunnel.

Now that my rig was squared-away, I turned my attention to Steve who was pouring bloody chum-water over the side. He smiled a devilish smile, as the blood stained the water, and I actually found myself wondering which one of us was the crazier of the two.

We watched the oily chum sink down into the water column, and as we did, I think we both realized that the chum slick was a bit of an over-kill. But it was way too late to worry about any of that, as the water was darkly stained, and the deed had already been done.

As the blood drifted downward, Steve readied one of the lighter rigs that we'd brought along. He hooked some squid to a five hook ganyon, then, with a flip of the rod, he sent it down to the fish gods below.

We figured that while one of us monster fished, the other could fish for more conventional species. I liked that idea, for in the unlikely event we didn't bring The Devil Fish to shore, at least we'd have something to show for our efforts. So we just sat there, soaking a couple of baits as a seagull bobbed next to the boat.

While we waited, I felt a few light tugs on the rod, and as the rod-tip bobbed up and down I figured it was most likely a small fish trying to bite off more than it could chew. There were hundreds of Catalina Blue-perch down there, and from the way the rod tip was shaking, they were the most likely suspects.

We were nearly in a trance, as the lap, lap, lap, of the early morning water rhythmically massaged the skiff's fiberglass hull. We'd only been fishing for a few minutes, when Steve got a bite that nearly pulled the rod out of his hands.

"Whatcha' got?" I asked, as he reared-back to set the hook. "Reel the bugger in, and I'll tell you when I see some color!"

Steve reeled in the fish, and as he did, I looked down into the blood-stained water. There was nothing to see yet, but as the fish came up from the depths, I knew that sooner or later I'd begin to see some color.

"Nothing yet," I told him, "Just keep on reeling and I'll tell you what I see."

Steve pumped and reeled, and as he did, I was sure to keep a firm hold on my own rig. I stared down into the water, until after a minute or so, I saw the tell-tale flash of a bright red rockfish.

"It's a Boccaciao!" I shouted, "and a really nice one too!"

That was cool, for even though we hadn't caught The Devil Fish, the medium-sized rockfish was a great way to start things off.

Steve horsed the fish over the gunnel, and as he wrestled it into the gunny sack, I was taken by surprise as my own rod began to bend quite severely.

The rod bent until the tip was nearly in the water, and I let out some line to give the bait some breathing room. It felt like I'd snagged the bottom, which was a common occurrence in SoCal's rocky waters. I didn't want to lose the bait, or the precious leader. So, after I ran the slack a bit, I pulled up really hard, against something huge that pinned the rod to the gunnel.

I'd snagged into something. Something so big, it had to have been the bottom. With my feet on the starboard gunnel, I pulled against the rod, but no matter how hard I pulled, the thing below just wouldn't budge.

The rod was bent like a giant fish hook, with the tip in the water and the butt between my legs. It didn't move or quiver in any way, and from the way it was bent dead still, I was certain the bait was in the rocks. For a moment I just sat there, not saying a word. Until the line's pull changed direction, and I began to feel waves of energy, as they bled off something's monstrous tail.

"What's wrong?" Steve asked, as I put on my best poker face. "Are you snagged-up?"

"Must be…" I muttered. "It can't possibly be something else."

But it was something else. And if it happened to be what I thought it was, it would have served us best to throw our gear into the water and head straight home.

Something alive was down there. But it wasn't just any old fish, and it wasn't The Devil Fish either. This thing had a tail that swept like a broom, and as the line on the reel pulled away at an angle, the broom felt like it was half the size of our boat.

It began to pull line from the spool, several rotations at a time, as each beat of its immense tail pulled the rod tip into the water. Thank God Steve had reminded me to set the drag . . . For had I not done so, I'd have taken a Nantucket Sleigh-Ride straight to the bottom.

The thing pulled hard, as if the bottom had suddenly come alive. At first it took line one click at a time, but then, as the beast shifted gears, line began to peel off the reel with a shrieking howl. Trying to look calm, I fumbled for the reel's clicker switch, and with a push of the small chrome button, the howl turned into a hum.

Now that I'd silenced the drag, all we could hear was the smooth rolling sound of line being torn from the reel's massive drum. Whatever I'd hooked into was monstrously large, and as it pulsed with strength I'd never felt before, I began to wonder if I'd hooked into a submarine.

There was no use reeling in, for with the current drag setting, it took all my strength to keep the rod from being pulled from my hands. Steve knew I was struggling, and he reached over the top of my reel, rolling back the star-drag until the pull on the rod lessened significantly.

"Thanks," I mumbled, as I leaned back a notch. "The thing's so big, all I can do is hold on!"

"What do you think it is?" Steve said, as he stared into the water. "Do you think it's The Devil Fish?"

"Could be," I told him. "But I really don't think so, because The Devil Fish is supposed to be a ray, and this thing doesn't feel like it's swimming with wings."

"Besides," I told him. "There's something else I'm feeling down there… Something in the line that's giving me the creeps!"

When I said that, Steve began to look a bit freaked-out. He knew I was spooked, and quite frankly, I had every reason to be. Because something was scary wrong, and I could feel it in the palms of my hands.

At first I denied what I knew all along, but then, as I felt sweeping pulsations running down the creature's back, I knew for certain that it wasn't The Devil Fish. This thing had a tail -- a tail as tall as a man. And as it swept back and forth in a twelve foot arc, I could feel the shape of its body in the wire-tight line.

None of this was good, for I was hooked into a fin fish, and a monstrous one at that. As I sat on a thwart with my feet pressed against the gunnel, I thought about everything we'd done thus far. I thought about the blood, and the deep canyon below, and how we'd seen a monstrous shark from our airplane, as it swam in the direction of the island.

We were into a monster alright, one that we had no business tempting, regardless of the size of our boat. What it was I really didn't know, and quite frankly, I really didn't care, as long as it kept swimming away from us, while I revised the game-plan.

As I saw it, we had only two options. I could cut the line and get outta Dodge. Or I could attempt to turn the beast, and see what it was really made of. The fisherman in me wanted to fight the thing, but as I felt the hellish strokes of its sickle-shaped tail, I was overcome with the feeling that we needed to cut and run.

I reached for the fillet knife, with every intention of cutting the monster free. "Maybe this isn't the greatest idea after all," I thought. "And maybe, after I cut the line, there might still be enough line left on the reel to scare up a rock cod or two." I liked that idea. So, without bothering to ask if Steve shared my point of view, I leaned forward with a quivering hand, placing the blade next to the line.

I was just about to cut the line when, out of the blue, the rod lost its bow, nearly flipping me backward over the gunnel. "WHOAAAH!" I yelled, as I boat rocked back and forth, "HANG ON!"

It was a scary moment, but thanks to Steve's grabbing my jacket, I didn't go over the side.

"Did you cut it?" Steve asked, with a trembling voice. "Did you cut the line?"

"No," I told him, as I sat up in my seat. "I think it bit through the leader. It must have been a Big-Ass shark!"

"Wow," he said. "Maybe we should fish closer to the island. There might not be any sharks there."

"Let me see if there's anything left of the leader," I said. "When we see what's left, we'll know a lot more about what I was hooked into!"

That made sense for the most part, and as I cranked in the slack line, I wondered what the end of the leader was going to look like. Was the bailing wire going to be cut in two? Or was the hook going to be straightened out? I was curious as hell on both accounts, but more than anything, I was wondering if we'd find some tooth marks.

Those questions ran through my mind as I reeled in the slack, and as I began to catch my breath, things seemed to have returned to normal. The fish had broken off, and he'd swam away. And he was never, ever going to come back.

And that's what I chose to believe, even as the two-ton killing machine raced toward us like a missile, with my hook hanging out of its razor-tipped mouth.

I imagine now, that had I looked over the side as its grinning face rose up from the depths, I surely would have screamed. But instead, I just reeled in the slack, while the slate-gray death machine raced toward the surface, looking to kill whoever it was that fed him the bogus Bonita.

There was a strange calmness in the air, where everything

seemed to fit into place. I was about to suggest moving closer to shore, when suddenly, a few yards North of our boat's starboard gunnel, the monster rose from the sea as if it was thrust up by the Gods.

The shark broke the surface like a missile, shaking its gills as twenty five feet of killer came out of the water. I gasped as the monster hung in the air, then, as it reached the apex of its leap, it looked me straight in the eye, with the cold stare of The Devil.

Time stood still as the shark gave us the you'll-both-be-dead-in-a-moment look. Then, as if God had granted the beast a little more hang-time, it lingered in space, while staring at us, as if we were a couple of steaks at the meat counter.

We looked at it, while it looked at us, until it fell from the sky with a sick arcing twist. As its slab-like body entered the water, a huge wave rushed toward us. We would have been thrown into the drink, had it not been for Steve, who'd rolled up like a pill-bug in the deepest part of the boat. Somehow he changed the boat's center of gravity, and by becoming a wad of human ballast, he kept the boat from capsizing.

Not that we didn't roll… for I know with certainty that our port gunnel was just a hair's width from scooping into the ocean. But that didn't happen, and now that we were alive only one thing seemed to matter… getting the hell out of there!

Where the shark was I hadn't a clue. Other than he was somewhere nearby, flossing his teeth with my fishing line.

I scrambled for the knife, which had fallen between the rear thwart and the boat's fuel tank. Within seconds I cut the line, and with a *snap!* we were freed from the thing below. Steve looked at me from his balled-up position, as blood-red chum water sloshed all around him. He was lying next to one of the bloody tunas, and at that moment I have to say that he pretty much looked like bait.

Our boat was covered in blood, and seeing that, I knew it was only a matter of seconds until the shark came back. Scrambling like a madman, I pumped the fuel tank's primer bulb, then, after standing up, I pulled the motor's T-handle for all it was worth.

As I stood at the edge of the transom, I stared deep down into the crystal clear water. I pulled on the starter-rope time and time again, until, with a loud *pop!* the engine roared to life.

"GET TO THE FRONT OF THE BOAT!" I yelled to Steve, as an enormous boil broke the surface. "We need to get out of here NOW!"

As I twisted the throttle, I fully expected to be eaten before the skiff got up on plane. But as the prop dug in, and the bow flattened out, we screamed with joy, as we narrowly made our escape.

Steve looked at me with the widest eyes I've ever seen. It was as if he'd been riding a roller coaster all day long, and there was no getting the look off his face. I just smiled as we motored along, feeling the sun on my face, and the wind in my hair. We'd hooked a monster, that's for sure. And although it wasn't the exact monster we'd set out to find, there was a sense of satisfaction just the same.

I looked at Steve with a smile, and as he looked back, he uttered the words I'll never forget:

"Dude... THAT WAS FUN!"

We never did catch The Devil Fish. But we did catch a heavy dose of optimism. We felt like we really could take on a monster if we put our minds to it, and that even though we'd lost the first round, there would be many others to come, in many different arenas.

The next day, I returned to the sea with my father. And in that very same skiff, he and I had the best day of our lives.

There was no talk of monsters, or of The Devil Fish. It was just he and I, spending a day together that was absolutely priceless. I took a picture of him that day, as he sat in the boat with his fishing rod in his hand. He looked so happy and content, as if he didn't have a care in the world.

Many things have been lost over time, but I'm happy to say that I still have that old, dog-eared photo. It's all yellowed now, but I don't care, because to me, it just makes it look as if the sun is shining on him.

And what of the Devil Fish, you ask? Well, that in itself is a whole different story...

You see, I chased the creature for years, nearly to the point of obsession. And although we eventually met face to face, prior to that magical moment, I was able to piece together a time-line that told me of his origin.

He *was* a ray, a gigantic manta ray, arguably the largest of his kind left on earth. Having been born in the deep, abyssal canyons of the Pacific's blue water, he was a creature from another world, a place where light and luminescence are the fodder of kings, and where he reigned supreme like a magical angel with wings of gold.

Spanning over thirty feet from wing-tip to wing-tip, his skin was adorned with billions of bio-luminescent diatoms. Microscopic creatures that made him glow brightly, as if he was shining like the moon. On rare occasions, the gentle beast would rise from the depths, glowing like a beacon, in truly amazing glory.

During the 1970s, The Devil Fish was seen many times by a great many people. Some saw just a flash of light in the water, while others, such as a good friend of mine, were privy to a spectacle that was nothing short of amazing.

It was a summer night, when my friend was ferrying a group of rental boats between Catalina's Twin Harbors and Avalon bay. His skiff was moving slowly as he traced the island's shoreline, when suddenly, he noticed a bright glow, deep down in the water column. The glow intensified, and as The Devil Fish swam up from the depths, it seemed like there was a spotlight under the boat.

According to my friend, the creature that rose up beneath him was over thirty feet wide, and as he flew beneath the small skiff, he banked and rolled, like a child at play.

When I heard the story I was amazed, but saddened, too, by the fact that I wasn't there to see him that night. I'd searched for him for so very long, and, sadly, I was beginning to sense that the window of time was closing.

I was beginning to lose hope, feeling like my nighttime trips to the island were quickly becoming the fodder of a fool. I'd searched for him everywhere, while anchored in the harbor and offshore on the banks. We'd raised many a beast, mostly giant squid, and although they glowed like the moon, they paled by comparison to the creature that I sought.

I'd begun to think I was never going to see him, when one day, roughly a year after my friend's sighting, I was diving on a wreck near Catalina's East end. It wasn't much of a wreck, other than a short piece of hull and a few rotting deck plates, so we did the best we could, poking around for lobsters near a narrow, open doorway.

My dive buddies were in the hull when, just as I was about to join them, the water lit up around me, as if I'd been illuminated by a giant spotlight.

For a moment I paused, not knowing what to think. Then, as I turned toward the source of the light, I nearly gulped in my regulator at the sight of what was before me.

It was Him! It really, truly was. The creature I'd searched for all those years. He was just a few feet away from me, so very close that I could reach out and touch him. I looked into his eyes as he glided toward me, and I ran my hand along his wing in a gesture of friendship.

He looked at me as if to say, "Hello," his giant wings glistening with sparkles that looked like fairy dust. There was so much life within him, and something more that I can't quite describe. The creature was magical in every way, and as it softly stared into my soul, there was a kindness in its eyes that I'll never forget.

Many times since that magical day I swam in his home waters, and as I did, I could feel his wings beat as they resonated for miles. He was there, that I knew, and as he filled the water with life, I felt a sense of welcome that can't be described.

I went back one day, to visit my old friend. But as I slid beneath the water's surface, something felt amiss. He was gone. Gone forever. And, sadly, in my heart, I knew his wings beat no longer.

Goodbye Devil Fish. Goodbye to you.

My curious, gentle friend.

Him

When I first met Him, I was just a little boy, at an age where innocence, simplicity, and complete trust ruled my world. He came to me as a mentor I suppose, grooming me in ways I never could have imagined. Why he chose me I don't really know. Nor do I fully understand his mysterious ways. But I do know this… He is infinitely wise. And I've grown to learn that following his lead, is always the smart thing to do.

It was a typical Saturday morning, when I found myself elbow-deep under the hood of the worst car I've ever owned. The '69 mustang was a complete pile of crap. And despite the thousands of dollars I'd spent on race motors and the like, my futile attempts at making a Ford as fast as a Chevy were quickly proving impossible.

I should have listened to my friends, and sold the car before it fell apart in the garage. But I was stubborn, and even though I knew I should have bought a Camaro, I kept wasting my money on the thing, as if it was somehow worth the effort.

You wouldn't have known the car was a dog by looking at it. In fact, with its full roll-cage and twin Holley carburetors sticking out of the hood, the thing looked fast as hell. But looks alone weren't enough to take out some of the street rods we ran against. Especially those clustered under the freeway bridge at two o'clock in the morning.

So there I was, trying desperately to milk a few extra ponies out of an increasingly hopeless cause, when my father burst into the garage like a deranged jack-in-the-box.

"Let's go to the car-wash!" he said. "And let's get some hotdogs too!"

Startled by his entrance, I slammed my head on the car's hood as he popped through the doorway. I saw stars for a moment, then, as the birds stopped chirping, the idea of getting a bite to eat began to sound pretty good.

"Change out of those greasy clothes, and meet me in the car in ten minutes," he said. "After we get her clean, we'll grab a couple of hotdogs at Brooklyn's Finest!"

He didn't have to twist my arm, as I loved eating at that place. And besides, the concept of going to the car-wash on a Saturday morning did have a nostalgic ring to it.

Cleaned and combed with minutes to spare, I hopped in Dad's '70 Chevy, adjusting the A/C vents so the air blew on my face. The cool breeze felt good, and as we drove down our sun-lit suburban street, tall queen palms reflected upside down on the Impala's side windows.

"So, what have you been doing lately?" My father asked, in a casual tone. "What's up?"

I looked at him with a typical teenage grin, filling in the blanks with the usual stock answers that all teens give their parents. He muttered "Oh, alright," as we settled into the drive, with nothing more to do than wash the car and get something really good to eat.

I don't remember how my father first broached the subject, but somewhere along the line he began to wax philosophically about several things he'd never mentioned before. As he spoke, there were references to his mortality, and mention of things occurring "after" he was gone. This all seemed quite odd, especially coming from a man who kept his innermost feelings to himself.

Just as I was about to ask if everything was alright, he started in again, saying, "There's something I need to talk to you about that I've been putting off for some time. It's something important we need to discuss, before it's too late."

Sensing an uncommon urgency in his voice, I half expected to hear he was terminally ill. That thought was chilling, but before I could get a word in edge-wise, he asked me something that seemed completely out of context.

"Have you ever heard of "Signs," he asked. "Have you ever heard of them?"

I didn't know how to answer that, other than by saying, "Yeah Dad, there are signs all over the road!" But somehow, as I said those words, I knew there was much more to the point than just the obvious.

"I'm not talking about THOSE kinds of signs," he said. "I'm

talking about the kind of signs you can't see."

Confused, but intrigued, I kept quiet as he explained further. As he went on, not only was I shocked by the complexity of the subject matter, but also by the urgency in his voice, which suggested that time really was conspiring against us.

He had my complete attention, to the point where I actually listened for a change. There was so much I wanted to know about the strange signs, but before I could learn anything more, he said "Hold that thought," as we turned into the car-wash parking lot.

After parking at the end of a long line of cars, we left the keys in the ignition before walking toward the main building. As we walked in, the smell of car wax and stale cigarettes filled the air. It reminded me of the smell that old airliners used to have, where cigarette smoke had been cycled through the air vents so many times, there was no getting rid of the odor. Everything smelled like that back then. From the A/C vents of my aunt's new Bonneville, to the coffee shop downtown, where the smoke never stayed in the smoking section.

While my father paid the cashier, I perused the assortment of pine tree air fresheners that hung like leaves from a wire display. There were many scents to choose from, and by the time he'd paid the woman behind the counter, my nose was clogged up from sniffing every tree on the rack.

Just as I'd moved from the air freshener isle to the custom floor mats, I heard my father call out from down the way. "Come on down," he said with a wave. Then, following his lead, I walked toward the long, glass corridor that ran the length of the automated car-wash.

When I reached his side, he pointed to one of the soap covered cars on the conveyor line, saying, "There's the reason we come to this place Sonny Boy. This is the only place in town where we can see our car during every stage of the wash. And it's the only place where the machine scrubs the white walls!"

"That's great," I told him. "Just great. But what about the signs?"

"Oh yeah," he said, "The signs… Well, in essence, they're the type of signs that tell you something is going to happen."

"In fact," he said. "These kinds of signs are so significant, that

168

if you don't follow their lead, you may never, EVER come home again!"

Shocked, I asked, "You mean die? Do you mean that if we don't follow these signs, we might actually die?"

"Maybe," he said, with a weird look on his face, "and maybe worse."

That didn't sound good at all, especially the, "or worse," part. Pondering it all, I watched our Impala roll past on the chain driven conveyor, before it stopped in place beneath a spinning red light.

Everything about that moment seemed so surreal, as the red light spun like a cherry atop a police cruiser. Dad seemed mesmerized as the soap wands splattered the car with greenish ooze. And as it dripped to the ground like protoplasm, I imagined the ride to the hotdog place, was going to be anything but ordinary.

Not wanting to discuss the signs until we were back in our car, my father said "Hold that thought," as he pointed to the cars down the line. He looked like a little kid as he stood there, watching the soap rain down, as the fluffy, cloth rollers tumbled over each of the cars. He carried on about how awesome the new, automated car-wash was, and as he did, there was a magical look in his eye that's hard to describe.

It made me happy to see him act that way, sort of like a kid who wants to go on the same carnival ride over and over again. For some reason the car-wash had captured his fancy, and while I don't know exactly what it was about the place that grabbed him so, I'll never forget how happy he was.

As our car moved forward, I pressed my nose to the glass, fogging up the window with my hot breath. I was just about to draw on the glass with my finger, when I glanced over my shoulder, to where the cashier was glaring back at me. Rather than incur her wrath, I shuffled to my right, before following my father out the building's back door.

The sun was bright, and I shielded my eyes as a man with a red towel buffed the Impala's hubcaps. He shined them to a luster, then, as he spritzed blue solution all over the windows, my father stuffed a couple of dollars into my pocket, which were intended for the man with the towel, just as soon as he was done.

The guy did an extra good job because we were watching him.

Going over everything twice just for emphasis. Then, as he held the towel up high, I walked across the tarmac, before handing him the two dollar bills. We hopped in the car, and just as I closed the door, the fragrant scent of strawberries hit my nose. "Another reason we come here," my father said. "The car always smells so good!"

Our wet tires screeched as we pulled onto a side street. Then, after my father adjusted his side-view mirror, I asked him to continue with the "Signs" story before he lost his train of thought. He held up his finger a moment as he set the A/C on high, then he glanced in my direction before continuing.

"Okay," he said. "I'm going to tell you something now, and it's going to sound really weird. But I'm going to tell it to you anyhow, because it's one of the most important things you'll ever hear."

I was intrigued, and as he began, I listened intensely, as if he was going to bestow upon me the great secrets of The Knights Templar.

"I'm starting to fear for you," he said, with a surprisingly serious look. "You're at the age where terrible things begin to happen."

"Terrible things?" I asked. "What kind of terrible things?"

"Well…" He said. "I'm talking about the kind of things that can't be fixed by anyone. No matter how hard you try. Like death for example."

"DEATH?" I blurted out. "What do you mean by death? Do you think I'm going to die or something?"

"No, no, God forbid!" he said in an apologetic tone. "I don't think you're going to die. I'm just worried that some of the things that you and your street racer friends are getting into, may lead to one of those late night phone calls that parents never want to get."

What he was implying shocked the hell out of me, but as shocking as it was, I suddenly realized what he'd been trying to say all along.

"So," I asked, "You're saying that these signs are indicators that things are getting a bit out of hand? Is that what you're trying to say?"

"Well, yes, and no," he said. "It's much, MUCH, more than that."

On that note, we pulled up beside the hot dog place, where my father gave me a very serious look. Putting the car in park, he said very slowly, "The signs are everywhere. And they litter the road where a man ends up, who failed to heed the warnings set before him."

You see, according to my father, at the exact moment when someone chooses to do either this or that, the clock of fate begins to tick. Once the clock has been set into motion, each and every choice made thereafter must be chosen wisely, lest disaster may ensue.

He then went on to give a few examples of people he'd known who failed to heed the signs. And before he was done, he mentioned that they were all dead, just for added emphasis.

I learned of his army buddy in Korea, who's headless corpse ended up laying in the snow after he repeatedly brushed aside the signs. Apparently the guy had seen them, but he was too foolhardy to respect anything or anyone. Sadly, disrespecting the signs was the wrong thing to do. And because he didn't heed fate's warnings, he was alive one minute, and headless the next.

The story was sobering to say the least, as was the mental image of a body-less head rolling around in the snow. I wondered if the head came clean off, in such a way that you might have been able to put it back on with a jar full of salve. But I'm sure that wasn't the case, or my father wouldn't have seemed so worked up about it.

As he went on about this guy, and that guy coming home from the war in a rough-pine box, I began to think the signs he spoke of were simply a metaphor for common sense. To make sure I'd gotten the point, I asked, "So, are you saying that these signs are moments in time where decisions are laid out before us? And that the signs are there to guide us in the proper direction?"

"Sort of," he said. "Except that in many cases the signs aren't posted beside the road. Sometimes there's someone standing there, holding them in front of you."

I was like, "Who are you talking about Dad? I don't really understand."

"I'm talking about Him," he said, with an unusually scary look in his eye. "The Shadow Man who shows up at the most inopportune times."

We stared at one another as the implications of what he said sunk in. I knew exactly who he was talking about. But up until that moment, I sort of figured that my association with the Shadow Man was pretty much just a byproduct of my own personal madness.

"Uhhhhh… I think I know who you're talking about," I said. "I think I know."

"I KNOW you know!" he said. "And I also know that you've heard Him, too!"

I had heard Him of course, knowing perfectly well who and what my father was talking about. Yet even then, as someone was finally lending validation to the voice I'd heard all along, I downplayed what I really knew, for the sake of my own sanity.

At that moment, it's hard to say if my father knew I was bluffing, or if he simply figured I was too wrapped up in being a teenager to have given it much thought. So, rather than nitpick who and what we were talking about, he leaned across the Impala's bench seat, before telling me something I'll remember for the rest of my life.

He said, "Sonny Boy, I'm going to tell you something I never, EVER, want you to forget. It's the most important thing I've ever told you, and you've GOT to listen to me!"

"It's simple," he said. "Now that you're older, you'll be doing certain things you really shouldn't be doing. Things that both you and I know you'll be doing, but you won't dare admit that you do. Sometimes these things will be dangerous, and sometimes they'll be immoral or illegal. But regardless of which, somewhere along the line you'll have to make a choice."

"What kind of choice?" I asked.

"The kind of choice that will determine just how deep a pile of crap you're willing to get into," he said. "The kind of choice that will make the difference between whether or not you come home in one piece, or in several little boxes!"

He went on to say, "As situations unfold, and you allow yourself to become more deeply involved, signs will begin popping up that rate the life expectancy of your choices."

"Regardless of where you are, or what you're doing," he said, "There will be a window of opportunity that presents itself should

172

you need to pull your chute. Seeing this "Bail-out" moment for what it really is, pretty much makes the difference between whether or not someone lives or dies."

"You've got to get out before the whole plane goes down," he said solemnly. "And the only way you're going to know exactly when to jump, is when the signs tell you to."

He was completely right about all of this, and as he extrapolated further, I knew with certainty that he'd done every one of the crazy things I was doing. As he spoke, it was as if I was talking to myself, only an older, more mature version. Then, as he began wrapping things up, my father told me something that I hadn't ever considered.

"Not everyone gets to see the signs," He said. "Nor would they know what they were seeing if it was held up in front of them."

I asked, "Do you mean that not everyone sees these signs, or not everyone is given the opportunity to see them?"

"The latter," he said. "For some reason, not everyone is privy to these signs. And furthermore, most people are so stupid, they wouldn't know how to save their own hide if given the opportunity."

"Maybe that's why so few people get the opportunity to see Him," he said. "It's almost as if some people are worthy of saving, while others aren't worth the effort. That's probably why he doesn't bother to show himself that often. Because most people are so clueless, they really aren't worth the time of day."

As draconian as that seemed, he was dead-on in his assessment. I had to admit there had been many times when I watched people do the stupidest things, while knowing all along, that soon enough, one of them would be carted off in an ambulance.

"It's all about respect," he went on to say. "It's as if someone holds out a sign just to see if you're looking. Then, if you're too much of an idiot not to appreciate the helpful hint, you'll be left on your own, to drive right off the cliff!"

"The Shadow Man does this," he said. "Some of my army buddies said that they'd seen Him, but they didn't think he was the real-deal. So they sort of brushed Him off, disrespected Him in a way. And for doing so, they paid the ultimate price."

The conversation was getting deeper by the second, yet as cool as the concept of signs was, what I really wanted to know more about was the Shadow Man. Coming clean for the first time since we'd begun talking, I admitted I'd seen Him a time or two, and that I really needed to know more about who he was.

"You'll see Him," he told me. "You'll see Him out of the corner of your eye, just as things are starting to get out of hand. Then, when you do see Him, you need to understand he's not there to visit with you, but rather, he's there to "collect" something . . . Something you definitely want to keep!"

"Whoa…" I muttered under my breath. "That sounds really ominous. Is this Shadow Man like some kind of a ghost?"

"It's not a ghost," he replied. "He's just someone who's there to retrieve something. And the thing he retrieves, better not EVER be your soul!"

"So he's The Grim Reaper then?" I asked. "Is that what you're saying?"

"That's far too simple an answer," he said. "Just promise me that if you and your friends do something that brings Him around, you'll heed the signs, and high-tail it out of there before it's too late, okay?"

"I will Dad, I promise… I really, really will."

It was roughly ten P.M. Late enough for a few beers to have gone to my head, but not nearly late enough to call it a night. We'd already been to one house-party, maybe even two. And now it was time for a short break before we ventured out any further.

We were lying on the hoods of our cars, staring up at a star-filled sky. "There's a satellite!" my friend Mark exclaimed, as he pointed to a light in the sky. "It's taking pictures right now, and the cops will be here within minutes!"

He may have been right about the satellite, but as far as the cops were concerned, they had far better things to do than drive onto the ridge and worm us out of a far-away cul-de-sac. Besides, we were harmless for the most part, far more content to sneak onto the golf course at midnight, than we were to cause any real trouble.

I knew Mark was full of hot air, but I humored him anyhow, saying that if the cops did come, we'd blame everything on him.

We all laughed for a moment, then, as a strange calm settled over us, I crossed my legs over the top of my hood scoop, staring deep into the cosmos.

Mark was right about one thing, the satellite sure did seem as if it was hovering above us. It just hung there, many miles high, flickering like a pulsar, as it zig-zagged left and right.

"Is it supposed to do that?" I asked my friend Charlie, as he sat on the hood of his Challenger. "Is it supposed to jump around like that?"

"Yeah, it is," he said. "Only it isn't the satellite moving, it's moisture in the atmosphere tricking your eyes into thinking it is."

"Do you guys think with your eyes?" Mark said, before laughing like a hyena.

"Well, it's better than thinking with YOUR DICK, like you do!" I told him.

We laughed aloud, lighting up the cul-de-sac with the kind of joy you rarely see these days.

It was a special time, and as I stared up at the sky, I felt as if that moment was something we all needed to cherish. None of us said a word, as our silence said everything. Then, as the distant sound of a car's engine echoed through the canyon, I slid my legs off the fender, before jumping to my feet.

"Someone's coming," Mark said. "And I don't recognize the sound of that engine."

"Well, it's not the cops," I told him. "Those are definitely headers and turbo mufflers. And the thing's got a built motor of some kind."

"Probably a Dodge," Charlie said. "You know why?"

"Why Charlie? Why?" I asked, humoring him.

"Because if it was a Ford," he said with a laugh, "The thing would have blown up long ago!"

I should have known that was coming, but before I could reply with a dig of my own, the mystery car rounded the corner, revealing that it wasn't a car at all.

It was a van, a blue and yellow Chevrolet van that we all recognized immediately.

"Oh Christ," Charlie said with a look on his face. "It's that Bob guy from the football team. He's such an asshole!"

175

Yeah, it was Bob. And he had been on the football team. But lately, the guy had become a major stoner. The likes of which made me and my alcoholic buddies look like altar boys.

Ordinarily I wouldn't have waved, but as the van pulled up beside me, I had no other choice. I gave a thumbs-up to Bob, just as the van's side door flung open, releasing a sizable cloud of smoke into the night air.

The pungent smell of cheap, homegrown weed wafted toward me as the passengers in the rear of the van shuffled toward the door. I could tell someone was in there, but until the smoke cleared, who they were was anyone's guess.

I mulled around as a couple of my buddies leaned into the doorway, then, as I heard someone call my name, I jumped to attention at the tone of her voice.

It was a girl, and her voice sounded very familiar. Except for some reason, I couldn't quite place who she was. With my curiosity piqued, I asked "Hey, who's that?" as I leaned closer to the doorway. "Who's in there?"

At first there was no reply, until a moment later, when the mystery girl jumped from the van, straight into my arms.

Had I not been leaning forward, I'd have been bowled over when she leapt. As it was, however, I caught her in mid-flight, just a split-second before she wrapped around me like a monkey. At first I had no idea who she was, other than she had long brown hair that hung way down her back. I played along as she hugged me, thinking it was a joke, until she pressed her ample chest against mine, while looking me straight in the eye.

"It's Cathy," I suddenly realized. A friend of a girl I'd dated some time ago. I hadn't seen her in a year. And wow, had she grown up.

I smiled back as she blubbered something about "Always having liked me, and never having told me so." Then, as I set her down on her feet, I could tell for the first time just how drunk she really was.

The girl was plowed, so wasted, that had she not been holding on to me, she would have fallen dead-away. She hung on me like a circus monkey, smelling of stale pot and the kind of perfume that clings to your clothes long after the night is over. She felt good in my arms, and as I clasped my hands behind her back, four guys exited the van who appeared to be as stoned as a person could be. I couldn't imagine anyone being more wasted, until Bob piled out of the driver's seat, making the others look stone sober.

"Holy Crap," Charlie whispered. "These guys are plowed, especially the driver."

"Yeah, they are," I replied. "And they're also one step away from killing themselves."

Right then, it all came flooding back to me. The way my father had forewarned me of just such a thing, and how at that very moment, Bob seemed to be ignoring all of the signs.

Sadly, I felt that Bob and his friends probably weren't worth saving, for had I bothered to intervene, they simply would have found another mindless way to off themselves. But the girl was different. She was a good girl. A smart girl, who was simply too drunk to know any better.

Charlie and I shook our heads as Bob stumbled around like a drunken sailor. I don't think either of us had ever seen someone so remarkably high, nor had we ever seen someone in his condition attempt to drive down the road. It was a miracle he'd made it up the canyon without driving off a cliff. And now that he had, there was no way I was going to allow Cathy to drive back down with him.

Before it was too late, I took her to one side and told her point blank. "I'm going to drive you home tonight. These losers are way too wasted for you to go anywhere with them!"

She smiled at the notion of my taking her home, knowing full well that we wouldn't be getting back until the wee hours of the morning. We were just about to walk toward my car, when out of the blue, one of the idiots she'd arrived with grabbed her by the arm and pulled her back into the van.

"WAIT!" I yelled, as the others pushed in behind her. "Where are you taking her?"

"Anywhere but here!" One of the guys exclaimed. "We're gonna find a party, cause this place is lame!"

At that moment, I didn't care where any of them were headed, as long as they were heading there without her. Trying my best to pull Cathy from the van, I could see her reaching out for me, but as she did, one of the idiots blocked the van's doorway while laughing his ass off.

"GET AWAY FROM HER!" I yelled out. But he was too wasted to do anything other than sit there giggling like a moron.

I saw red. The likes of which made me want to drag him from the van and stomp on his head. I was about to reach for him, when I glanced over his shoulder to where something dark began to materialize.

At first there was a blur, something moving in the fabric of space and time that had no business being there. It's a wonder it caught my eye at all, given how angry I was. But something within the living shadow called out to me. And as it began to take solid form, I gasped, as there was no doubt as to who sat before me.

It was Him, sitting in the back of the van as if he was taking a family road-trip. I froze in place when I saw Him, babbling as if I'd just survived a train wreck. While he stared into my soul, as ice water coursed through my veins.

"Are you going to get in?" he asked, in a low, metallic tone. "Will you be joining your friends tonight?"

I said nothing, as the others in the van began to move in slow motion. Their words strangely garbled, as if they existed in another dimension.

"They don't know I'm here," he said. "They rarely ever do."

I looked into his eyes while his form phased between shadow and substance, asking, "What are you doing here? Why are you here tonight?"

"Do you have to ask?" he said. "Do you REALLY have to? The signs are everywhere you know."

As he said that I peered through the smoke, suddenly realizing the interior looked as if it was on fire.

"Very good," he said. "Now that you've seen that, what else do you see?"

Looking to my right, I followed a sound, to where the turn signal of the van was stuck in the on position. As it clicked over and over, the red indicator light on the dashboard glowed brightly. I watched the light flash on and off, its lens illuminating the smoke with a fiery red tinge. Then, as the flasher stayed lit just a moment too long, I could see a burning ember in its core.

It glowed like fire. And as he looked over my shoulder with a shadowy smile, he asked, "See it? Do you see what's inside?"

"Yeah, I see what's inside." I told Him. "There's fire inside." "Very good," he said. "So what do you conclude?"

"I conclude that the van is going to burn!" I said in nearly a cry, "That's what I conclude!"

"Maybe," he said. "That's always a possibility."

When he said that, I broke away from his shadowy gaze, looking into the eyes of a girl who seemed frozen in time. "You aren't going to take HER?" I asked. "Not after we've spoken this way!"

He said nothing, as he sat there smugly in the smoke filled shadows. I glared back at Him, with an angrier look than I probably should have given. But he said nothing, content to just sit there, as if he had a bowl of popcorn in his lap.

"Don't disappoint me," he said. "I've learned to expect great things from you!"

I didn't know what to say to that, for it involved much more than I dared to consider. All I could do was stare at Him, as I pondered his statement, while questioning my sanity at the very same time.

"Am I hallucinating from the pot fumes?" I wondered. "Is the stuff THAT powerful?"

But it wasn't the fumes, for as he began to vanish into the night, he pointed toward Cathy, who was beginning to speak normally again.

At first her words seemed garbled, all strange and fuzzy, as if she was speaking under water. Then, as my head began to clear, a voice spoke out, from somewhere within the van.

"Are you going to get in, or stay out?" One of the stoner idiots asked. "Are you coming with us or not?"

I would have answered him, had I not been in that hazy nether-region between consciousness and God-knows-where. Trying to call out to Cathy, I found my own words slurred, just a second before the van's door slammed shut, as if a steel guillotine had sliced down in front of me.

Pulling on the door with all my might, I realized that one of the idiots must have locked it from the inside. I could hear someone giggling within the van, then, as Bob spun the tires, I jumped back

179

as they rumbled off into the night.

Just as the van's taillights disappeared, I felt a reassuring hand on my shoulder. "What's wrong?" Charlie asked. "What the hell just happened?"

"I don't know." I told him. "I just have the feeling that something terrible is going to happen. And there's nothing I can do about it!"

"Have another beer," he said, "I'm sure you'll see her again soon. And everything will be just fine."

I suppose I have Him to thank for my not being in the van when it rounded a corner at over one hundred miles an hour. And I also have to thank Him for my missing out on the moment when eight tons of metal compressed into a blazing furnace.

Years later, I still wonder about the crash that took seven lives, such as whether or not he had a hand in the accident or whether or not he spilled his popcorn when the van swerved to cross the center line.

Perhaps I'll never know the answer to either of those questions. But I do know this . . . He threw me a bone. Tossing Cathy clear of the crash, just a millisecond before everyone else perished.

Grim Reaper? Maybe not at all.

Putting thought into it all, I wondered whether or not he was there to collect souls, or if there was another reason for his being. He had a purpose; that was evident. But whatever that purpose was, it seemed much more complex than simply taking out the trash.

I knew there was a lot more to Him than the shadowy front he put on. And besides, had he been all that bad, why would he have guided me to safety time and time again?

Considering that, and a whole lot more, something my father had said really rang true. "It's all about respect," he'd said. "It's ALL about respect."

Several years passed since the dark conversation in the van. And although I hadn't seen Him as of late, I knew he was out there somewhere. Figuring he had more important things to do than follow me around, I assumed we'd catch up later. And besides, with college classes, a new job, and everything else that was going on in my life, I didn't have time to look over my shoulder.

One Spring night, between the rush of final exams, and the call of the fraternity, Charlie and I slipped away for a nostalgic trip down memory lane. It was a beautiful evening, and we'd taken my Corvette roadster out to Van Nuys Boulevard, the cruising mecca for anyone and everyone living in Southern California.

Back in the day, especially on Wednesday nights, the boulevard was choked with all manner of hot-rods and muscle cars. It was a magical time, when streetlight drag-races were the norm, and just about every teenager in the valley showed up to make the scene. The fun lasted for decades, until one night, when road-blocks went up unannounced, abruptly ending an era that seemed to be eternal.

Charlie and I hadn't been back to the boulevard since that fateful night. But now, years later, we'd heard that a small group of diehards had staged a renaissance of sorts a couple of streets away. Hearing the news, we were eager to investigate, as both of us had mourned the loss of the boulevard as if it were the passing of a friend.

I figured the best way to approach the strip was from the South, as driving up from Ventura Boulevard would seem the least conspicuous. As we neared our old haunts, I expected to see the flashing of police cruiser lights. Yet as we drew close to our old hot-spot, the police presence appeared to be long gone.

"They're here," Charlie said, "just not in plain sight." I knew he was right, as the feel of hidden eyes raised the hair on the back of my neck. "Drive slow and steady," Charlie said. "Look as if you've got somewhere to go, because if you don't, they'll pull you over in a heartbeat!"

"Where do you think they are?" I asked. "Do you think they're still around?"

"They're all around us," he said. "You do the driving, and I'll spot one for you."

We stopped at a four-way intersection on a street so deserted you could hear the lights change. I slowly let out the clutch, as Charlie pointed to a narrow alleyway half a block down. "There's one," he said. "You can see the nose of his black-and-white tucked away in the shadows.

"They're everywhere," he said, "not as many as there used to be, but several just the same."

He was right, they were everywhere. And if we wanted to stand half a chance of slipping into the secret parking lot undetected, we were going to have to make a few left turns, before coming in from the West.

We swung off the boulevard, driving a half mile or so before doubling-back down a side street. After weaving down a sequence of alleys, I turned off my headlights as we neared our destination. I could see a crowd up ahead, standing beside a couple of car hauling trailers that were positioned for a quick getaway. One of the trailers had a street rod strapped to its deck, its windows numbered with white shoe polish, which was a tell-tale sign that the car had just come from the drag strip.

As we rolled past with the Vette's top down, some guy yelled "WANNA RACE?" from the peanut gallery. My ego wanted to take him up on it, but from the look of the car on that trailer, it would have eaten my roadster alive.

I revved the small-block just to screw with the guy. Then, as I saw a parking space near a large dumpster, I pulled in close before shutting off my engine.

Leaving the top down, we headed toward a crowd that had assembled near the trailered drag cars. At first I didn't recognize anyone, but then, after spotting someone we knew, it didn't take long before it began to feel like old times. It was good to see the old crowd, and within short order, we got caught up on all that was happening with the street racing scene.

Apparently there was quite a renaissance going on, with this get-together being one of several pockets of resistance that had sprung up in the valley. The police had successfully ended the cruising movement, but as far as street racing was concerned, that was an entirely different story. Sure, they'd closed down San Fernando Road, which was the best place to run cars to their limit. But the racers had adapted to change, moving toward the desert communities, where they could run fast and long, without any interference.

All of that was interesting, I suppose. But as I stood there listening to some guy drone on about the nefarious use of nitrous oxide, I began to think about heading over to Tommie's for a couple of chili burgers.

I was just about to mention the burgers to Charlie, when some guy in a lowered El Camino skidded into the parking lot. He jumped from his car, looking a bit frazzled, before running toward a group of people who were standing beside the savings and loan. As they huddled in the shadows, we could hear only bits and pieces of what the driver was saying. At first his voice was muffled, but then, his voice cut through the night air, as he said something that made the hair stand up on my neck.

"HE DROVE STRAIGHT OFF A CLIFF!" the driver exclaimed. "RIGHT THROUGH THE GUARD RAIL!"

"Jesus Christ!" Charlie said. "Some guy drove off a cliff! We've got to check it out!"

I was about to second the motion, when the driver of the El Camino bolted toward his car as if it was the beginning of the Grand Prix at Le Mans. Several others took chase, and within seconds, a group of cars skidded from the parking lot. As we ran toward my car, Charlie had the jump on me, but as he swerved to cut around a dumpster, I gained on him as we sprinted down the alley. "FOLLOW THE GUY IN THE EL CAMINO!" he yelled. "HE KNOWS WHERE THE CRASH SITE IS!"

That was easier said than done, as the guy who'd started the ruckus, was already half way down the boulevard. I backed onto a side street, before spinning sideways as I laid on the throttle. "WHAT THE HELL ARE YOU DOING?" Charlie yelled, as I spun the wheels into second gear. "THE COPS ARE EVERYWHERE!"

He was right; I had gotten caught up in the moment. Listening to the voice of reason, I backed off a bit as a primer gray Chevelle sped past like we were standing still. Looking in the rear-view mirror, I could see a group of cars that were closing in fast. Some were content to follow single-file, while others thundered past as if they were asking for a speeding ticket. I figured that the safest bet was to fade into the pack, much like an antelope does when a predator appears. Besides, with as many cars that were speeding down the boulevard at that moment, the chances we'd be pulled over were practically zero.

That made perfect sense, as the lead cars were running red lights three-abreast. I rolled through the light at Ventura Boulevard. Then, as we began to weave up Mulholland Drive, I fell into the groove, running the pack single-file.

The growl of my small-block echoed through the canyon as I downshifted into the turns. It felt good to turn the Corvette loose. To give her some room to stretch after spending way too much time on the straight line blacktop. She was made for the canyons, and I pushed her hard, quickly narrowing the gap between ourselves and the lead pack.

We'd gained considerable altitude, twisting past a dirt turn-out that had been nicknamed "Grandstands" by the local canyon racers. This was a place of legend, where those in the elite road racing sect would convene on weekend nights. It was a natural over-look, a viewing point of sorts, which served as both a grandstand and a meeting place for the gilded few of the road-race sect. Only a select few ever parked at Grandstands. And from what I'd been told, unless you drove a Ferrari, or a tricked-out A/C Cobra, it was best you kept on going.

As I glanced toward the turn-out, I saw that only one car was parked in the shadows. That seemed odd, considering it was such a warm, moonlit night. But with a car over the edge, I figured the rest of the canyon racers had joined in on the hunt.

We crested the summit, heading downhill toward a serpentine line of glowing brake lights. Slowing markedly, we followed single-file toward a headlight-lit, hair-pin curve at the end of the road. The curve was severe, bent in such a way that the road nearly doubled-back on itself. I slowed as we entered the turn, seeing a crowd that had gathered beside a fresh break in the guardrail.

Some stared back, while others looked like ghosts in the shrill headlights. Smoke was in the air. And as we rolled past like we were on a carnival ride, the orderly precession of cars soon digressed into a melee of roadside gawkers.

Cars were parked everywhere. Some in roadside turn-outs, while others parked on patches of dirt that were mere inches from the cliff's edge. I passed them all, preparing for a quick get-away just in case things went sour. Besides, if there was to be a dead body or two rounding-out the evening's festivities, we didn't want to become any more involved than we needed to be.

Looking for a sane place to pull over, I rolled a hundred yards until a dirt turn-out appeared on the road's inner edge. With no opposing traffic, I drove across the oncoming lane, parking the Corvette with its nose down the road. It was the perfect place for a quick getaway, and no sooner did I turn off the engine, than Charlie jumped out of the car, ready for action. "Grab a couple of flashlights from the car's boot," I told him. "It's gonna be pitch black down in the ravine."

Charlie secured the lights, while I grabbed a couple of ratty sweaters that I'd stowed behind the seats. It wasn't particularly cold, but the going would be thorny, especially down in the canyon. I tossed Charlie one of the sweaters, saying, "Dude, put this on. You never know what we're gonna to be getting into." He nodded as he put on the sweater, before we briskly walked beside the rusted guardrail.

Our shoes scuffed on the bristled asphalt as cars rolled by. Some hung out the window, while others hid from the smell of blood in the air. I could see the look in their eyes as they idled past. They wanted to look, and they wanted to see. But I think they also hoped that the window glass would be thick enough to shield them from the horror.

One by one they passed, like a macabre, drive-through funeral precession. I stared through the windows as we walked against traffic, until we reached the area where most of the crowd had congregated. No one said a word as we arrived, although they stared at us as if we had a solution to it all.

"Nobody knows what to do," Charlie whispered, as we moved through the crowd. "No one's in charge, and none of them have a clue what to do next."

He was right, as this was yet another example of a hundred people watching, while one or two did all the doing. We gracefully horned our way through the crowd, toward a spot where a teenage girl stood with tears in her eyes. She didn't say a word, nor did she need to, as the twisted guardrail did all the talking.

"It's down pretty deep," I said, as I pointed into the canyon. "Let's have a better look."

We turned on our lights before leaning our knees against the guardrail. It was a long way down to the canyon floor, but there in the moonlight, I could see that the ominous "cliff" wasn't nearly as vertical as I'd imagined. I pointed my light into the canyon, and from the look of things, I began to think that climbing down was a viable option.

"Someone's already down there," Charlie said. "See the lights? They're way down in the canyon."

He was right, there were lights down below. Enough of them that it seemed as if someone may have had the situation under control. A shrill voice echoed up from below, and as it did, I asked, "Where are the police and firemen? Don't you think someone would have called them by now?"

"I suppose so," Charlie said. "Though it may take a while, considering the nearest pay-phone is way down on Ventura Boulevard."

That was a disquieting thought, as was the notion that the guy in the El Camino had driven half way through the valley without calling the authorities.

"Why didn't that guy call for help?" I asked Charlie. "What's up with that?"

"Go ask him yourself," Charlie said, as he pointed toward a group of cars. "He's standing right over there!"

Not sure what I was getting myself into, I walked toward the El Camino, where the driver was leaning over the edge of his tailgate. He was reaching for something, and as I approached, he said "Hey man," as he lifted a long, red toolbox from the vehicle's bed.

"What the hell happened?" I asked. "Who drove off the cliff?"

"It was one of the canyon guys," he said, with a hurried response, "a guy in a tricked-out Mustang."

"Is he alive?" I asked, as he secured the latch on the toolbox. "Have you been down there yet?"

"Uh... no," he said, with a weird shrug of his shoulders. "I haven't been down there yet. And as far as whether or not he's alive, I dunno."

He gave me a nod before crossing the street with the toolbox in hand. He was heading into the canyon, and as far as I was concerned, we were too. Besides, with no flashing lights to be seen, I figured that Charlie and I were the most competent rescuers on scene.

As the guy with the toolbox side-stepped down the slope, I looked at Charlie as he stared into the abyss. "It's not really a cliff," I told him. "It's sort of a semi-cliff. Just tell yourself that." Charlie rolled his eyes, laughing at my assessment of the slope. "A semi-cliff," he said sarcastically. "Does that mean you'll only be semi-dead if you fall off of it?"

I looked at him with a smile, saying "Well maybe it is a cliff, and maybe it isn't. But let's not worry about that. Because there's someone down there that may still be alive, and we might be able to save him."

Charlie tugged on the bottom of his sweater, saying, "You lead, that way your body can cushion my fall!"

"You're welcome to fall on top of me," I told him. "Just make sure I'm dead first!"

We jumped the guardrail a few feet from the crowd, searching for the best place to climb down. With flashlights in hand, we navigated by feel, grabbing the tops of sagebrush bushes as we skidded down the slope. The hardy bushes held fast, and before we knew it, we'd climbed down to a large impact crater that had been formed when the Mustang pitch-poled into the canyon. It looked as if a giant spatula had shaved away the canyon wall, and as I stood on the rolled edge of an avulsed pile of dirt, a weird chill ran down my spine.

"This is where the car first hit," I said to Charlie. "It flew all the way here before it nosed into the ground."

There was a pause before Charlie asked, "How long ago do you think this happened? Do you think there's a chance that the guy's still kicking?" I looked into the darkness, saying, "It's anyone's guess." But deep down inside, I felt that the only kicking the driver was going to do involved the proverbial bucket.

Perhaps that's why I felt the way I did. Sort of the way you feel when there's a body to recover and the chance of saving the day is pretty much out of the question. I felt like we were doing the right thing as we climbed down the slope, yet somehow there was something wrong about it all, something that transcended the obvious several times over.

Charlie sensed it too, and we stared at one another while the strangest feeling settled over us. We both knew something was wrong, but at that moment, there was no telling what that might have been. We could have turned back, and driven home as if none of this had ever happened. But it was way too late for that. As with each tentative step, the journey down below was becoming more about our needs than it was the ill-fated driver's.

We were roughly half way into the canyon, when the micro-thin game-trail ended at a cluster of sandstone boulders. "Great," I thought, "We're going rock climbing. And we're going to have to do it with our flashlights in our mouths."

I wasn't sure if we'd gone the right way, especially now that we'd come face to face with a steep wall of boulders. Charlie shrugged his shoulders indifferently, saying "There's, no way that guy came through here. I mean, he could have gone this way, but not with that heavy tool box in his hand."

"Let's find our own way," I told him. "That dickhead probably tripped and killed himself long ago!"

"If we find him dead can we keep his tools?" Charlie asked. "I mean, he may have some cool sockets in that box!"

I laughed as I probed the side of a boulder, looking for a hand-hold I could lock into. "Hang on a sec while I find a way around this thing," I said. "There are plenty of cracks, I've just got to find the right one."

After a bit of recon, I found a deep slot between the boulders that was the ideal place to shimmy down. Charlie held both lights as I crammed the toe of my boot into the narrow slot. Then, as I locked into the crack with my fists, I descended while Charlie lit the way from above. The going was good, except for the nagging thought that I was about to poke a rattlesnake in the eye. Maybe I would have, had the damned things been awake. But aside from shooing off a scorpion or two, the climb down was easier than anticipated.

Charlie waited up top, before tossing me the lights one by one. With the crack lit from below, he moved quickly, following my line step by step. We then regrouped atop another boulder, where I leaned forward to look over the edge. Below us was the abyss, and right in the center of it all was a dull, orange glow. Something was on fire, that's for sure, but I had no way of knowing if it was the entire car or just a portion of it.

"That's just great," I thought. "We're on the wall of a brush-filled canyon, and there's a fire burning below us!"

That was the last thing we needed. But seeing that the mysterious glow hadn't grown any brighter, I figured we were in reasonably good shape for the time being. Skirting the fire, we moved to our left, as the acrid smell of burning oil thickened the night air. I could smell burning plastic too, and in that moment I had no doubt that a significant portion of the car was on fire.

We moved carefully, navigating the canyon wall until the wreckage of the car came into view. "Oh, Jesus," Charlie said. "The thing's pancaked flat." That it was, and now that I'd moved close enough for my light to cut the smoke, I could see what was left of someone's arm, protruding from a small, triangular opening near the car's roof-line.

From the rubbery look of that arm, to the way a bone protruded from its skin, there was no doubt its owner was dead. But since we'd come all that way, it stood to reason that we needed to yank on it a time or two.

Crouching down low, we crawled commando-style toward the smoldering wreckage. From what we could see, whoever it was that had beaten us down there, hadn't done much of anything. In fact, aside from the lights we'd seen earlier, and the mysterious El Camino guy, who'd disappeared into thin air, Charlie and I seemed to be all alone.

"Where the hell is everyone?" Charlie asked, as he poked at the arm with a stick. "And what were those lights all about?"

I was about to hazard a guess, when a beam of light flashed out from under the car's front end. Pointing my own light in that direction, I could see the El Camino guy, along with two others, kneeling in front of the car. They looked up a moment, before one of them slid under the front-end, as the other two disappeared around the side.

What they were doing had me baffled, as did the notion that not a single person seemed to care about the driver. "Maybe it's because he's dead," I thought. "Or maybe they've crawled under the car because someone's pinned beneath it."

We couldn't yet tell, as the blue smoke grew thicker by the

second. I pulled back a bit, while Charlie slid his hand along the car's rocker panel. "It's a GT," he said in a soft tone. "A GT-350. This is a damned shame!"

I looked back in agreement, just as the dead-arm twitched a tragic farewell. "HOLY CRAP!" I yelled out. "The guy's arm just moved... Maybe he's not dead after all!"

We sat back on our knees, lit by the glow of a small oil fire that burned beneath the buckled hood. "Poke at the arm," I told Charlie. "Yank on it a couple of times just to see what happens."

"You yank on it," he said. "You saw it move. So it's your turn now!"

Ducking the smoke, I leaned close to the flattened roof-line, before yelling into the car's interior..

"CAN YOU HEAR ME? I asked loudly. "ARE YOU ALIVE IN THERE?"

There was no verbal response, nor was there a twitch of flesh that suggested a glimmer of life. I called out once more, while shaking the wrist of the rubbery limb... But as expected, there was no reply. That's probably when we should have headed back up the hillside. Yet for some unknown reason I felt compelled to try one last time.

I called out again, when a sharp voice rang out from beneath the car, saying, "QUIT YELLING, DUDE! THE GUY'S BEEN DEAD FOR HOURS!"

I shut dead-up when I heard the voice, immediately realizing that something was very wrong. What it was I didn't know, other than it wasn't the body, or the dead arm, or the smell of burning insulation that bothered me. There was something more in the man's voice, the twisted realization that he actually didn't care.

Had this been the first corpse we'd ever stumbled upon, perhaps it would have explained the queasiness that was welling up inside of me, but there was much more at work here than just the obvious. Something sinister that transcended the severed head we'd seen rolling on the ground last summer, and something much darker than the bloated corpse that washed ashore at our riverfront campsite. This wasn't just death. It was death mixed with something else... something that definitely shouldn't have been.

Sensing we'd overstayed our welcome, I pointed the beam of

my flashlight far into the inner recesses of the car. I needed to. Half out of perverse curiosity, and half out of the notion that I might have recognized the driver. There's a possibility I would have, had his head not been crushed between the steering column and the forward portion of the roof-line. "Whoa…" Charlie said, as my light illuminated what looked like a splattered cockroach. "That thing used to be his head!"

"What is it about heads?" I asked. "This guy's head is pinched off, and that other guy's head was chopped off, and for all we know, next week someone else's head is going to roll!"

The dismembered head thing was beginning to look like a trend, but before we could ponder why that was, another question begged to be answered.

What were the others doing under the car?

We looked at one another as that question rolled through our minds, until the zipping sound of a socket wrench broke through the crisp, night air.

Charlie tipped his head as the sound welled up. Just a moment before the El Camino guy slithered out from under the wreckage with the bounty in his hands.

He smiled in the fire-fueled glow, holding something in his hands that I couldn't quite see. "What's he got there?" I asked Charlie, as I peered through the smoke. "What the hell is that?" I couldn't tell for sure, until he held the prize over his head as if he was holding the Stanley Cup.

"Oh my God," I stammered, as the prize came into view. "I can't believe this!"

But I had to. As he held up the car's custom, Shelby oil pan for all the world to see.

He held it high with a sickly smile, and at that moment, there was no doubt that they were parting-out the car.

That they were. They were stripping the car of its custom parts, without giving the slightest thought to the dead driver inside.

The whole scenario was horrifying, and it became even worse when one of the guys under the car started laughing like a jackal. Perhaps one of them had told a joke. Or perhaps they found something amusing about the way the driver's head had been splattered like a pumpkin. Why they laughed I'll never know, and who they were I don't know either. But I do know with certainty that, as they laughed beneath a blood soaked grave, something dark looked down from above.

Feeling like we'd witnessed a grave robbery, I turned away with a heaviness in my heart. "Let's get out of here NOW," I said. "Before something terrible happens!"

We began to climb, as if we knew we'd seen something that we never should have. I climbed quickly, thinking there was more to come than what we'd just witnessed. It wasn't going to fall upon our shoulders, that I knew. But as I scrambled up the slope, I was overcome with the urge to escape with my life.

Charlie followed suit, and within minutes we'd reached the boulder-jam. I scrambled to find a foothold, and as I did the words of my father rang loud and true. "Promise me that if you ever get involved in something that brings Him around, you'll high-tail it out of there!" he'd said. And as I looked down upon the bluish-orange glow of an unknown man's funeral pyre, those words burned with renewed urgency.

We climbed without saying a word, and as we did something became glaringly apparent. The Reaper had been there all along. And he'd been showing us the signs since the moment we drove past Grandstands.

I'd seen the signs of course. But like everyone else on that road that night, I chose to drive on by. It had been easy to pretend the signs weren't there, and even easier to ignore them by assuming they were intended for someone else. "This one's not for me, and that one's not for me," is what I'd been telling myself. "As long as you're careful, the signs won't apply to you." That may have been true on any other night. However, on this particular eve, it would have done me well to slow down and read the fine print.

Had I read the sub-text, I would have headed home, thankful for my coddled, happy life. But it felt as if we were voyeurs. There to observe. As if we were combat photographers, with no political interest at all.

The whole scenario was unnerving. Both the fact that I was there, and the notion that we'd stumbled up to Hell's window. Now that we'd seen things for what they really were, all I wanted to do was high-tail it out of there. The guy was dead, and there was nothing we could do about it. Especially now that the fire was spreading, and his crooked, dead arm would soon be reduced to a charred chicken wing.

Climbing the final pitch, I looked up toward the guardrail, where the silhouettes of those above were back-lit with an ominous, orange glow. We could hear their voices, drawn long and thin in the late night air. Some were speaking in whispers, while another, according to his tone, seemed to have found something amusing about all of this.

I listened to the laughter as my boot-tips found their mark, wondering who it was that felt the need to laugh in the face of death. "It's just some idiot," I told myself. "Just some guy who's had too much to drink on a night that's most unsettling." I was willing to let it go, and chalk it up to a bad night out, when the drunken idiot threw an empty beer bottle that nearly hit me in the head.

Whether or not he meant to hit me, I'll never really know. For as I climbed the hill with a taste for vengeance, something materialized beside the guardrail that made my blood run cold.

It was Him, standing on the hillside between the glow of the headlights and the rusted guardrail.

"Go home NOW!" The Reaper said, with a low, metallic rattle. "Go home, before it's too late!"

I didn't dare reply, for the tone in his voice had said it all. It was time to run, as everything else that had just transpired seemed woefully unimportant.

Charlie hadn't heard the voice, but he had sensed the urgency in my stride. Climbing quickly, we cut past the guardrail, onto a road that was littered with empty beer bottles. "They've turned it into a party," I thought. "a sick, twisted party with a Grim Reaper pinata."

I was beginning to see the irony in it all, when the words of The Reaper resonated as if they'd been sent on a wire.

"GO HOME NOW!" he said. "NOW!"

"We've got to move, and we've got to move fast!" I told Charlie. "Trust me… We need to move NOW!"

Whether or not he'd seen Him, Charlie felt his vibe. So much so, that he took the lead as we hurried down the road. "Let's head down to Sunset, and come back up on the 405," he said. "Lets just get the hell out of here!"

We did just that. Running down the road to where the Corvette waited in the shadows. I could have kept running, and never looked back. But something begged me to turn, and see why it was he'd come to call.

I paused mid-stride, on the double-yellow line, twisting in place to look back on the road. The crowd had thinned... while beside the El Camino stood The Reaper. As if he was waiting to get in.

"That's going to be one hell of a ride," I thought. "One HELL of a ride."

I paused mid-stride, on the double-yellow line, twisting in place

Five years passed, and it was time to move on, time to look past the expectations of others, and finally time to do what was best for me.

I'd been driving through the desert for hours. Chasing a copper strand of sunlight, that clung to the distant mountains. My eyelids had grown heavy, and a refreshment stop was definitely in order. Squinting through the oncoming headlights, I could see the dull, yellow glow of a truck-stop sign a quarter mile off in the distance. The turn-off was rapidly approaching, and I down-shifted to bleed off some speed. "You'd better stop here," I told myself. "This may be the last gas station for the next two hundred miles."

As I rolled onto the off-ramp, I was surprised at how short the exit road was. "DAMN!" I yelled, as I stood on the brakes. "This ramp is short!"

I suppose it was. Or perhaps I'd been traveling way too fast, for far too long. The sudden stop had jarred me awake, and now, as I idled at the intersection of nowhere and God-knows-why, I reflected upon the words my mother had spoken earlier.

"It's not safe for you to drive all night in the desert," she'd said, "especially all alone!"

She was right of course. But with my friends waiting for me at the Colorado River, the long desert journey seemed almost requisite.

"I'll be okay," is what I'd told her. "I've driven through the desert many times, and I know the road quite well."

That sounded alright I suppose. Yet as I attempted to placate her fears, deep down inside I could sense that something was amiss.

It had all started when I left work earlier that evening. Everything seemed to be conspiring against me somehow, as if for some reason an unseen hand was trying it's best to hold me back. First it was the long line at the gas station. Then it was the bungee cords that had disappeared into thin air. And finally, it all came to a head when my bank closed an hour earlier than normal.

That would have been the cog in the wheel that stopped me for sure, had my father not ponied-up a couple of hundred dollars to float me through the weekend. And besides, the IJSBA Jet Ski Racing World Finals came but once a year, and I was qualified for a spot in the Modified Division. There was no way I was going to miss out on racing at the big-show. And no way I was going to disappoint my friends who were waiting for me at the end of the line.

I pulled forward, driving down a narrow road that smelled of scorched brake linings. There was an overpass up ahead, and I drove up and over before pulling into a truck-service parking lot.

To my right was a shantytown of battered motor homes and broken-down semi's that looked as if they were being reclaimed by the desert. In one of the old travel-trailers, I could see the sallow, yellow hue of a low wattage lamp, glowing through smoke stained curtains. It was as if the people inside were just waiting to die, and as I rolled past the shadowy rows, the pull of unseen eyes was unmistakable.

I drove toward the rear of the complex, passing a long row of diesel pumps that weren't going to do me any good. There was a shoeless man with a cowboy hat standing beside the pumps, who stared at me with darkened eyes, as the cherry of his cigarette glowed bright red.

This was a place where you'd best be passing through. A place where if you lingered too long, whatever it was that infested those molded trailers, would likely worm its way under your skin. I could feel the malice between the rows as it reached out for me, and I shivered at the thought that it was hungry for my soul.

Hooking around the back of the truck stop market, I saw a row of old-school gas pumps that reminded me of the days when I worked at the filling station. Some of them were missing their cowlings, while a tall pump at the far end of the row, looked as if a bird had made a nest inside of it.

I pulled up beside a working pump, before shutting down my engine. Stepping out of my pickup truck, I stretched my arms toward the sky, where dozens of bat-sized moths fluttered wildly around the fluorescent lights. I'd never seen moths that big, and as they crashed their bodies against the light fixtures, it seemed as if they were bent upon killing themselves.

There was a madness to their flight as they raced to their doom, as if there was something within the light they needed more than life itself. I watched them dive-bomb the fixtures, feeling like the same thing that had gotten into them, was reaching out for me as well.

I looked far to the West, where the reddish glow of the Indian sun fast faded. There in the desert, I could feel the earth's energy all around me. And even though the air rumbled with the sound of idling diesel engines, a magical presence pressed through, with a force that was unmistakable.

"You'd better get her gassed-up," I thought. "And you'd better check the trailer's tie-downs one more time."

As I walked beside my tandem trailer, I checked the transom tie-downs to make sure everything was cinched down properly. Each of the two race-prepped Jet Skis was securely held in place, but I pulled down on the ratchet straps anyway, just to be doubly sure. The rig was tight, and ready for the final haul. So, after shuffling some gear around in the pickup's bed, I walked into the truck-stop store for a cold drink, and a quick bathroom break.

It was a quick stop really. Just long enough to stretch my legs and fill a sixty four ounce soda cup to the limit. I walked into the store where I was greeted by the smell of vinyl floor-mats and stale cigarette smoke. My head began to spin as the scent hit my nose, while memories rushed forward that nearly overwhelmed me.

"The signs are everywhere!" my father's voice said, as it cut in like a razor. "And they litter the road where a man ends up, who failed to heed the warnings set before him."

Where that came from I hadn't a clue. Other than it seemed like my father was watching me from afar. The memory of his words seemed to fall from the sky, and as I stood in the entryway the strangest chill rolled down my spine.

I collected my thoughts, while a crusty old codger looked at me like I was some kind of drug addict. I stared back for a moment, before my feet guided me to safer waters. I took a few steps as my head cleared, before shuffling down the store's center aisle. "What the hell just happened," I thought. "Was that some kind of a message, or was it an omen?"

I stopped at the isles end-cap, where a rickety stack of shelves did its best not to fall over. On the top shelf was a dusty display of old fishing hooks beside a jar of salmon eggs that had yellowed long ago.

Scuffing around a bit, I poked through bins of knick-knacks that brought back distant memories. "Oh my God," I thought, as I picked up an old bait-casting reel. "This is the very same model I caught my first fish on!"

After turning the star-drag back just a bit, I spun the reel's handle with a broad smile. "Now cast it like THIS," my father had said long ago. "The hungry fish are waiting!"

That memory came out of nowhere, thrust from the annals of time that seemed to be stored on those dusty old shelves. I placed the reel beside a jar of catfish bait, thinking, "When I get back, I'm going to spend some quality time with the old man... before it's too late."

That thought resonated as I walked past the motor oil, toward a long, narrow aisle that looked like it was abandoned. "Where's the food?" I thought. "It's got to be here somewhere."

I was about to lose hope, when I caught sight of a loaf of bread and a can of sardines, perched atop the aisle's end-cap. "Ah-Ha!" I said aloud. "I've found the food section!"

It didn't take long for me to scoop up a bag of pork rinds and a beef stick or two. Then, after stealing a few sips off the top of my fountain drink, I topped her off before humping the load to the register.

I suppose that as I headed toward the check-out counter, I expected to see a weather beaten road-hag standing there. But as I looked up at the clerk, I was greeted by a girl with the most beautiful blue eyes I'd ever seen.

Her name was Debbie. And somehow, there in the most unlikely place, she and I made a connection. I don't remember which one of us spoke first, but before I knew it, our chance meeting had lasted more than an hour.

She was a beautiful girl, with sandy blonde hair, and the curvy kind of figure that drives me wild. We talked about anything and everything as I leaned against the check-out counter until her dinner break arrived, where we moved the conversation to an old, wooden bench just outside the store a ways.

Moths swirled like fairy dust as we sat there, neither of us knowing what just happened, but knowing it was magical just the same.

"I'll come back and see you," I told her. "I promise I'll see you just as soon as I can!"

She smiled as she sat atop the bench, her legs swaying back and forth as if she was sitting on a swing.

"You'd better come back," she said. "Cause I like you!"

I didn't want to leave, but I knew if I didn't get out of there soon, I was never going to. Taking her hand, I looked into her eyes, saying, "Hey, I've really got to get going, but I PROMISE I'll be back to see you soon!"

Debbie knew I meant it, and she smiled as if it might actually happen. Then, with her hand in mine, we walked back to my truck where we stood there looking at one another.

"Have fun at the river," she said, before kissing me with lips that tasted like bubble gum. "Be very, very safe. And come see me!"

I brushed her hair away from her forehead, telling her I'd be extra careful. Then, just as I was about to leave, I remembered the most important thing of all.

"I don't have your phone number," I said. "I don't want to take a chance of losing you!"

"You're not going to lose me!" she said, as she slipped a folded gum wrapper into my pocket. "Cause my phone number will be right here!"

She paused a moment, with her fingers tucked into my jeans. Then, just before she spun around teasingly, she said, "You'd better come back and see me, or I'll come find you!"

I was thinking "Hell yeah, I'll be back," as Debbie cat-walked away from me. But before she'd made it half way to the door, she spun around with the most awkward look on her face.

"DON'T GO!" she said as she rushed up to me. "I just got the strangest feeling… as if something TERRIBLE is going to happen to you!"

I didn't know what to do, other than hold her as she seemed ready to cry. She'd sensed something, that was for certain. And whatever that thing was, it was causing fear to roll off her in waves.

As she shook her head back and forth, I asked, "Tell me exactly what you've seen, it's very, very important!"

"I… I can't say exactly," she said. "It's like I saw something for a moment. Something terrible!"

She calmed a bit as I held her, until she looked up with tears in her eyes. "I don't want you to think I'm crazy," she said. "It's just that sometimes I have these weird visions, and the one I just had scares me to death!"

"It was just a flash," she said, "where I could see someone walking down the highway, while a fire burned all around. I don't know if that person was you, but I do know that if you do go down that road, I'm never, EVER going to see you again!"

It would have been nice to have told her that her vision was just a random thought. But I'd seen the signs too. And now, more than ever, I needed to pay careful attention to them.

Speaking softly, I told her, "You know what? You're not crazy at all, because I've had a bad feeling about this trip from the get-go. It's almost like something out there is warning me to dig in and hunker-down low, before a big storm comes my way."

"And what do you think that big storm is?" she asked.

"I don't know," I said. "I only know that I'm going to meet it head-on, somewhere between here and the river."

"That's why you need to stay here!" Debbie said, with a pleading tone to her voice. "Don't you see that?"

"I do," I told her. "I do see it. And now that I have, that bit of knowledge is what's going to keep me out of harm's way."

"Well, that does make some sense," she said. "But it's too great a warning to leave to chance. What if the thing you do to save yourself ends up making things worse?"

"I can't think like that," I told her. "If I start second-guessing myself at every step, it'll do nothing more than weaken the magic that's saved me time and time again. Besides, there's no way I'm going to let something bad happen to me, because that would mean I couldn't come back here to see you!"

"You'd better be careful," Debbie said. "And you'd better call me from the river, or I'll forever worry that something really did happen to you."

"I promise I will." I told her. "I really, really promise."

A hundred miles passed like they never existed. And as I gripped the wheel, my head swirled with the implications of all that had happened. Had fate sent me to that forgotten truck-stop so I could meet the girl of my dreams? Or was the unexpected side-trip simply fate's way of speeding me up, or slowing me down?

It would have been nice if the delay had altered the equation in my favor, but for some reason it didn't feel that way. In fact, as I drove down the desolate stretch of road, the voice in the back of my head suggested quite the contrary.

"You're heading straight for disaster," The voice kept saying. "Now that you've taken a break, you're lined up in the cross-hairs more than ever."

There was no denying that, for I knew that fate had simply adjusted its scope for windage and distance. I had the weirdest feeling as I rolled down the highway, almost as if I was a trophy deer that had been spotted from a mile away. My fur was bristling, and I could feel the eyes upon me. But I had no idea where the hunter was… no idea at all.

Intuitively, I knew to keep a couple of ridges between myself and whatever it was that was stalking me. And in order to do that, I needed to keep moving. "No more stops," I told myself. "Not even one, especially on this lonely stretch of road."

It sure as hell was lonely, save for the endless line of semi-trucks that blasted by in waves. I imagined that inside each of those tractor cabs was a good-old-boy, strung-out on Marlboro Reds and a hand-full of uppers. There were human beings driving those machines, yet as they thundered past like rolling monsters, I was as far from humanity as I could possibly be.

As the white lines in the road shot past like glowing tracer shells, I couldn't help but wonder, "Why does everything seem so symbolic? And why does it feel so literal?" I couldn't quite put my finger on it, other than it must have had something to do with the words my father had spoken years earlier.

"The signs are all around you," he'd said. "And the decisions you make when you see them will determine whether you come home on the boat, or come home in a box!"

I pondered those words as a double-trailered semi bore down on me at ninety miles per hour. The truck was way over the center-line, perhaps a tire's width or more, and as it thundered past on the two lane highway, my trailer was nearly sucked under its carriage by the powerful suction vortex.

"HOLY CRAP!" I yelled out, as my trailer swayed wildly. "Why do those assholes always have to wander over the line? And why do they always do it when an car is approaching?

I was seeing red, but before I could vent my anger over his careless head-on pass, another trucker did the exact same thing, nearly jack-knifing my rig in the process.

The truck came so close that we must have swapped paint. Then, as the first of two trailers clipped alongside, I ducked down, fearing decapitation. How the Jet skis didn't end up under his rear wheels I'll never know. But I do know that the second I cleared the end of his trailer, my entire rig veered wildly into the oncoming lane.

As I swerved across the line, there was little time to think. I only knew that if I didn't regain control, I was going to hit the next semi head-on. I fought the wheel as best I could, nearly pitching my truck on its side. Then, as I accelerated rapidly, I pulled her true, just seconds before the next monster approached.

I shook with adrenaline, knowing far too well that if those long-haul assholes kept it up, one of them was going to kill me. They were driving like they couldn't care less, and in that moment I realized that if they did kill someone, they'd probably have kept on going.

That thought was chilling, as was the notion that death had

stepped up to the plate. "What do I throw Him," I thought. "Maybe low-and-tight, or high-and-wide on the outside." Either way it was a gamble. Unless I walked Him... which was my only hope.

The only way I could make that happen was to get as far away from the trucks as I could. With no hard-shoulder and a steep pitch to the sand, pulling to the side wasn't an option. I was going to have to run the gauntlet, at least until the next turn-off three miles ahead.

I gripped the wheel with sweaty palms as one truck after another thundered past. A couple of times they came close, but not nearly as much as the two had earlier. Counting my blessings, I turned onto an intersecting highway that seemed deserted, save for a few large tumbleweeds that were rolling across the road. "Thank God," I thought, as the tumbling bushes rolled aside. "I'm off the truck route. Now all I have to do is count coyotes for the next hundred miles."

It took a while, but eventually, the feeling of doom that had permeated the trip gave way to an eerie silence. The radio was on, and the music was playing, but for some reason it felt like I was driving through a sound-free vacuum. Looking to both sides of the road, all I could see was the inky blackness of endless desert. There wasn't a pin prick of light to be seen, other than the red glow of a radio tower far in the distance.

"Wow!" I thought, as I rolled down the highway. "There's absolutely nothing here. Nothing, but nothing."

That thought was dead-on. For where I was, not a person could be found, except for the unlucky few, who'd taken up residence in shallow, unmarked graves.

There were plenty of those folks out there, people who'd taken a one-way ride, back when The King was still doing Vegas. Things were a lot different back then. When a man would sling a water filled bag over his car's radiator, before taking a trip down a road without a name. Somewhere along the line he'd make a stop, to lighten the load a bit, careful to kick the dirt off his shovel, before getting back on the road.

That's just the way it was out in the desert, a place where you'd never stop unless you absolutely had to. There were things out there you didn't want to see. And things you were better off never finding. All of them left behind by those who parked just a wee bit off the road.

I learned about that the hard way. Back when we'd roam the desert canyons, in search of God knows what. There were old refrigerators out there, old, rusted relics that had no business being that far off the road. I always wondered why someone would drive that far just to dump an old appliance until we started opening the doors, and quickly found out why.

Yeah, I knew what was out there. And I also knew it was best to look straight ahead. "There's no sense looking for something you shouldn't be seeing," I thought, "especially tail lights, way off the road."

Taking my own advice, I kept my eyes on the road, as an occasional truck flew by. The trucks were just as big, and just as dangerous as the others had been, except for the fact that the undulating, hilly road had slowed them down quite a bit. Additionally, the sandy shoulder that had abbreviated the main highway, had now given way to packed dirt, creating a run-off zone, that was hard enough to drive onto, should someone cross the line.

I was breathing easier, with a bit of room to maneuver, and fewer morons coming my way. It was a beautiful night, with a sky full of stars, and the sweet smell of sagebrush in the air. I flipped on my high-beams to brighten things up a bit, and as I did I could see a huge jackrabbit standing beside the road. The thing was big. Really, really big. So much so that it looked more like a small kangaroo than anything else.

"Maybe it was a jackalope," I thought with a smile. "I should have looked for some horns!"

Now that I think about it, I believe I'd become complacent, lulled by the softly undulating road, and the song that was playing on my cassette deck. I was nearly in a trance, chomping ice from the bottom of my cup, while counting jackrabbits along the way. Aside from a tumbleweed or two, there was nothing else to see, until glowing lights rushed up behind me, that seemed to have come out of nowhere.

It was some kind of truck. Or at least it looked like a truck, with narrow-set headlamps that shook with the road. It had crept up on me like a predator, and now that it had, I felt as if it wanted to devour me. The driver flashed his high-beams, over and over again, while revving his engine like he wanted to run me off the road. I tried to see who or what was behind me, but as the truck's headlamps beamed directly into my rear view mirror, all I could see were two balls of light, that seemed to be free-floating in space.

Where the truck came from I hadn't a clue, nor did I know how he managed to sneak up on me the way he had. Sure, I may have been lost in thought for a moment, but not so much that I would have allowed something that aggressive to creep up on me.

I gripped the wheel tightly as I slowed down a bit, hoping the truck would pull around me. That would have been the sensible thing to do, but rather than do that, the driver seemed more interested in driving up the rear end of my trailer than anything else.

"I'm afraid something terrible is going to happen!" echoed through my mind, as his headlamps pressed closer. "Something TERRIBLE!"

I didn't want to think about that, but I also knew that if I didn't find a safe place to pull over, Debbie's prophecy may very well have come true.

Toggling my rear-view mirror, I looked ahead in the fleeting hope of seeing a turn-out. There were a few flat spots, but as I blew past at speed, there wasn't nearly enough time to react. Whoever this idiot was, he was pressing me, much too fast, and much too close for me to do anything about it. All I could do was look ahead, in the hope of seeing a semi truck's taillights far in the distance.

"That's what I'll do," I thought. "I'll just bleed off a bit of speed, until we come upon a slow moving truck. Then he'll have no choice but to drive around us!"

That thought was comforting, but as I looked ahead, there wasn't a tail light to be seen. "There's got to be a truck up there somewhere," I thought. "With these frequent hills, I'm bound to creep up behind one of them."

I looked far ahead as I feathered the gas, but every time I backed off, the deranged trucker pushed even closer. I had no idea who he was or what he wanted, I only knew that he was there, and that his vehicle stood nearly twice the height of mine.

"What the hell is this thing?" I thought. "It's not a semi, and it's not an R/V. The headlights are way too dim, and too closely set for that to be the case."

All I could do was wait things out, while hoping he'd pull around before he crawled up the ass-end of my trailer. What I really wanted to do was slam on the brakes, sending both Jet skis through his radiator. That would have been satisfying as hell. But, being that I was all alone in the middle of the desert, that kind of thing was probably best avoided.

Hoping the driver would respond to reason, I rolled down my window, waving him around. I expected he'd jump at the chance to pass, until he raged up behind me, solidly ramming his bumper against my trailer.

When I first felt the impact, I couldn't believe what he'd done. It no longer mattered who he was, for he had threatened my life, and now, all bets were off. With the realization that he could kill me, I found myself in a precarious position. There was no one around who could help me, save for the truckers who blew past as if they were on rails. None of those guys gave a rat's ass about what was happening to me, nor did they care about anything other than how quickly they flew down the road. All I could do was stay focused, and hope that he wouldn't run me into the soft sand, where my truck could easily flip over.

With one eye in my rear-view mirror, I stabbed the throttle as he tried to ram me again. My counter move worked for the moment, buying me inches of room as his teeth missed their mark. Over and over he tried to tag me, but as I slowed one moment, and sped up the next, he was finding it difficult to impact me with any real success.

There was a moment of breathing room. Not enough to get away, but enough to gather my thoughts and put together a game-plan. He wasn't going to let up, that I knew. But I had no idea how far he was willing to push. Would he press me to the point where I'd need to retrieve my shotgun? And was I going to have to shoot someone, who seemed like he was begging for just that?

The more I thought about it, the less sense any of this made. The mystery driver seemed bent upon ramming me, and if he didn't let up, he'd be dead for his troubles. I'd had enough of his bullying, and if he did manage to run me off the road, I was going to come out shooting.

Things had passed the point of reason, and in a moment of rage, I leaned out the window, shaking my fist at the moron. He gunned his engine as I did, and beneath its guttural growl I heard something I hadn't expected. It was music, loud, rock and roll music blaring from his stereo speakers as he charged up behind me, time and time again.

I froze for a moment, with my head out the window and a wheel on the broken line. I knew that song… I knew it. And in a moment of clarity, everything made perfect sense. This wasn't some crazed long-haul trucker, or a belligerent farm-boy. It was a drunken river-goer in a jacked-up pickup truck. A pure asshole, who couldn't bear the thought of slowing down a notch.

Realizing who he was, I yelled out "YOU ALMOST KILLED ME, YOU ASSHOLE!" before sliding back into the cab.

I was already pissed, but now that I knew who the idiot was, I nearly blew my top. "I'm going to slam on the brakes, and beat his drunken ass!" I yelled out in the cab. "I'm going to put both Jet skis through his radiator, before I beat the crap out of him!"

God, that would have felt good. And I was just about to make it so, when I saw something in the rear-view mirror that made my blood run cold. It was his lights. Or at least something in those lights, that glowed with an unnatural fire. Something about them was all wrong. As if their core was a glowing flame, the kind that's fueled by hatred, and the type of rage that's got no business being on this earth.

I could see the embers glowing brightly, flickering like the turn indicator of the doomed van. The lights seemed to be on fire, and as I stared into them, I felt as if The Devil was behind the wheel.

"Don't do anything stupid," I told myself. "Something's happening here that's not going to end well."

I could see it of course, just as clearly as I'd known all along that someone would be dying that night. This guy wasn't going to slow down for anything, and if I wanted to save my own hide, I was going to have to find a way out of the theater, before the grand finale.

As I figured it, the best way to get him to pass was to pull onto the shoulder. Besides, if I could find a wide enough area, there was still the possibility of keeping one set of wheels on the road. So I gave it a try, fading to my right until my tires sounded loudly, with the hum of the drainage grooves on the road's beveled edge.

He could have passed, but rather than end the madness, the maniac followed me onto the shoulder, purely out of belligerence.

I held my course, tracking along the shoulder until my trailer was struck with a neck-snapping blow. First, I flew forward, as my right front tire bit solidly into the soft sand berm. Then, as the front end seemed to float above the ground, my tires castered uncontrollably as the steering wheel was ripped from my hands.

Had I been driving just the truck, I would have pitch-poled end over end. But thanks to my trailer's extra weight, the rig held straight and true. I'd survived the worst blow by far, and now, with one tire on hard-packed sand, I looked over my shoulder to where the madman shadowed me.

"THIS IS THE FARTHEST YOU'RE GOING TO PUSH ME!" I yelled out to the faceless driver. "PUSH ME AGAIN, AND I'LL SHOOT YOUR ASS!"

I half hoped he'd push his hand, but as I pulled farther onto the shoulder, the monster-truck swerved to the left, half way across the center line. What he was doing I'll never know, other than he began swerving back and forth like a snake in the road. His engine roared and the music blared, and in that moment of madness I sensed my only option.

Holding the wheel for all my life, I feathered the brakes on the hard-packed shoulder. My wheels bit hard, rolling one moment and skidding the next, until I'd slowed considerably. For a moment I thought the truck would pass, until I heard his engine race, as he down-shifted to keep pace with me.

He braked as hard as he could, but with as much mass as he was hauling, the best he could do was roll up beside me. As his tires chirped on the asphalt, I looked to my left, seeing for the first time what I was really up against.

It was a truck alright, but not the typical Chevy or Ford that I'd expected. Rather, it was a jacked-up Willy's farm truck. A monster of a rig that looked like it could pull the hinges off the gates of

Hell. The thing was huge, with giant off-road tires and a push-bar made of steel. It was nothing short of a monster, and behind its iron bed was a boat trailer, loaded with a tricked-out pickle-fork race boat, primed and ready for the river.

The cab was so high that I couldn't see the driver. But I could see a group of idiots who were sitting in the bed, all of whom were shaking their fists at me. I stared at them as we rolled side-by side. Three guys and a girl, all sitting in lawn chairs with beers in their hands. The girl was laughing hysterically, as if there was something funny about all this, while the men sat glassy eyed, with a haunting, vacant stare.

They cursed me up and down, then, in a shocking move, one of the men hung from the truck's roll bar like he was preparing to jump onto my vehicle. My blood ran cold at the thought of that, knowing the last thing I needed was a murderous idiot in the back of my pickup.

Wanting no part of that, I pulled as far onto the shoulder as I dared, widening the gap as best as I could. He could have jumped, but as drunk as he was, there's no way the guy would have made it. I think he realized that, as he postponed the jump, in favor of side-arming a half empty beer can at my head.

I have no idea how I saw that one coming. But somehow I did, and I pulled my head out of the way just a split-second before the can exploded against the driver's-side window post.

Beer foam was everywhere, covering the dash and steering wheel like I'd rolled down the windows in a car wash. I turned on the wipers, but as the cheap beer mixed with red clay dust, it created a slurry that nearly obscured my vision.

"This is SO wrong," I thought as a second beer slammed against my rig. "How far is this guy going to take this?"

I couldn't answer for him. But I do know I was about ten seconds away from stopping in the middle of the highway to take care of business. I didn't want to do that. But with six of them, and only one of me, their actions constituted deadly force.

So that was the plan I suppose. I was going to jump from the truck, and unlock the gun box, before any of them got the jump on me. That would have worked I guess. But in order to do that, I needed a bit of breathing room. That would only come with distance, and at the moment, the shadowing vehicle didn't leave much room at all.

The only way I was going to shake this guy off my nine was to speed up quickly, before slamming on the brakes. Sure, it might have run me into the sand, but I really didn't have another option. All I needed were ten precious seconds. Just long enough to level the playing field.

I dropped down a gear with my foot to the floor, nearly floating my valves on the red-line. My truck responded well, and with the element of surprise, I pulled ahead of the beast by at least five car lengths.

His engine roared, and within seconds the truck from Hell pulled alongside. I could see a young woman in the passenger's seat who was hanging half way out the window. She looked like she was floating in air, while the jumper was locked and loaded with a fresh can of beer in his hand. The girl screamed at me, then, as she tried to spit in my face, I slammed on the brakes for all they were worth.

My tires skipped on the rutty shoulder, before finding their mark on a hard piece of ground. I expected to plow through the sand, but by the grace of God, a dove-tailed turn-out appeared in my headlights. I swung wide onto the tarmac, steering far from the road, where the monster truck idled, with the long boat in tow.

"He can't back up!" I suddenly realized. "It's pitch black out, and he won't dare back that boat into the soft sand!"

Skidding to a stop, I jumped from the cab, before leaping into the back of my truck. The small, rear-facing cab light illuminated the tool box just enough that I could see the keyhole. And after I fumbled with the keys for a moment, the latch flew open, as the diamond-plate lid popped up.

"Oh, yeah," I thought, as my shotgun came into view. "Don't you dare follow me into the desert unless you never plan on coming out again."

They must have heard my thoughts, because now, as the monster truck idled in place, one of the morons in back, pulled down his pants and mooned me.

Seeing him act that way, I suddenly realized this had been nothing more than a joke to all of them. I was just someone to terrorize, just another helpless person on a long stretch of road. I was horrified by it all. And the more I thought about it, the angrier I became.

I was livid. Angered to the point where I failed to notice a dark shadow that had quietly crept up on me.

"So... what do you think?" He said, as he popped out of nowhere. "What do you think about all this?"

At first I couldn't think, as his impromptu appearance nearly gave me a heart attack. But then, as I quickly regained my composure, I faced Him while I tried to catch my breath.

He stared at the road, while asking again, "What do you think?

"I think you've got to stop jumping out of the dark like that!" I told Him. "You're going to give me a heart attack!"

He just looked at me with the look he gives when he's feeling quite smug. Then, he asked again. "What do you think?"

"You know EXACTLY what I think!" I told Him. "They're a bunch of ASSHOLES!"

He just stood there, agreeing with me in his all-knowing silence. Collecting my thoughts for a moment, I asked, "Why are you really here? Why now, and not earlier?"

"You saw why," he replied. "You could see it in his headlights."

"You mean the fire?" I asked. "The glow in his headlights?" He could have answered, but he chose not to, preferring, instead, to let me figure it out on my own as I had that fateful day on the bay.

I could hear what he was thinking, and as his thoughts mixed with mine, I half wondered if I was losing my mind. "Aren't you going to follow them?" he asked, as the monster truck rolled away. "Aren't you the least bit curious about what's going to happen to them?"

The answer could have been, "No." But that would have been a lie, for as I wiped the windshield with a musty sweatshirt I knew damn well that I didn't want to lose sight of them.

I turned to answer, but he was gone. Off into the night as if there was someplace more important he needed to be. Maybe he'd be back and maybe he wouldn't, that I didn't know. But I did know that I needed to catch up to the monster truck, before it got too far down the road.

Sliding back in the cab, I pulled onto the highway amid doubts of my own sanity. I didn't feel insane, but then again, I'd never really lost my mind before. The Reaper seemed real, and others had seen Him too. But the way he kept phasing in and out of reality, made Him a bit hard to nail down, and even harder to figure out.

I pulled onto the highway, as an oncoming truck roared past like a freight train. The imminent threat was gone, at least from behind anyway. But as I sat on a seat full of sour beer foam, I could still sense danger, relatively close by.

I'd barely gotten up to speed, when He appeared again, this time in the cab of my truck.

"SHOTGUN!" He called out from the passenger seat. "I've always wanted to say that!"

I nearly swerved into the oncoming lane as he popped out of nowhere, while smiling smugly, without his seat-belt on.

"Better catch up!" he said, with an nearly childlike tone to his voice. "There's death in those headlights, and you know what THAT means!"

Yeah, I knew what that meant. But not wanting to concede kinship with The Grim Reaper, I played dumb for a moment, as he pointed through the beer stained windshield.

"Just sit back and watch," he said, as his pointy death-finger traced a line to the horizon. "Just watch!"

Following his finger line, I looked ahead, to where the monster truck had pulled up behind another vehicle. This time he was tailgating a semi-truck, a sixty-five footer that had geared down to negotiate some hills. You'd have expected the idiot would have given the semi some room, given the size difference and all. But in keeping with his moronic behavior, he was breathing down the trucker's back, just inches from his bumper.

From where we sat, it looked as if both vehicles had become one. I could see the boat trailer's lights flashing on and off as the driver rode the brake, while surging as close as he could to the fifty ton behemoth.

"He's doing it again," I said. "He's on another God-damned rampage!"

"It's got nothing to do with God," my shadowy companion

added. "It's got everything to do with respect, or, in his case, the lack of it."

I glanced toward Him as the trailer's taillights flickered in the distance, nodding in agreement as we rolled down the road.

"Your father taught you well," he said, in a rusted, metallic tone. "He understands respect, and he recognizes the importance of passing that on to you."

I just rolled along, staring at the brake lights while everything he'd said hit home.

"I've got so many questions," I said, "There's so much I need to know."

"Not now," he said. "Right now you need to slow down, in order to give IT some room."

As he said that, a chill ran down my spine that nearly yanked my foot off the gas. Staring straight at Him, I asked, "What the Hell is IT? Exactly what are you talking about?"

"You know damn well what," he said, as brake lights flickered in the distance. "You can see things before they happen... Yet you're afraid to admit you're just like me."

He was right. I was troubled by something that I'd known all along. Probably more-so than the fact that I was sitting next to The Grim Reaper.

"Yeah, I do see things," I admitted. "It's just that I can't process what I'm seeing as quickly as you do."

"I've had time to work on it," he said, "an awfully long time."

I slowed to ponder it all, rolling onto the shoulder as gravel crunched beneath my tires. I was about to ask Him more, when he pointed down the road, as if time had suddenly run out.

Ahead of us, we could see the monster truck cut into the oncoming lane. Its engine roared as it began to pass the semi, then, as both vehicles dropped into a deep dip in the road, I lost sight of their taillights for a moment.

At first there was darkness, until the taillights reappeared on the next cresting hill. Up and down the taillights went, as they pushed forward on the narrow two-lane road. I watched them from afar, seeing crimson dots rise and fall as the road sought its level. The semi slowed, as the shrill sound of distorted rock and roll wafted through my air vents. He pointed, and I waited, as both vehicles disappeared, into the deepest dip of all.

There was nothing but darkness, mixed with the acrid smell of ozone that wafted off my passenger. He seemed like he was going to ignite, when suddenly, from deep within the dip in the road, there was a screech, and a crack . . . Just a second before an enormous ball of fire rolled skyward.

"OH MY GOD!" I gasped, as the night sky turned to day. "OH MY GOD!"

He said nothing, as we stopped short of the largest explosion I'd ever seen. It looked like a gasoline tanker had just exploded, and as the first heat wave hit my truck, I leaned away from my window to shield myself from the blast.

My mouth was agape as he basked in the light of his craftsmanship. And I could see Him smile a wry, fickle smile as the flame-ball rose skyward like a fiery mushroom.

I shielded my face, but not so much that I couldn't see something emerge from beneath the fire ball. At first it looked like a shadow. Maybe even a gas pocket that hadn't ignited. I didn't know what to think, until the form crept closer, and I gasped at what I saw.

It was a semi-truck, free-rolling over the crest in the road, with its crushed front end completely consumed with fire.

My mouth was agape as the flaming hulk approached, and as it did, I was overcome with the uneasy feeling that no one was behind the wheel. It was freakish the way it rolled down the highway, the flames of its burning cab melting the black-top like it was a gigantic blow torch. Below the cab, the ground shimmered with heat, and as droplets of molten metal rained down from above, the beast hissed like a locomotive.

I should have driven forward as the behemoth crossed the center-line, but as it veered toward me, I held fast, compelled to stare down the dragon's throat. "MOVE OUT OF THE WAY!" My mind screamed out as the truck rolled closer. "It's coming for YOU!"

And that it was. Perhaps in the hope of adding one more soul to those who were cooking on the asphalt. I stared down its throat until my face felt its fire. Then, as if I was on autopilot, I let out the clutch, pulling clear of the beast without a moment to spare.

My truck lunged forward, as the super-heated window glass began to singe my arm. "OWWWWW!" I yelled, as my skin began to fry. "GET AWAY FROM THIS THING, BEFORE IT TAKES YOUR LIFE!"

As I pulled away from certain death, the semi plowed into the soft sand berm. The truck yawed a moment as its front wheels left the highway. Then, with a shudder, its molten mass pitched forward, as the front end dug in like the blade of a bulldozer.

For a moment I thought the entire rig was going to flip, especially when its high-boy trailer stacked up against the king-pin. But the pin-clip held, and the trailer shuddered violently as its mass settled to the ground.

I pulled to a stop, far enough up the road where I felt reasonably safe. Sure, I could have driven farther. Maybe even to the point where I'd have kept on going. But we weren't even half way done with the show, not nearly to the point of intermission, nor anywhere near the part where the plot twists were disclosed. So I just sat there, with one foot in the cab, and another on the blacktop, hoping the flimsy pane of glass behind my seat would shield me from the blast when the flames reached the semi's fuel tanks.

The fire hissed angrily, and as it did, an odd cracking sound began to emanate from within the truck's melting cab. It sounded like someone was banging a wrench against solid steel. And as I sat there in shock, it suddenly occurred to me that the driver of the semi may have survived the impact.

I suppose that up until that moment, I hadn't considered that the trucker might still be alive. It just didn't seem feasible, given the flaming cab, and the noxious cloud of fumes that was closing down my throat. The thought of his survival wasn't even an option, until the crumpled door flew open, and the driver threw himself onto the freshly melted black-top.

At first he rolled on the ground, just feet away from the flesh-searing flames. I couldn't tell if he was doing a death-roll, or if he'd been blinded by the smoke and fire. All I knew was his clothes were beginning to burn, and if he didn't roll clear of the flames, he'd surely be consumed by the fire.

"RUN THIS WAY!" I yelled. "RUN TOWARD MY VOICE!"

Perhaps he'd heard me. Or perhaps it was instinct that drove him from the flames. But regardless of which, he seemed to be on auto-pilot, as he slowly staggered in the direction of my voice.

He tripped over the roads cut edge, staggering sideways like a drunken sailor. I stepped toward him, while all around us were fires, set on pieces of debris I'd not yet recognized. Squinting into the smoke, I could see the truck driver standing by the side of the road, back-lit with the crimson glow of burning diesel fuel.

As I approached, it was so hot that I feared my clothes would ignite. "COME HERE NOW!" I cried out, as I reached for his shoulder. "YOU'LL BE SAFE HERE!"

The trucker stumbled toward me like he had nothing left to live for. I led him to my truck, where I faced him, before doing a quick assessment of his injuries. The guy's face had been scalded, but not much worse than if he'd opened up a barbecue at the worst possible moment. He was obviously in shock, but aside from a few burns on his palms and a sweater that was half melted, he'd definitely dodged a bullet... health-wise that is.

He stared straight into my eyes, with the look of a man who'd just seen The Devil. "It came right at me," he said, in almost a whisper. "That THING came right at me."

There was nothing I could say that would change any of that. So, after steadying him with my hand, I reluctantly turned to face the highway. Something burned brightly in the dip in the road. And although I hadn't yet seen what it was, there was little question as to what was lying in wait.

I began the walk. The kind of scuffing, stumbling, tripping walk you take when you'd rather not be walking at all. The road rose before me, and as I neared the crest of the hilltop, I was nearly overcome with the sickly-sweet smell of burning death. The stench swarmed like bees, its long fingers reaching out as I pulled my shirt collar over my nose.

Skirting a fiery pool of diesel fuel, I traced a smoldering divot that had been cleaved deeply into the ground. Far below, in the road's deep depression was a fireball, burning brightly with a glow that seemed fit for The Devil. I walked toward the flames, not sure why, other than they seemed to be calling out to me. I could have sworn I heard a voice as I neared the burning wreckage, then, as the soles of my shoes began melting to the ground, I stood dead in place as the horror began to unfold.

The roadside was empty with not a headlight to be seen, nor another soul to stand beside me. I was completely alone, standing before something that had been compressed into a hideous, flaming box. To my left was a steaming lump of metal, lying half on the black-top, and half way off the road. Walking past it, I saw it was an engine block, attached to what was left of a transmission that had been sheared completely in half.

Down the center of the highway was a long trickle of flame which had caramelized the black top into a thread of onyx glass. The flame-thread stretched a hundred feet or so, toward the body of a vehicle, that was completely consumed in flames. I moved toward the fire, as if there was something I could do, and as I approached the wreckage, I watched things burn that I'd rather not describe.

I spun around, needing to do something other than stare. "Surely someone's been thrown free," I thought, "There's got to be someone alive. There's just got to be." But there wasn't. There wasn't a thing on the road that reeked of humanity, except for a severed arm, that twitched beside an open beer can.

Across the road, I heard a shout, a voice from the living that had come out of nowhere. It was another truck driver, probably the guy that the monster truck had passed just before the explosion. It felt good to feel a human presence, and as his voice cut through the night air, I began to feel whole again.

The man walked to my side without saying a word. He didn't need to, as there was nothing to say that hadn't been said by the invisible hand of doom. I suppose there was beauty in it all, although at the time, it was hard to reconcile that understanding.

I nodded to the trucker as I ventured into the desert, side stepping a barbed wire fence that had been sheared in two during the crash.

Fifty feet out were the remains of the boat trailer which was in surprisingly good condition aside from being bent in half like a giant jack-knife. I walked around the trailer, scuffing through the sagebrush as if the rattlesnakes didn't matter. "Someone might be alive," is what I kept telling myself. But as I came across what was left of the ski boat, I knew for certain that no one had survived the crash.

There was nothing left of the thing except for a motor that had been fixed to the transom with three inch lag-bolts. Splinters of fiberglass lay everywhere, sprinkled throughout the desert in testament to how far the thing had been thrown.

"Somewhere between here and there is the rest of them," I thought. "They've either been torn to pieces, or they're in that ball of flame."

While I kicked through the sagebrush, headlights scattered across the road as several more big-rigs arrived on-scene. Their drivers began the grisly tour, and, as they did, I took a step back into the shadows.

They stumbled across the road, each of them looking like they'd been shell shocked by a bomb. While they walked the walk of death, The Reaper appeared by my side.

"Caught you standing around in the shadows!" He said. "You know, if you keep that up, you might just scare the life out of someone!"

I looked at Him as he stood there like an artist at a gallery opening. "Now all they need is a tour-guide," He said, "someone to show them the finer points, such as, here's the flaming truck body, and there's someone's arm! Although we don't yet know rightly whose…"

I'd have been sickened by his humor had we not shared the same sartorial wit. "You've really outdone yourself this time," I said. "Don't you think you've caked on the horror just a little bit thick?"

"On the contrary," He said, "this has nothing to do with me. I'm just here to sweep up the popcorn. Besides, you saw for yourself what an idiot that guy was. Do you think that was the first time he pushed his luck?"

I knew it wasn't. And as I stared into the wreckage with the sickly taste of copper in my mouth, a black twist of smoke spiraled skyward.

"What do you think?" He said, as droplets of blood boiled on the ground. "What do you think of all this?"

I didn't know what to think other than God-knows how many people were dead, and whatever was left of them was cooking just a few feet away.

"Tell me what you REALLY think," He said. "Don't you think they got what they deserved? I mean, I sorta do…"

I stared into his shadowy eyes as a popping hiss emanated from the charred wreckage.

"You know what disturbs me the most about our little friendship?" I asked.

"No," he said. "What's that?"

"The fact that I'm starting to agree with you."

The Hell Cat

The turn-out was littered with shattered beer bottles and the flattened remains of countless shotgun shells. I rolled past a forest service gate, before parking my truck nose-in, beneath a buckshot peppered dead-end sign.

There were no other cars in sight, meaning that for today's ride, I would be the only person on the mountain. I liked that a lot, and I smiled as I unloaded my mountain bike from the pickup truck's bed.

Beside the truck's wheel-well was a large duffel bag, and I unzipped it before rummaging through its contents. "Better pack heavy," I thought. "And you'd better bring the gun… just in case."

It was probably best I did, given the nature of where I was headed, and what I was likely to encounter. After all, things had a way of getting weird on my deep-canyon runs. And whether it was wild animals, or God-knows-what, I liked knowing that I wouldn't be going down without a fight.

As I stowed my gear, I packed for the worst, knowing a day's training ride could easily turn into a freezing over-nighter. Double checking everything, I made sure my tools and repair items were in their proper place, along with a few energy bars that would sustain me if things went sour. Lastly, I packed my survival bag, which included a lightweight exposure suit, matches, and a thing or two that would come in handy if my life depended upon it.

I cinched down the straps on my pannier bags, feeling assured that the hand-packed load would easily allow me to weather a night in the bush. That gave me solace, for on the dirt back-roads that I frequented, breakdowns occurred regularly, and when they did, it was often at a time when there wasn't enough daylight left to hike back on foot.

The last thing I packed was my gun, a small, capable automatic, with just enough punch to dissuade a hungry predator. It may have seemed I was over-prepared, but this was coyote country, a place where I'd been attacked more than a time or two. The last attack had been the worst, and now I carried a bit of firepower, just in case the brazen mini-wolves got any wild ideas.

Packed and ready, I shouldered the bike, swinging it over the steel-tubed gate that punctuated the road's dead-end. I adjusted my helmet, then, after a glance up the road, I began my ride at a casual warm-up pace.

Winding up the mountainside, my heart-rate held steady, as my legs caught their rhythm. I climbed higher and higher, well above the haze, to where the clean mountain air smelled of Pinion Pines and Junipers. I rode beside a low, scrub brush hedge, until I came across the ruins of a Nike Missile installation that had been decommissioned in the 1970's. It had been several years since the base was manned, and now, all that was left of the entrance was a tin-roofed guard shack, and a rat's nest of phone wires that protruded from a steel pole.

I passed the base within minutes, climbing toward an area where the road became less accessible. Gone was the hard-packed dirt, while in its place, was a rutty, uneven trail that was fit for only the hardiest of hikers.

Climbing higher, I soon rounded the curve that marked my entry point. To my left was an overgrown hiking trail I'd located some time ago, and now that I was prepared for almost anything, it was time to explore far into the uncharted interior. I was excited to say the least, with the promise of adventure, and the very real possibility of discovering something unknown.

Banking left, I gathered speed before thundering onto the hidden trail-head. Once I'd passed the bushy entrance, I traversed the roadside berm, before dropping onto a hard-packed game trail that ran perpendicular to the side of the hill. I picked up speed, following the trail as it wove along the mountain's upper rim. The going was good, until I came across a large cluster of Manzanita bushes that had completely blocked my way.

The bramble was thick, and I dismounted the bike, before looking around. The trail was completely overgrown, which was probably due to the fact that no one had been there in years. I was beginning to become discouraged, when I caught sight of a distant area where the trail began once again.

It was a stretch, but I figured I could scuff my way through the waist-deep brush if I held the bike over my head. The idea was sound, except for the fact that the bushes were crawling with rattlesnakes. I wasn't thrilled with the idea of stepping on one, so I shuffled my feet with the bike overhead until I'd thrashed my way through the briar.

I survived the gauntlet without being bit, and as soon as I pulled a few fox-tails from my socks, I was back in the saddle. Moving fast, I'd soon covered ground that would have taken a seasoned hiker half a day or more. I rode briskly as I followed the natural trail, out-pacing the possibility that anyone could have ever been where I found myself. I was in no-man's-land, an area of wilderness that was completely unmolested by footfall or otherwise. This was where real discoveries could be made. A place so remote it wasn't even on the map, save for a large blot in the Santa Monica Mountains labeled "Wilderness Area."

As I traversed the mountain ridges, I looked deep into the canyons, where the creeks and stream beds lay. To my right was a chasm, a sheer-drop cliff that led to a cluster of old-growth Oaks that looked like heads of broccoli in a vegetable bowl. The tree tops were very closely knit, forming a large canopy hundreds of feet below. I was amazed at how closely the trees had grown, and from my vantage point high on the ridge, not one piece of canyon floor could be seen under the thick carpet of overgrowth.

I rolled to a stop near a sandstone cliff, while reaching for my water bottle. It was such a beautiful place to be, and I dismounted the bike before walking toward the cliff's edge. A lizard ran for cover, its feet sending tiny grains of sand tumbling downward like a mini-avalanche. I sat near the edge of the ridge, with my back to a boulder, and the sun on my face. The lizard looked at me with the strangest look, before scrambling away as if I was a monster. I smiled as he scurried off, while gazing into a canyon that sprawled like a stadium.

As I turned my head to sip water from the bottle, I gazed into the distance, where the giant broccoli heads seemed to fade into eternity. At first, all I saw was the canopy of trees, but then, as my eyes fixed on an object far in the distance, I froze in place, as something fascinating came into view.

It was a monolith of some kind . . . A dark, red monolith, that protruded through the canopy like the nose cone of a rocket. "What the hell?" I muttered, as I stared slack-jawed. "What the hell is that?"

With my eyes on-target, I walked the cliff's edge, hoping for a better look at the strange object. The thing was far away, just far enough that I couldn't tell what it really was. The only thing I knew for sure was that it was man-made, and that, in the strangest way, it seemed to be hiding from me.

But it was too late for hiding, for now that I'd seen it standing in the shadows, I wasn't going to rest until I found out what it was. That was going to take a bit of work, however, because lying between myself and the canyon floor, was a near-vertical drop, of perhaps three hundred feet or more.

As I looked over the edge, it seemed much too sheer a cliff to hazard a drop on my own. I didn't have any ropes, nor did I have my climbing gear. So, I walked along the ridge-line, in hope of finding a safer, less direct route down.

Everywhere I looked, the cliff-side seemed impassible, and as I traced the ridge-line I began to feel discouraged. The sheer drop was daunting, and given that there were few bushes to hold on to, viable passage seemed out of the question. That sucked, but being determined to find out what the mysterious object was, I furled my brow, knowing I'd figure something out, as long as I put my mind to it.

As I scanned the topography, I noticed something that seemed to hold promise. To the South, where the canyon narrowed, it appeared as if the cliff's walls were a bit more forgiving. They'd lost the sheer edge that the other cliffs had, and on the side closest to me, there appeared to be a series of game trails that had been etched into the canyon wall.

I was reasonably optimistic that I'd found a way into the canyon, especially after spotting the game-trails. They looked large enough to provide a good foothold, and with any luck, I had all intentions of following them into the canyon. Otherwise, if that didn't pan-out, I figured I'd return a few days later with a couple of friends and a sack full of climbing gear.

After a bit of recon, I spied a sizable game-trail that cut its way down the cliff's sloping face. Securing the bike, I grabbed a few supplies, before packing them smartly in my large fanny pack. What I'd packed would do in a pinch. So, after stashing the bike in a thicket of bushes, I headed into the canyon, with measured, cautious steps.

With each step I paused, sure to secure a foot-hold before advancing any further. I ventured down the cliff-side, to an area where the brush had grown so thick, I couldn't see beneath it. Moving tentatively through the bramble, I could feel the sharp bite of scrub brush as it scraped against my legs. I'd expected this, as the bushes were quite common, so I sucked-it-up, feeling my way down the slope, one step at a time.

The bushes were thick, but the going was easy, and soon enough, I found myself bounding from one foothold to another. My pace increased considerably, until a razor sharp spike dug deeply into my leg that seemed to come out of nowhere.

I cried aloud as the spike found its mark, frozen in mid-step by a shooting pain that was nearly incapacitating. Whatever had impaled me, it burned like fire, and as I fought to maintain my composure, I looked deep into the thicket to see what the culprit was.

I knew it wasn't a snake, because snake bites don't hurt. And even if it was a snake, it would have had to have fangs that were ten inches long. This was something else entirely, some kind of fixed object that had pinned me to the ground. I carefully bent down, while moving the thicket aside, until I saw a long, black spike protruding from the ground.

The tip of the spike was needle sharp, and it had penetrated deep into my calf muscle. I held dead-still, knowing that if I broke off the spike, I was in for one hell of an infection. I stood completely still . . . Then, after taking a deep breath, I jerked my leg up high, pulling free of the jagged needle.

"AHHHHH!" I yelled, as the spike pulled free. "OWWWWW!"

It burned like hell, tearing-up my eyes with pain that wouldn't quit. As I stood there, I knew exactly what I'd stumbled upon, and as the reality of my situation came to bear, a cold chill ran down my spine.

Looking down through the short scrub brush, I could see

multiple rows of the deadly spikes, lined up as far as the eye could see. There were hundreds of them on the hillside, all clustered together like a mat of toxin-tipped death spears. They were everywhere I looked, and I knew that with one false step, I'd be a goner.

As slowly as possible, I retraced my steps until I'd climbed well above the reach of the deadly spines. I'd lucked out, that's for sure, and as I crested the top of the ridge, the burning reminder of my near-death carelessness, slowly crept up my leg.

"Wow!" I thought, as blood pooled against my sock. "I should have seen that one coming!"

Indeed I should have. For what I'd stumbled across were the burned remains of countless Manzanita plants whose roots had been scorched into sword-like barbs by an errant wildfire.

They were once hardy plants, but thanks to the fire, now all that remained was a carpet of razor sharp spikes. I'd dodged one hell of a bullet, but now that I had, there were other problems on the docket. Such as the weeping hole in my leg, and the plum-sized hematoma that had already formed at the puncture site.

The wound looked angry, but I'd seen worse. And given my background in trauma medicine, I knew it wouldn't be trouble. Opening the frame-mounted pack on the bicycle, I grabbed a few things from the first aid kit that were sure to do the trick. I sat down on a rock, before squeezing most of the toxin from the wound. Then, after irrigating it well, I topped it off with some antibiotic salve and a clean bandage. The field dressing looked pretty good, so I figured as long as I didn't bleed to death, there really wasn't much more to concern myself with.

Now that I'd learned my lesson, it probably wasn't the best idea to hike on down by myself. I conceded it was most prudent to head back to the truck, where I could plan a return trip sometime soon. It was frustrating to make that call, but I knew it was for the best. So, I reluctantly reloaded the bike, before turning around, in the direction of home.

As I looked back one last time, I couldn't help but feel dejected. Sure, the monolith would be there when I returned. And sure, it had probably remained hidden from prying eyes for fifty years or more. But I wanted to see it right then and there, and the thought of going home with more questions than answers just didn't sit right with me.

"Whatever," I thought. "Just forget about it. There's nothing you can do until you come back with some climbing gear." There was no use beating myself up over it, so I set my sights on a return trip, with a lot more gear and a lot more manpower.

I felt cheated, but with nothing more to do, I rode along with the sun in my eyes and the mysterious structure behind me. The narrow ridge twisted and turned, commanding my attention to the point where I nearly passed a well-worn game-trail that headed down the slope. This trail was larger and wider than the previous one I'd chosen, and seeing that it was nearly all hard-packed dirt, I slammed on the brakes, stopping just a few feet short of its inception.

The single-track trail was wide enough to ride upon, and from what I could see, the hillside seemed devoid of the toxin tipped death-spikes. Now that I'd found a suitable trail, the only question was whether or not it headed deep enough into the canyon to make the trip worthwhile. I circled a moment as I pondered my options, then, throwing caution to the wind, I stood on the pedals, as I lined-up for the drop into the canyon.

The first drop was soft, and somewhat predictable. But not wanting to be too reckless, I slowed my descent by skidding sideways like a downhill skier. Lizards scurried for their lives as I slid down the mountainside, while the soft, knobby tires stretched to the limit as they gripped the sandstone cliff.

Half skidding, and half free-wheeling, I dropped in elevation as the trail led the way. Out of the saddle I rode, until I reached the tops of the trees I'd seen from above. There was a natural cut in the canopy, a space where the trees moved aside and the trail carved downward. I dropped into the slot, slipping through the canopy as if I'd flown under a cloud. The transition between light and dark was immediate, and as I rolled under oaks that were centuries old, a landscape of awe and wonder unfolded before me.

I was in a place like no other, a twilight world that must have been the realm of fairies.

There was dust in the air, or at least I think it was dust, and from the way it glimmered in the diffuse sunlight, I half expected a magical rabbit to jump out of a hole and greet me.

Relaxing my grip, I free-wheeled deep into the ravine, where the towering canopy filtered the light. Darkness was everywhere, save for a few breaks in the canopy, where beams of light shone down like spotlights. I rode from light patch to light patch, occasionally looking up, while feeling as if I'd been shrunk down to the size of an ant.

I was overwhelmed by a sense of discovery, and as soon as the trail became level, I hopped off the bike to look around a bit. It took a moment for my eyes to adjust to the diffuse light, and as I stood beside an enormous Oak, I could see a long row of trees that seemed to have grown in an unexpectedly symmetrical pattern.

"What the hell is this place?" I wondered, as I walked the line of Oaks. "What is it? And why does everything look so uniform?"

Slinking along like a trespasser, I came across an area that deepened the mystery. It looked like a city park, but not the kind of park that any of us have ever seen. This one looked as if it had witnessed The Apocalypse, with the remains of sidewalks, service roads, and planter boxes, appearing as if they'd been burned in a nuclear blast. One of the planter boxes looked as if it had been thrust straight out of the ground, cast aside by a giant tree trunk straight out of Jack and the Beanstalk.

I stared wide-eyed at the carnage, not knowing what to think. Most of it had been burned, in a wild-fire no doubt. But there was something else going on that didn't make sense. There was an eery feel to the place. And from what I could see, most of the damage appeared to have come from the hands of men.

Something had gone horribly wrong, and I needed to know how a place so utterly beautiful, could have been turned into a landscape of twisted concrete and metal. The need to know weighed heavily on my mind, but before I ventured any further, I walked back to the bike to set things up a bit differently. This was exactly the kind of place where my special training might come in handy. And knowing that far too well, I removed two sheathed knives from the frame-mounted pack, placing one on my person and the other easily within reach.

Locked and loaded, I buttoned things up before hopping on the bike once again. Weaving down the blistered asphalt of an old service road, I rolled past twisted metal railings, and jagged drainage pipes that protruded from the roadside. The road looked like an obstacle course, its surface littered with a mine-field of broken metal. I wove around the debris, while skirting several medium sized bushes that had broken through the asphalt. Everywhere I looked I saw something of interest, until I spied a structure in the distance that was especially intriguing. It was an old single story farmhouse, standing adjacent to a stable-like barn that rose to nearly twice its height.

Stopping short of the property, I dropped to a knee in a field of waist high grass. I laid the bike on its side, scanning the landscape from a relatively obscured position. The abandoned home was overgrown with vines, but despite that fact, the structure's whitewashed siding was remarkably well preserved. It seemed odd that a perfectly good home would have been abandoned in such a manner, but I knew deep down inside there was nothing normal about what I'd just discovered.

I drank from my water bottle, before walking toward a beam of sunlight that had broken through the canopy. As I lingered in the spotlight, I knew the farmhouse would have to be explored. But with daylight at a premium, it would have to wait until another day.

As I bent down to check the bandage on my leg, I caught sight of something large as it moved in the shadows of the stable area. I ducked below the weed-line as I panned to my left, but just as I did, it dropped to the ground as if it had seen me as well.

"Oh GREAT!" I thought, as I commando-crawled toward the bike. "I'm not the only hunter here. And now I've got this thing to worry about!"

The tall grass blew like wheat in the wind, blurring all things into the distance. I knew for certain I'd seen something move, yet despite its appearing near the door of the barn, it definitely wasn't human. This thing was different, and although I hadn't seen but a flash of its profile, it immediately gave me the creeps. I could sense that it was a predator, and I knew quite well that it was best if I put some serious distance between the two of us.

I waited a moment before standing, seeing only the wave of grass, and the glimmer of pixie-dust that hung heavily in the air. I definitely wasn't alone, yet I wasn't going to get too worked up

228

over it, unless the creature became aggressive. Besides, for all I knew it was probably just a mountain lion, or a bear that had no business poking around in the daytime. If that was the case, we'd go our separate ways. Yet as comforting a thought as that was, I just couldn't shake the feeling that something dark was watching from the shadows.

Fending off a case of the willies, I rolled past the farmhouse toward whatever lay ahead. The asphalt was blistered and uneven, so thin in parts that it had almost crumbled to sand. I traversed a wash-out or two, before the pavement ended in a rough transition to a hard packed dirt road.

The road twisted in an S-shaped pattern, and I rode out of the saddle as I wove from turn to turn. All around me were the remains of household items, as if a home had been gutted, and its contents had been strewn across the landscape. I couldn't imagine what had caused such chaotic destruction, and as I rolled along, I looked down upon history that practically screamed to be heard.

Some of the debris was pedestrian, the usual bottle caps, rusted cans, and pull tabs that litter the roadside in Anywhere USA. That was no surprise, other than all the debris I was seeing dated back several decades, perhaps to before the Second World War.

I could tell that no one had been there for a very long time. And with the absence of tire tracks, recent trash, or any other signs of human intervention, I surmised it must have been decades since a living person had been there. It was so damn eerie the way everything seemed to have been forgotten on purpose . . . Which was all the better to fuel the imagination of a guy like myself, who had stumbled way too far, into a very dangerous place.

But I didn't care about any of that. Nor did I care if I had gone too far. This was the find of a lifetime, a discovery as intoxicating as any drug on earth. I wanted more, and I needed more, even if it meant putting myself in harm's-way.

Resigned to doing just that, I tossed all caution to the wind, as I headed toward a group of houses on my right. Unlike the farmhouse up the road, these homes were of a more generic type, looking much like those that were built just prior to the war. The roofs of the homes bore rounded shingles, while the walls were finished with the type of heavy stucco that was popular during the nineteen thirties and forties.

One of the homes was nearly intact, while the other two had been badly burned in the fire. "How many people died here?" I wondered, as I stared into the burned-out entry of one of the homes. "And why is it I can't shake the feeling that there are several sets of eyes upon me?"

As I pondered the unthinkable, something within those burned confines reached out with the cold touch of death. I reared back as the icy fingers wrapped around me, sensing a wisp of smoke that had long lay dormant.

I couldn't help but wonder if I was feeling the call of those who had been immolated as they slept. Unaware that just outside was a fiery wall of death that was about to consume them. I pondered that as I stared into the pulsing blackness, until something occurred to me that sent a chill up my spine. The homes hadn't been burned in a wild-fire. They'd been set on fire on purpose, as was evident by the burn patterns all around them.

"What the hell?" I thought. "What would compel a person to do such a thing? And moreover, what madness brought this all about?"

The questions were too numerous to ponder, especially now that I was certain something was watching me. Every nerve in my body could sense a nearby presence, and as I was painted by the radar of unseen eyes, I juiced the pedals before the thing had a chance to run me down.

With my head on a swivel, I rolled past several burned-out homes as I tried to make sense of it all. "Why doesn't anyone know about this place?" I wondered. "And why, even more-so, did everything have such a sinister feel to it?"

All those questions would be answered in time, but for now, all I had were clues. The clues were old and rotted, perhaps just a few years away from vanishing all together. I'd found them just in time, and now that I had, I'd soon discover the burned-out town wasn't so much a place long forgotten, as it was the resting place of the damned.

I wanted to know more, when, as if on cue, the largest clue of all revealed itself as I rounded the next corner.

When it first came into view, I slammed on the brakes as if I'd seen The Devil. Then as the landscape of Hell unfurled before me, I gasped at what I saw.

It was a house, but nothing like any house I'd ever seen. Built entirely of heavy steel plates, the rusted monstrosity rose toward the sky as if it had been thrust up from the depths of Hell. It had been horribly burned... Burned beyond description, in a fire so hot, much of its structure was now warped and twisted.

I stared at the rusted hulk, and it stared back, while holding the melted remains of a child's tricycle under its wing. I was mesmerized by the sight of the toy, its tortured frame melted beside twisted spokes that protruded from the ground. I tossed my bike to its side, before walking toward the trike as if in a trance. I was drawn to the thing, as well as the ghost of someone who stood beside it. As I touched its rusted handlebar, a vision flew through my mind . . . Of a child, as it ran screaming . . . Just steps ahead of a crimson wall of flame. The flames rushed forward, enveloping the tricycle, then, as its   paint popped and blistered, the image faded to ash, as did the screams as well.

There was something so wrong about all of this . . . Something that tugged at my soul as I knelt in the shadow of the rusted building. The shrill smell of burned metal rose up in the mid-summer air, and in that moment, I should have run as if The Devil was chasing me. But for some reason I stood my ground. Not sure why, except for the strange feeling that something was calling out from within the building's burned confines.

"What if someone's body is in there?" I thought. "What if they never took the bodies out?"

I didn't dare consider that, nor did I want to find a child's skeleton curled up in a melted toy chest. That would have been the gruesome discovery of the week. So I shook off the thought, while walking around the structure, in order to get a better look at it.

As I walked toward a sun-bleached patch of concrete, I could see that the building was constructed of flat steel plates, each of them featureless and raw. There wasn't a window to be seen, a feature that gave the building a curiously macabre appearance. Everything felt so wrong, from the strangely sinister architecture, to an advanced thicket of bushes that conspired to consume the place.

I stood at the base of a concrete stairway, beside a steel pipe handrail that had warped in the fire. The stairs led to a small driveway, which played host to an old, oval-windowed Volkswagen that had been burned beyond description. I walked toward the car, crunching through a rusted mat of debris that crackled with each footfall. The car had nearly melted to the ground, its rims fused into an onyx-like glass that seemed to have been poured over the wheel hubs. There was nothing left of the car but the body, and the requisite seat springs that always stand at attention after a car fire.

Leaning forward, I craned my neck into the car's scorched shell. The air was dead still, deafeningly so, until a guttural, metallic hiss shot through the interior that almost made me leap out of my skin.

I jumped back, hitting the rusted roof-line with the edge of my scalp. A droplet of blood ran down my temple, and as it did, I could have sworn the car itself had spoken, with a hellish, fire-scorched tongue.

I didn't want to hear any more, nor did I want to linger beside something that felt like a portal to Hell. There was a lot more to see, and a lot more to learn. So I backed away from the car, before heading up the stairs to the lower patio terrace.

Three crumpled steps led to a parched flat of concrete that was littered with burned toys. I stood and stared, as I sensed something odd about the way the toys had been scattered all over the ground. They were nearly everywhere, almost as if someone had placed them there on purpose. I sensed a perverse calculus in their placement, intervention of the type that seemed born of The Devil. He'd been there, that I knew. And while he was, he just couldn't help but make things a touch more macabre.

The place was damn creepy, and not just on the merit of what I could see. There was something that was hidden in my midst, something palpable that lay just beneath the rust, and the ash, and the things left there to draw one's eye away.

I needed to keep moving, for I was beginning to feel as if I was being herded into a trap. Sure, the things I'd found were compelling. But the way they were strung along suggested my movement was being regulated by something that wanted to slow me down. "Break it up," I thought, "Head your own way, and determine your own direction." I was right. It was time to move beyond the obvious, toward whatever it was that waited behind the proverbial shed.

I climbed the stairs, fearful of touching the rail, as if it was an electrode filled with bad memories. The rail-pipe was rusted, and bent in the center, as if something had sat on it while the rest of the town burned. I could only imagine what that something was . . . In a thought that was quickly dismissed, as I ventured further into the yard.

As I stepped through the charred remains of other people's lives, I felt a rush of emotion that's hard to describe. The town was a burned-out tomb, and with every step I took, I felt like something angry was about to blister out of the ground.

I blotted away that thought, along with the realization that there were whispers all around me. After reaching a crumbling stack of steps, I transitioned to an upper terrace that was cut into the hillside. Lying by my feet were the remains of many things, all burned beyond description. The place looked as if there had been some kind of explosion, and what hadn't been vaporized by the initial blast, had been melted by the heat wave that followed.

Looking up, I saw an old wire-framed basketball hoop that had been melted in the fire. Bent around its rim was the warped frame of a bicycle that looked as if it had stepped straight out of a Salvador Dali painting. The bike had been thrown onto the hoop, not by the hands of man, but from an explosion that seemed to have scattered everything.

Whatever it was that had exploded, its remains were nowhere to be found. And as I scuffed my feet across a large, star-shaped blast mark, I began to wonder if something had fallen from the sky.

"What the hell," I thought. "The only thing that could have done this was an incendiary bomb. But those are airborne... aren't they?"

None of it made any sense, so I turned my attention to the strange metal building, hoping that somewhere inside, I'd find some answers.

To my left, a doorway led to the home's main floor. I stood under the scorched header for a moment, staring into the burned-out interior as my eyes adjusted to the darkness. The remains of many objects filled the home, most of them burned beyond recognition. While rising above the ash, was an old gas-fueled oven that stood hauntingly in the corner. It stared at me as if it was alive, and as I looked down at its burned, clawed feet, I could have sworn it was ready to pounce…

I turned away from the oven as I scanned the rest of the room. The walls were black and burned, yet there was enough left of the structure that it began to tell a story. It had definitely been a home, although from the looks of what was left, I wondered why anyone would have chosen to live in such a place.

The building was completely constructed of raw metal, and as I stared at the smoke tinged walls, I couldn't see a fastener or rivet that suggested there had ever been any wall boards. That seemed really strange, because a cold steel structure seemed like the last place that anyone would have wanted to live. I supposed there might have been paint on the walls at some time, but that notion did nothing to negate the pulse of the place, which was nothing short of unsettling.

Something other than the fire had gone horribly wrong. Something evil that set the tone for everything that came after it. Sure, the fire must have been horrible, and that in itself must have been Hell on Earth. But for another reason I hadn't yet put my finger on, something wasn't quite right. It was more than just the visual horror, or the implications of everything I'd found. There was something else in the air… something that bristled my fur, in a way I hadn't felt in a very long time.

What I sensed was still a bit off the radar, yet I knew enough to realize that I faced danger of the highest degree. Hyper-sensitized by a rush of adrenaline, I walked softly upon the ash, hearing each footfall, while sensing every vibration. I sensed danger with every step, but compelled as I was to find God-knows-what, there was no other option but to explore the home further.

As I pressed onward, I found the building both disturbing and enigmatic, while with each footfall, the echoes of the past swirled with a touch of vapor. There were emotions mixed in with those echoes, feelings trapped long ago within the walls of that hellish place. I could feel the ashes stir, almost as if the ghosts were about to rise into solid form. There was a pulse as the room swirled with the vapor of death, before something dark reached out from within the burned-out oven, running a long, pointed fingernail down my spine…

I nearly jumped out of my skin as the hellish finger found its mark, spinning wildly in place as if I'd been touched by The Devil. "WHAT THE HELL!" I yelled, as a shadowy hand drew back into the fire-box. "WHAT THE HELL IS IN THERE?"

Rust rained down as I stared at the oven, its blackened core hissing as if it had suddenly come to life. I faced it like a gunslinger, half ready to run, while something within its blackened confines dared me to come closer. Compelled by madness, I inched toward the oven, as its burned-out faceplate started to glow. "Don't open it," I told myself. "Just get on the bike and ride like hell… THAT'S what you need to do!"

That made perfect sense, but nothing about any of this had anything to do with sensibility. Needing to know what burned within its core, I approached the oven, before tentatively reaching for the flue's rusted latch. As expected, it had been welded shut in the fire, so I kicked the latch a few times, as a thick cloud of rust rose into the air.

The oven taunted me, as it hid its true self behind a wall of blackened steel. Something evil lay beyond its vented grin, and in that moment, I'd have done anything to see it, even if it drove me to madness.

Taking a knee, I crouched as close to the oven as I dared, while an acrid stench wafted through the rusted face-plate. I turned my head to one side as I peered through the slots, just a moment before a sound emanated from its throat, that threw me backward with a bolt of fright.

It sounded like a sigh, a coarse, metallic sigh, that slid from the stovepipe as if The Devil had just spoken. I stood bolt upright, as the sigh morphed into a whisper. Then, as a voice echoed through the room, I was nearly anchored to the ground with fear.

The oven spoke with a demonic shrillness, and as it whispered to me with rusted words, I began to feel as if a long tongue of fire was about to reach out and touch me.

"Fire… Fire…" The stove hissed and cried. "Won't you start a fire in me ONE MORE TIME?"

235

I bristled with chills as I stared at its slit-like eyes, before the oven from Hell spoke once again. "I started the fire that burned them to death," the hellish monstrosity whispered. "Would you like to burn to death too?"

"YOU'RE NOT GOING TO BURN ANYONE!" I yelled out, as ash crunched beneath my feet. But it didn't care what I said, as it just looked at me, with its evil, vented grin.

"This place burns with insanity," I muttered to myself. "Now I've really gone off the deep end, to the point where I'm talking to stoves!"

The oven shifted as I backed away, shaking rust from its fire-box as it began to hiss and growl. "GET AWAY FROM THIS THING!" My inner voice yelled. "GET AWAY BEFORE ITS GRIP BECOMES TOO POWERFUL!"

Heeding the voice of reason, I stepped through a doorway, beside a buckled wall of steel. There I waited, for a moment or two, as I paused to gather my senses. The pull of the oven had been strong, but now that there was a wall between us, it seemed to lie dormant, at least for the time being. I looked around the room, a roofless place, where the incinerated remains of a coil-spring mattress stood in muted testimony of what had once happened.

There were bits and pieces of many things mixed in with the mattress springs, mostly debris from the rotting roof, which had collapsed many years ago. I leaned over the mattress frame, staring down through the coils at something almost unrecognizable. "There are bones in there!" the oven called out. "A child's bones, don't you know…"

I knew damn well what had been burned into those springs, and the fact that the oven did too, was even more horrifying. Whether or not the oven had actually started the fire wasn't my concern. The only things I cared about was that it wanted to start another one, and it was unmistakably alive.

It was time to go, which is laughable, considering it was time to go before I'd even arrived. I scanned the room one last time, and as I did, something within those rotted confines began to call out to me. It wasn't the oven, or the bones, or the patch of dead skin that had melted onto the bed-springs. This was something else entirely, something that called out from above, somewhere near the roof-line.

I stepped toward the center of the room, looking up through scarred I-beams that had buckled in the fire. There was something scribed into the wall roughly three feet from its apex. Near the point where the beams originated, and a mass of cables and wires hung like rusted dreadlocks. I looked at the markings, and the way they seemed to have been carved into the wall by a cutting torch. "What the hell?" I muttered, as I squinted in the twilight. "What the hell is that?"

At first it was just a jumble of lines, shapes carved into a steel plate that was horribly scorched and scored. But then, as my eyes focused in the shadows, a shape emerged that made my blood run cold.

It was a swastika, a carved, metal swastika that had been burned into the wall-plate by an acetylene cutting torch. The Nazi symbol was at least three feet square, with artistically rolled edges that suggested it was part of the home's original design. I stared at the symbol, mostly in disbelief, wondering how anyone could have purposefully adorned their home with the universal symbol of cruelty and hatred.

Being both repulsed and fascinated by my discovery, I stepped closer to the wall as the smell of burned steel filled my nose. "Oh God," I thought. "Everything about this place is SO wrong."

It was beyond wrong, and as I stared at the edges of the melted Nazi cross, a chill ran down my spine that was one for the record books. It was the kind of chill you get when you're somewhere you don't belong, and you've pushed your luck way beyond the stretching point. Sensing a quantum of danger, I realized I'd been seduced by something that had taken me far beyond the brink. Before its grip became unbreakable, I stumbled backward, just as the rasping feel of a wire noose touched the back of my neck.

I leaped forward, before spinning in place to face my attacker. I expected the fight of my life, but rather than seeing a madman with a noose, all I saw was a frayed, rusted cable hanging from one of the ceiling beams.

I paused dead in my tracks, as the cable swayed before me, until a metallic voice broke the silence with a most unwanted narrative.

"It's only a cable," the oven said. "What's the matter? Afraid you might get burned?"

"GET OUT OF HERE!" I told myself, as the oven hissed and rattled. "You've got to get out of here NOW!"

Taking my own advice, I quickly moved toward the outer doorway. I'd had enough, and whether the oven had actually spoken, or I'd simply lost my mind, it was time to get the hell out of there. As I headed toward the door, I kept one eye on the claw-footed menace, just in case it decided to get up and run. There was burned debris everywhere, so much so, that the carpet of ash caused my footsteps to echo with a loud crunching sound. I hadn't given too much thought to the noises I'd been making, but now that I was on the move, I chose to recognize something I'd known all along.

"I'm being shadowed," I thought. "I'm not the only predator in this canyon, and the damn thing's been on my six ever since I passed the barn."

Not being one to question intuition, I distanced myself from the oven, until its sickly pull no longer masked the feel of a predator in my midst. There was something else close by, something with the eyes of a hunter and the step of a killer. I could feel its presence as it drew closer, and now that I knew it was coming, it was time for the games to begin.

Using the oldest trick in the book, I crunched my footsteps, before breaking my stride in mid-step. I held my foot motionless, just inches from the ground, and as suspected, I heard my adversary's foot-fall just a moment later. He'd been shadowing me step-by-step, but now, as rust rained down in the sickly twilight, he knew I was on to him.

"GOTCHA!" I thought, as he gave away his position. "You got careless, and now it's YOU who's about to be stalked."

His footsteps had betrayed him, although for a while, he'd shadowed me quite well. Whatever this thing was, it was anything but a fool. And now that we'd tested one another, I began to wonder what I was up against.

"Definitely a top-chain predator," I thought, "and a stealthy one at that!"

As that thought hit home, I pressed my back to the wall, while drawing my knife from its sheath. There was comfort in its feel, the type of comfort that comes from years of weapons training, and the confidence to put it to the test.

I was ready for whatever this thing had to offer. Feeling confident in my ability to strike and neutralize, as well as kill if it became necessary. I was as ready as I could have been, given the circumstances, knowing all the while that given the terrain, and my remote location, even the slightest mistake could cost me my life.

But there wasn't time for concern, as it was now time to engage the stalker by taking the fight directly to him.

Standing as still as I could, I turned an ear to the patio, while my adversary moved toward the rear of the home. The thing was posturing for position, circling to my flank where it felt it had an advantage. I could feel its every move, yet despite its cat-like subtlety, it left behind a trace of ether that was nothing short of alarming.

Whatever this thing was, it was damn scary. And I knew if I was to better it, I'd need to get outside, where the playing field was much more level.

That was my objective, to meet him head-on and neutralize any advantage. It was a simple plan, but before I did anything else, there was just one thing that I needed to do.

Taking a step forward, I horse-kicked the wall with all my might. The force of my kick shook rust from the walls, and as a shock-wave pulsed through the building, there was now no doubt that my stalker knew I was on to him.

With soft, backward steps, my adversary moved toward the rear of the building. I could feel a cat-like softness to its movement, yet at the same time, there was an undeniable cadence of something that stood on two feet. I listened as it sought concealment, and as I did, I could hear a strange scratching sound as its claws scraped the ground. "What the hell is this thing?" I wondered. "It's definitely not human, nor is it anything I've ever encountered before."

I suppose it could have been anything, given that I was in the land of the hissing car and the demonic oven from Hell. But I guess none of that mattered, for whatever this thing was, the battle plan was the same. I needed to get outside and take the high-ground, while somewhere along the line, I'd need to fetch my gun.

It was time to move, so I crept toward the door while the creature quartered around the far end of the home. With blade drawn, I stepped onto the patio, circling backward as I surveyed the area. It was all-clear to the edges of the structure, while somewhere around the corner, my adversary lay in wait. It moved to the left as I moved to the right, in a weird stalking dance that kept us apart, just long enough to think things through.

I began to feel as if I was being herded, or at least controlled, until the coming of nightfall. There was no way in Hell that was going to happen, nor was there a chance I'd allow it to herd me in a direction I wasn't comfortable with. The dance needed to end right then and there. So, as I heard it move again, I rushed its position, in the hope of rattling its nerves a bit.

As I charged forward like a wild-man, I was banking on the fact that predators aren't used to being attacked by their prey. Luckily, my scare tactic worked, for as I rounded the corner like a freight train, something large and bipedal, bounded into the overgrowth just a few yards away.

I skidded to a stop as it disappeared into the brush, before doubling-back toward the upper patio terrace. The move was far from stealthy, but I'd definitely gained the tactical advantage. I now held the high ground, which was all fine and good. Yet as I scanned the shadowy landscape, I knew that if I spent any more time in the standoff, the valley would soon be cloaked in darkness.

The urge to root him out was strong, but despite my instincts, common sense prevailed. Besides, as my sensei had told me many times over, living to fight another day, was always the smartest move. It was good advice, and I knew I needed to give this thing some space if there was to be any chance that we weren't going to kill one another. So, I figured if he was content to lurk in the shadows, I was fine with leaving him be. As long as he stayed concealed, just long enough for me to slip away.

Down the hill rested my bicycle, just a few feet short of the weed-line. I needed to get there fast, not just for the gun, but for mobility's sake as well. Moving fast, I cross-stepped toward the bike, as my adversary bounded toward higher ground. As I ran downhill, it moved uphill, which suggested the standoff had cooled down a bit, at least for the time being.

When I reached the bike, I quickly unzipped the triangle pack where I'd stowed the small handgun. The sight of the gun brought me comfort, but somehow, I felt the coyote killer would merely piss the thing off. That was probably true, for I knew from experience that if the creature had been a wild boar or a bear, I would have done more harm by beating it with my shoes, than I would have with the small caliber handgun.

Whether or not I was under-gunned, there was some solace in knowing the weapon was close at hand. So I removed the gun from the pouch, before sliding a round into the chamber.

Now that I was locked and loaded, I was ready for anything that came my way. Stowing the gun in the triangle pack, I zipped it up snugly, so it wouldn't fly out on the road. "It's ready if you need it." I told myself. "It's all ready to go!"

Now that I was suitably armed, I scanned the landscape for any sign of the beast. Everywhere I looked, all I could see was the debris of death, yet as hard as I tried, I couldn't see hide nor hair of the strange, bipedal creature. "What the hell kind of a thing looks like that?" I thought. "It stands like a man, but it runs on all fours?" Whatever this thing was, it certainly wasn't human. And even more-so, despite its partially human attributes, there wasn't a human on earth who would have chosen to live in such a place.

Collecting my thoughts, I wondered what I'd just seen. The thing had only been visible for a moment, and in that moment all I could tell was that it was the weirdest looking thing I'd ever seen. It wasn't a man, and it wasn't a bear, nor was it any other type of common forest creature. This thing was different in so many ways I didn't know what to think, other than it was deadly, and it definitely had the home-field advantage.

"It's not over yet," I told myself. "Just like the great Yogi Berra once said, 'It ain't over, till it's over!'"

Yogi was right, and I knew I needed to be extra cautious, especially now that the canyon was growing dark. I didn't know of the creature's motives, nor did I know what it really was. I only knew that I wasn't done with the thing, and I needed to get out of the canyon before dark-fall. Remounting the bike, I rolled onto the trail with a glance over my shoulder. I should have headed back up the canyon, but needing to know what that strange monolith was, I decided to explore just a few minutes longer, before getting the hell out of Hell.

I rolled down the road, skirting the remains of several homes that had been completely burned to the ground. In the center of the group, was a fire-ravaged structure, with an enormous, kiln-like chimney. It thrust through the trees like a missile in a silo, and as I craned my neck to see its apex, I had no doubt the chimney was the monolith I'd seen earlier. "That was easy," I thought, as leaves rustled by my side. "Maybe not as fascinating a discovery as I'd hoped for… but satisfying just the same."

Having found the monolith, I was now satisfied that I'd seen enough for one day. The place was awesome, and there was much more to discover, but with the sun lying low, I needed to get out fast, before it was too late.

Back in the saddle, I rolled past the chimney, toward a natural roadside clearing. I turned around quickly, before heading up a side road that paralleled the town. I rode fast, racing past the burned-out remains of several more homes. Most had been reduced to chimneys and foot-pads, interspersed with an occasional wall that had defiantly refused to burn. One by one I passed them by, until I reached a home that had been spared some of the fire's wrath.

I stopped beside the home, straddling the top-tube with one foot on a pedal. The home stood perhaps twenty yards away, and as I stared into its blackened core, shadows shifted as if they were alive. I was about to stand on the pedals and ride for my life, when a whisper called out that made my skin crawl.

"They burned them out," the wisping voice said. "They burned them while they slept, so no one would know."

I'd known that all along. Yet as horrifying a notion as that was, hearing it spoken on the wind, nearly pushed me over the edge.

"I know, I KNOW!" I barked out toward the house. "I know what they did… I can see it all around me!"

The place crawled with a collective of ghosts that stirred ash by my feet. It was high-time to leave -- time to leave a place that was haunted by something horrible. Something that had been there long before the fires had been set.

The voice whispered, but I didn't listen. Rather, I sped up the road with The Devil's eyes on my back. There were other homes along the way, all of them burned by the hands of men. I refused to stop, even as I passed a large metal structure that looked like a burned-out bunker. The buckled structure reminded me of a Nazi pillbox, while all around its doorway were blast marks that looked like they'd been caused by a flamethrower.

Out of the saddle, I flew past the structure as a strange magnetic pull beckoned me to come closer. I pedaled like a madman, not wanting to imagine what I'd find within its rusted confines. I wasn't going to stop, no matter what. Nor would I follow a whisper that would ultimately lead to my demise. For all I knew there was another stove in there. Or something worse, like a boiler room, filled with a hundred Thumping Men.

Preferring the course of sanity, I shifted onto the big chain-ring and rode like hell. The plan was simple really. I was going to ride like The Devil was chasing me, until I reached the canyon wall, where somehow, given enough daylight, I'd climb my way to the top.

My plan was sound, and within one hundred yards the small accessory trail merged with the main road. I was in my zone, moving swiftly as The Hell House came into view. As I neared the burned monstrosity, I stepped it up a notch, while the smell of its acrid walls filled the air. Dead fingers reached out from beside the melted tricycle, but I dared not glance their way, for my eyes were fixed in the distance, where the tall grass blew like wheat, while shadows walked beside the road.

As I scanned the trail ahead, all seemed clear, until something large broke free of the brush fifty yards to my right. It moved wickedly fast as it bounded toward the road, quartering me in such a way that it cut off my advance.

When the creature broke from the shadows I immediately reacted, cutting to my left in an attempt to widen the gap. I couldn't tell what the creature was, other than it was an animal of formidable size and stature. It moved fast, bettering my speed by nearly double, until I planted my foot, fish-tailing to a stop, with roughly fifty feet between us.

A cloud of dirt hung in the air as we faced one another, as if we were about to engage in a freakish duel. I stared at the thing as I postured for position, and as I did, I couldn't believe what stood before me.

It was an animal, but nothing at all like any animal I'd ever seen. It was satyr-like in appearance, with the muscular legs of a dog, and the slotted eyes of a cat. The beast was large, easily the size of a full grown cougar, and its eyes pulsed with the strangest light, as if they were reflecting the glow of a wind-blown candle. Whatever this thing was, it was frightening as hell. And as it stared at me with glistening eyes, I had no doubt it was the creature that had been stalking me all along.

As I stared at the beast, it bared its teeth, before standing on its hind legs like a werewolf. "GET THE GUN!" Cried the voice in my head, as the creature spiked its ears. "PULL IT OUT OF THE POUCH AND KILL THE THING!"

That would have been nice, had there been the opportunity to fumble with the triangle pack. But this wasn't a pack of coyotes, that would have given me time to clean the gun if I'd chosen to. This was a deadly predator, one that barely allowed me time to draw my knife from its sheath.

I stared at the creature, seeing an intelligence in its eyes that was nothing short of unnerving. The thing was a demon by all accounts… monstrous in every way. Yet there was something more to the creature than just the obvious. It was smart as a man, and as it cocked its head while it looked into my eyes, I began to sense that it could be reasoned with.

I'd like to think that the two of us could have started up a conversation. But as it leered at me with the "Go for the gun, and I'll tear your throat out," look, it seemed as if diplomacy was currently out of the question.

The beast stared at my knife, while its glowing eyes summed-up my arsenal. "One of us is going to die," I thought, as shadows danced in the grass. "I'm going to have to kill this thing quickly, before it tears me to shreds."

That was possible, I suppose, but it was also easier said than done. For whether or not this thing was a werewolf, or a dog-man, or even The Chupacabra, it was all killer… and in that moment, I felt seriously outgunned.

With the bike positioned between us, I faced the beast as it bared its pointy teeth. From the look of its fangs and its cat-like claws, I had no doubt that it was capable of ripping me to shreds. Yet for some reason, it hadn't done anything other than block the trail, in an attempt to stop my advance.

Perhaps it was thinking things through, for had it been driven by instinct alone, the thing would have pounced long ago. But this creature was much more complex, showing glimpses of intelligence that really made me wonder. "Maybe it's hesitating because it's never seen a human before," I thought, "especially one with a shiny, metal bike."

It would have been nice to ponder that over a pint of chocolate stout. But now, with night-fall fast approaching, the hellish cat took to all four legs as its yellowy eyes glowed brighter.

"HOLY CRAP!" I thought, as the beast approached with an s-shaped saunter. "This thing is NOT going to be easy to kill... not easy at all!"

As it closed in on me, the creature swayed from side to side as if it was testing my perimeter. It now stood like a predatory cat, with its short, dark hair stretched ominously over a heavily muscled back. I could see its fur quite clearly, or perhaps the lack of it, as its skin shined strangely in the last glow of twilight.

It looked like it had been burned, although not from a fire, but rather by design. Its singed-fur skin looked like vulcanized rubber that had been stretched over muscles that bulged with each of its slow, circling steps.

I backed up as it approached, holding the bike in front of me as if I was a lion tamer. The move bought me some time, as the bike's frame and wheels formed a solid barrier between the two of us.

The thing allowed me to circle, but only in a direction that led away from the road. I didn't put too much thought into it given the circumstances, until the creature did something I didn't expect at all.

It looked over its shoulder... toward the old wooden barn.

Suddenly it all made perfect sense. The reason why the thing hadn't attacked me in The Hell House, and why, even now, it hadn't moved in for the kill: It was protecting something. Something in the barn that was near and dear to it. Maybe it was a litter of freshly born Hell-Cats. Or maybe it was just the comfy confines of a home that hadn't been touched by the fire. I didn't know which, and I really didn't care, as long as I could back far enough away, that the creature would stand-down.

Acting on a hunch, I stepped back slowly with the bicycle held between us. I moved in an arc, far away from the barn-house, as if to say "Sorry neighbor, I didn't mean to step on your lawn." The creature shadowed me step by step, with its head held low, and its angled back pulsing with power. It was planted like a sprinter, ready to pounce . . . Yet for some reason it spared me, allowing me room to back away, until I was no longer a threat.

Maybe it understood that I was just a traveler who had ultimately lost his way. Or maybe it just wanted me to leave, so I could go home with a new-found reverence for life. I don't know why it spared me that evening, but it did. And as it relaxed its posture while standing its ground, I slowly stepped away.

From a distance, I stared into its eyes in the last glow of twilight. Its face softened as I made my retreat, and now it just stared at me, with its head held high in the softly blowing grass. Time stood still as we stared at one another, before, in a nearly unconscious act, I was overcome with the need to speak to the creature.

"WHO ARE YOU?" I called out, as it stared into my soul. "WHO ARE YOU, AND WHAT IS THIS PLACE?"

I wish it would have answered, but the Hell-Cat didn't say a word. Rather, it rose to its hind legs, while standing silently at the property's edge, like a dark, demonic sentinel.

I looked back at the creature, feeling for it as if it was a child. "Maybe it doesn't know any better," I thought. "Perhaps it's much like a child of war, who still finds dandelions in a bombed out wasteland."

I felt sorry for the thing as it stood there, and strangely, as I slipped farther away, I wanted to say goodbye.

"Do I say goodbye, or do I thank you?" I wondered. "Or, do I simply run for my life?"

As I moved down the road, I didn't bother to ask, for it had decided to let me pass, and for that, I was eternally grateful. So I simply walked away, slowly and patiently, until I reached the trail-head, at the crest of the hill.

With one last glance I looked down the road, to where he stood in silent vigil.

"Goodbye, Hell-Cat," I said softly. "For what it's worth, I wish you well."

I never looked back. For once I'd reached the small game trail, I shouldered the bike, climbing like a goat toward the waning sunlight above. I nearly ran up the hillside, until an ethereal lightness came over me that slowed my heart-rate, and calmed my soul.

Way too much time had been spent in the canyon, and I was going to have to race what sunlight was left before the coyotes ran loose. As I saddled up, I imagined what it would be like to have a swarm of coyotes all around me, and as I did I chuckled.

"You think YOU'RE tough?" I'd ask, as they ran their silly circles. "Well, you ain't tough. Compared to THAT thing down there, YOU AIN'T TOUGH AT ALL!"

That thought amused me as I looked back at the chimney one last time.

"Coyotes? HAH!" I yelled out. "YOU DON'T SCARE ME!"

Then I got up and rode, on the thin thread of sunlight that lined the mountain tops.

"What the hell was that place?" raced through my mind as I pedaled furiously. "And, what really happened in the burned-out town of the damned?"

Well, as it turned out, many of those questions would be answered on the day that I returned, with a small army by my side.

The Wave

Her name was Annie, and she was one of the most beautiful things I'd ever seen.

She was a wide one, with a beam nearly a third her over-all length. And from the first moment I laid eyes on her, I could tell she was all woman.

Technically, Annie was a trawler, but she was built to work like a tug. With her hips flared on the surface, and her bow thrust toward the sky, there was no question she was built for seas that would swallow a lesser boat whole.

I walked the gangway that winter morning without a care in the world, tossing my bag amidships with a caress of Annie's rail. At first it seemed as if I was the only hand on deck, until I walked toward an open hatch, where the clanking sound of a cold wrench on hard steel bellowed up from below.

"Better get a bigger hammer!" I yelled down the stairwell. But before I could savor the pleasure of my sarcasm, someone poked me in the back with a cold, pointed object. I froze in place as a chill ran down my spine, then, as I slowly turned around, I saw Captain Tom standing there with a frozen mackerel in his hand.

"You're gonna have to be a LOT less jumpy if you want to work on this boat!" Tom said, as he shook the fish up and down. "These things have a way of showing up in the strangest places!"

I knew that far too well, especially after finding a small tuna flopping around in my bunk the week prior. I had my suspicions as to who had put it there, but according to the crew, the beast had found its way in there all by itself.

Smiling, I gave Tom a nod before heading toward the bunkhouse. As I reached the gangway that led to the lower decks, I stepped onto one of the bulkhead ladder rungs beside the water-tight door. Taking a few steps down the shaft, I jumped onto the lower deck, before heading down the tight corridor that led to the forward bunkhouse. The place was a mess, with clothes strewn about as if there had been an explosion at a laundromat. With that much mess, there was no telling whose bunk was who's. So I used my arm like a giant squeegee, dozing off a section of cot, while staking claim to a piece of territory all my own.

It felt good to be aboard, and it felt good to be a member of a crew that valued my position on deck. I had Tom to thank for that, for had it not been for his guidance and fatherly advice, I wouldn't have had the slightest chance of being grandfathered into a profession that almost always hired from within.

We'd worked out a deal, of course. One where he'd show me the ins and outs of working on a commercial fishing boat, while I'd pretty much work for free. There were a few hidden perks to be had, such as free beer, an occasional fish, and lots and lots of food. But overall I was slave labor, until I'd weathered enough storms to finally earn my wings.

After stowing my belongings, I donned my yellow overalls, crossing the straps of the farmer-john in an "X" behind my back. I pulled down hard on the twin chest straps, cinching the suspenders against my thick flannel shirt. I snugged the straps down tight, then, with my boots pulled up and my hair pulled back, I was ready for a day's worth of fishing.

Annie's engines roared to life, sending me scrambling up the gangway toward the upper deck. I worked the port lines, waiting on the Captain's call, before pulling in the fenders just prior to departure. The twin Caterpillar diesels burned cleaner with each second, then, amid shouting fore and aft, Tom throttled-her-up, pulling free of the dock.

The morning was foggy, as most tend to be in Southern California. But unlike most of the days we'd set to sea, there was a feeling in the air that something wasn't quite right. It was an intuitive feeling more or less, one I couldn't quite put my finger on. Other than deep within my bones I felt as if a storm was coming.

Leaning against the rail of Annie's starboard gunnel, I watched the slick gray water slip past her hips. "The boat's not even wet," I thought. "She just glides through the water like they're dancing together."

I was mesmerized by the stillness of the early morning air, until we rounded a channel marker, where my trance-like state was broken by the sight of something huge moving across the inlet.

"Oh crap…" I thought, as a lump formed in my throat. "It's breaking HUGE across the bar!"

That was definitely an understatement, as gigantic waves were breaking against the jetty with earth-shaking force.

"Looks like its breakin' BIG!" deck-hand Mike said with a half-toothless grin. "I'm going downstairs, where I can pretend those puppies aren't out there!"

Mike had the right idea. He was headed down below, to where he could put a pillow over his head until the shouting was over. Then, if Annie was still afloat after we'd run the bar, he'd simply climb back on deck, as if nothing had happened at all.

I would have liked to have followed him below. Except for the fact that below deck was the worst place to be. I was just about to mention that, when Mike slid down the tube, as a new set of waves rolled in.

Up in the wheelhouse, Captain Tom feathered-back Annie's Cat's, before setting her screws in neutral. He knew damn well what the ocean could do if you gave her an inch. And now, as Annie sat motionless, Tom whispered to the sea as he peered through the patchy fog.

At first glance, the inlet's waters looked flat and calm. Yet to any seasoned mariner, that was a sure sign it was anything but. Tom watched and waited for movement across the bar, until slowly, out of the back-drop, a giant gray curtain appeared. Tom watched from the wheelhouse as the curtain moved from right to left. Then, as it cut through the fog, a steep mountain of water appeared out of nowhere.

The wave rolled silently across the bar, cresting higher and higher as it drew into the shallows. I stood motionless as it rose before us, wondering if Tom and the rest of the crew were having the same second thoughts that I was. The wave was huge, much larger than any wave I'd ever seen, and as it crashed down upon the jetty, I heard Tom shout out, "DAMN! That one was BIG!"

He was right, it was damn big. Way too large a wave to start out the day as far as I was concerned. But Tom was the Captain, and the Captain made the call. So, I held tight to the bulkhead's hand-rail, as Annie swirled in her backwash, while Tom timed the set for our run toward the sea.

Side-stepping to gain my footing, I bumped into crew-mate Matt who had come up from the galley moments earlier. He'd been pretending not to notice the waves, but now that we were about to make a run over the bar, he grabbed the rail as he tucked in close behind me. We were about as ready as we could have been, swirling in the slack eddy behind the break-wall's rocks. One, two, three... we timed the set. Until Annie's Cat's roared to life, as Tom fire-walled the throttles.

I remember it all so well. The way I bit my lip as Annie cut through the water, and how I actually believed we'd slip through the gap unharmed. But that was the fodder of fools, for just as I was beginning to believe my own line of crap, a dark wall of water rose up that must have been thirty feet tall.

There's little doubt I gasped, knowing it was foolish to expect anything less than a deck-clearing hit. I was scared, and as Annie chugged forward toward the slate-gray wall, I scurried behind the wheelhouse, taking a last look seaward before I closed my eyes. Leaning against the bulkhead, I pretended the wave wasn't there. But just like all the other monsters that have come my way, it charged straight in, as if we'd been lined up in its sights all along.

As I held onto a rail with a death-grip, I wholly expected the monster to throw us onto the rocks. But then, just as I thought the wave was going to break, it rose up even higher, pulling Annie's bow up toward the sky. It was strange how the wave lifted us, as if we were being cradled for a moment. Then, after Annie teeter-tottered at the wave's crest, her bow dug deep into the following trough with a deep, sloshing vee.

"First wave down," I mumbled, as Annie pushed onward toward the sea. "Give her just a bit more room and we're gonna be home-free!"

And a bit more room was all she needed, for as Annie's props bit the green water, she churned past the remaining swells, heading out toward the open sea.

It felt good to be past the bar, where the backs of waves stood so high they made my skin crawl. I didn't want to think about dealing with those monsters on the way in. But knowing that returning with a following sea made running the inlet easier, I put aside thoughts of disaster, turning my attention to the smell of freshly cooked bacon that wafted up from the galley.

A hot breakfast sounded great, especially after the scare we just had. Hopping down the gangway, I made my way toward the galley with food on my mind. After unstrapping the bib of my overalls, I bellied-up to the grill where galley cook Mike was tossing around a half pound of bacon, and a mountain of O-Brien potatoes. Grabbing a few half-cooked morsels, I barely got my fingers out of the way before Mike chopped down with the edge of his spatula. "Hands off!" he grumbled, while trying to contain a smile. "I'll let you know when it's time to chow down. Until then, the grill is MINE!"

As breakfast cooked, I began to feel like things were looking up. We'd cleared the bar, and despite the touch of rainy mist that painted Annie's hull, we soon broke through the fog, heading toward the offshore islands, fourteen miles in the distance.

We ate like kings that morning, as if the meal we shared was the greatest bounty on Earth. Tom piloted as we crewmen ate our share, then, after Mike was done eating, he piled up an enormous breakfast on a paper plate, bringing it up to the wheelhouse where Tom was eagerly waiting.

At twelve knots of headway, the fourteen mile channel took a while to traverse, more than enough time to rig some heavy leaders before we reached the first fishing spot. I took my time, tying each loop of the five hook ganyons in one foot increments. Then, after I slid each hook onto the looped ends of the leader, I placed each unit in a single plastic bag so they wouldn't get tangled up with one another.

Once the leaders were tied and bagged, I placed them in my tackle box, next to some weathered old lures my father had passed down to me. Those lures were heirlooms of a sort, good-luck charms in a way. And although any of them would have risen a fish as readily as they had years ago, I'd never dare fish even one of them, for fear of losing it forever.

But that wasn't going to be the fate of any of those lures. There wasn't a chance in Hell of that happening. Rather, they'd simply come along for the ride. To smell the salt air, and be with me on a day when everything I was made of would finally be put to the test.

Our plan was to motor Northwest, past the shelter of the islands, before heading offshore, to where the ocean's shelf dropped off markedly. There we'd be in waters of tremendous depth, where we were assured a fine catch, especially with the few boats there were working the outer banks that season. All on board had high hopes for the day, and as we readied our gear, every man on deck was humming in anticipation of the best haul of the season.

We were in high spirits, that's for sure. So much so, that none of us seemed to notice the fog had turned to rain. Nor did we seem to notice the way it was falling sideways, as if it was running from something that was just over the horizon.

Feeling a cold splash on my back, I looked up to see water spilling off the cowling atop Annie's cabin doorway. "Damn, it's raining," I muttered, before stepping into the galley. "I'd better put on my rain gear before it really starts coming down!"

I walked toward the row of coat-hooks at the end of the hall, before grabbing a hooded slicker that hung by the watertight door. After tightening the straps of my farmer-john, I slipped on the outer jacket, buttoning it up with fingers that were much colder than I'd previously realized.

I was about to say something witty about how I looked like the Gortons Lobster Guy, when deckhand Matt chimed in, saying, "Dayumm! Are we getting into the snot, or what?"

He was right; we were getting into the snot, especially now that we'd motored past the last of the sheltering islands. "Everyone clear the decks!" Tom said over the intercom. Then, as he keyed the mike with a double "SQUAWK-SQUAWK!" each of us headed to our favorite hidey-hole to best ride out the storm.

My favorite hiding spot was the wheelhouse, where a hand-full of us hunkered down while the rain blew sideways. Luckily, we'd climbed into the wheelhouse before any of us got soaked. And that was a good thing, especially because the bunk that Matt and I were sitting on was going to be someone's bed later on that evening.

As I sat on the bunk's edge with my knees pulled up to my chin, Matt stretched out like he was going to sleep for the rest of the day. I guess I couldn't blame him, as the cot was the coziest place in the wheelhouse. But even as he cat-napped, Matt knew damn well that as soon as we reached the fishing grounds, Tom was going to kick his ass out, sleeping or awake.

Tom throttled back a bit, so Annie could make headway in the ever growing swells. Rising and falling with the seas, I began to feel as if I was being rocked in a cradle, as did Matt, who began to snore so loudly it sounded like something had broken loose in the engine room.

As Matt droned on like a bullfrog, Tom looked over his shoulder, pretending to dip his coffee cup over Matt's head. "I'd really love to do that," Tom whispered, before taking a sip of his coffee. "I'd do it in a second, except that the lazy bum is sleeping in my bunk!" We laughed as we huddled together like soldiers in a fox-hole, before slipping into a strange silence, as rain sheeted off the wheelhouse's front window.

Looking around, I saw each man adrift in his own thoughts. Tom steered, with his coffee mug between his knees, while Matt snored away like he didn't have a care in the world. To my left was Mike, who was hanging half way out of the wheelhouse, seemingly lost in the drone of his tape deck, and whatever cold medicine he'd taken the night before. He rocked side to side as he stared at the sea, hypnotized by the waves as rain sprayed noisily against the leg of his slicker.

Tom reached toward the console, speeding up Annie's wipers. The rain was coming down hard, and from the look of things on the radar screen, the weather was about to get a whole lot worse.

"Damn," Tom said, as he pointed to the wave-like bands on the screen. "It's really starting to stack-up out here!"

"Yeah, it is," I told him. "But on the long-range scan it looks like there are bands of calm following the waves of the storm."

"That's what I was thinking," he replied. "I don't want to turn her around and run a following sea if there's any way I can help it."

Tom was right, for as he and I both knew, Annie rode best when her high-pitched bow cut straight into the seas. And besides, Captain Tom had a good handle on things. So, rather than wonder if he'd made the right choice by heading out into a gale, I ran off a run on the weather fax, just to give him a real-time update.

Tearing the sheet off the printer, I held the chart against the side window so that Tom could see it as clearly as possible. On the hard copy, the oncoming weather bands appeared much sharper than they had on the radar screen. It was nice having a real-time view of

what was coming toward us, but it was also a bit disconcerting., for what we originally thought were bands of calm, now appeared to be something else... something neither of us had seen before.

Tom knew damn well that things had gone to hell, and he also knew that the farther offshore we ventured, the worse things were going to get. Not being one to take unnecessary risks, he made an executive decision, altering course toward the leeward side of the nearest island.

"I'm taking her behind the island," Tom said, as he cautiously changed our heading. Then, after quartering the seas to get us on track, he announced over the P/A system that we were running for cover. I didn't hear one complaint as he announced the change in plans, nor did I hear a peep out of anyone in the wheelhouse. Tom had made the right decision, we all knew that, especially now that Annie was plowing through waves that had rolled for thousands of miles.

As Annie turned, I could feel the change in her attitude almost immediately. In the oncoming sea, she'd been confident and assured, slicing through waves like a wedge. But now that we'd turned toward the island, the waves quartered us viciously, causing her hull to pitch and yaw in a much more unpredictable pattern.

"She's built for this," I told myself, as the swells rolled beneath us. "She's definitely built for the snot."

And that she was. Although as Annie did her best to stay her course, I felt deep down inside that she too was holding her breath. Tom felt this as well, for each time Annie paused atop one of the larger waves, Tom jumped to his feet, feathering her engines so she could briefly catch her breath.

It was scary watching Tom guide Annie over the back of one beast after another. But strangely, in that moment, I felt as if Tom had complete control. There was no way he was going to let Annie get out from under him, and no way she was going to let the seas take control. That was something I'd bet my life on. So, having faith, I cautiously watched the dance, while holding my breath just the same.

Up we rose... first to the left, and then to the right, snaking along on the backs of giants that seemed to have been sent by the gods. Things were getting rough, rougher than I'd ever seen before, which is saying a lot, considering I was used to working in seas that could swallow a commercial boat whole.

Not liking the way things looked, I closed my eyes while Annie swayed and yawed. Where I really wanted to be was below deck, where I could pretend everything was going to be just fine. But Tom had other plans for me, which involved my doing something that was much more important than hiding from reality.

"Do you see that blue box down there?" Tom asked, as he pointed toward the bow. "It's broken loose, and now the damn thing is smashing all over the foredeck!"

Squinting through the front window, I looked down to where a large wooden box was sloshing around in green water that we'd taken over the bow. "That's the one," Tom said, as it rasped against the gunnel. "Would you mind fastening it down?"

Always obeying my captain, I gave the thumbs-up, before climbing over Mike on my way out the door. I hurried down the rungs, taking a wide stance on the hard-deck just as four inches of water rushed past my feet. "Damn!" I yelled. "How the hell did things go south so quickly?"

There really was no answer to that, other than things had aligned in such a way, that it seemed as if the gods were conspiring against us.

Cinching down my hood and collar, I looked around as a second wave rushed past my feet. The deck-borne water was deep, and now that the seas were rising, it seemed like everything that hadn't been nailed down was sliding around the deck.

Timing the waves, I scurried forward each time Annie's pitch centered close to zero. Ahead of me was the large anchor pulpit, which poked into the mist like the bowsprit of an ancient mariner. Grabbing hold of the heavy anchor chain, I could see the loose cargo box sloshing between the forward bait tank and Annie's starboard gunnel.

I approached the crate gingerly as it smashed against the hull, not wanting to lose a finger when I grabbed it. The damn thing was slippery, but timing its movement just right, I grabbed hold of the box just as a cold stream of water shot through the hawespipes, soaking me from head to toe.

The water was freezing cold, and as it flooded the foredeck to nearly knee height, I knew that if I was to fall overboard, there wouldn't be a chance in Hell they'd ever find me. That was the sobering truth, one that was driven home by a mewling voice that was carried by the wind.

I spun around when the voice rang out. Not sure if it was another deckhand, or the wind howling through the superstructure. I didn't dare answer, as I held an ear to the wind, while hoping it was my imagination, as rain poured down all around me.

Annie's bow pitched into a trough, and I felt weightless as the floor dropped out from under me. I floated in mid-air a moment, until the bow rose up sharply, slamming against my feet. That spooked me a bit, and I scrambled to secure the box before I was battered and bruised any further. My fingers grew numb as I worked a small rope, lashing the box to the anchor pulpit as best I could. "Get it tied, and make-it-fast!" I told myself. "Make-it-fast, and get back to the wheelhouse before you're sucked over the side!"

I moved quickly, doing the best I could on the wildly pitching deck. The loops in the rope seemed right, but each time I cinched the head knot down, the box floated free of the deck, as if it had a mind of its own. Things seemed oddly out of focus, almost as if time was standing still. Then, as Annie pitched and twisted beneath me, I heard a voice in the wind that was decidedly feminine.

The voice called out. Not from the sea, but from somewhere deep within Annie's hull. At first I thought it was her propellers, howling on their shafts as they fought to bite the water. But then, as the voice rose to a near fever pitch, I heard Annie cry out, as she desperately begged me to look toward the horizon.

I didn't want to look. I really, really, didn't. Especially since boats aren't supposed to talk, and the sound of her voice was anything but reassuring. But I had to look. I just had to. So I did. And in a moment I'll never forget, I saw something unimaginable...

At first I thought it couldn't be real, that the line in the sky must have been a squall, or a low-lying inversion layer. But as the white foam lip of the great wall of death blotted out the horizon, all I could hear was the scream in my throat, as it raced to catch up with me.

Running toward the wheelhouse, I body-slammed the super structure as I leaped for the ladder's upper rung. I clamored for my life, scaling the rungs three at a time, before I burst through the doorway as if I'd seen The Devil.

As I pointed to the horizon, Tom reacted with amazing speed, wiping the sleeve of his musty sweat shirt against the fogged-up window. He said nothing as he pressed his face against the glass. Then, as an icy chill rolled off his back, he looked as if he'd just met his maker.

I didn't have to ask whether or not he'd seen it, for as he stood silently amid the rhythmic "Slosh, slosh, slosh," of Annie's windshield wipers, we both knew that death was upon us.

We were all going to die. Courtesy of a wave so tall, it looked like a mountain. There really wasn't anything to say as the black wall approached, other than a few gakking sounds and a gutteral "OH GOD..." now and then. The sky grew dark as the wave drew nearer, and as the clouds and sea reached out to touch one another, we were just about out of options.

In the back of my mind, I hoped that Tom had a trick or two up his sleeve. But as the wall of water rolled closer, I leaped from the wheelhouse, needing to face death on my own terms. Hitting the deck hard, I figured I'd give survival a shot as long as there was breath left in me. Where to go or what to do were of little concern. I only knew that I was going to have to play the moment by ear, and ride it out by the seat of my pants.

The wave was coming, and looking at it again wasn't going to change a thing. So, rather than spending my last moments gawking in terror, I pressed against the bulkhead, as I looked away from the approaching horror.

There was no way that I was going to look. No way in Hell . . . At least that's what I kept telling myself. In fact, for a brief moment I descended to that fool's paradise where Tom would magically steer us around the wave, and we'd all laugh about it later on. But that was wishful thinking. For as the wave bore down on us, there was no possible way Annie could make enough headway to avoid a direct hit. Tom knew that all too well. So, doing what any good captain would, he grabbed the wheel, and turned us into the wave.

There was a shudder as Annie's rudder swung full to starboard, yawing her fantail in a pitching roll that nearly flung Mike from the wheelhouse. I hung onto a handrail as we turned, biting my lip as I hid from the horror. Annie dug in hard, dipping her shoulder like a fullback punching through the line. She turned quickly, faster than expected, bringing us to bear with a black wall of water that seemed to reach up to the heavens.

As we turned, the wind stopped blowing, for what rose up before us blotted out everything, except for the horror. It was a wave of immense magnitude, one so large it seemed like the world had folded up on its end. It was black as night, standing sixty feet or better, rolling toward us with a white-lined crest that delineated it from the dark sky above.

I stared at the wave, and its hollow, cavernous face. Seeing long trails of mist dance like phantoms as they fell. There was death in that hollow, and as it approached, time slowed to half speed, so that the horror could build to the ultimate climax.

That moment was unforgettable, as everything seemed so unbelievably surreal. In the background, there was a "Tink, tink, tink," bell-like sound, emanating from somewhere within Annie's hull. And as she turned to face the wall, I had no doubt she'd taken all control.

Sure, Tom had turned the wheel, but even then, she was way ahead on the inside curve. Annie was alive, and now that her life was on the line, she was going to do things her way. So she feathered her engines as the wave watched and waited . . . Until they each took a breath, before charging toward one another with all their might.

As the wave drew nearer, I could feel a force within it that was nothing short of incredible. Energy filled the air as we were sucked into the hollow, and in that singular, terrifying moment, I felt strangely compressed, as if the physical properties of time and space had somehow been altered.

I sensed the change immediately, as nearly all sound and movement ceased to exist. Then, in a moment that was both horrifying and enlightening, the clock stopped ticking, as time began to stand still.

It started with a pause, a wonderful dream-like pause, where I stepped out from within my own skin to look upon the wave. Everything seemed frozen in time, except for an oily, black sludge that oozed down the wave as if it was melting. The sludge was gritty, sparkly in fact, and as it swarmed with particles that looked like atoms, I felt like I'd witnessed a force of nature I'd rather not be privy to.

Looking away from the living ooze, I gazed up toward the heavens, where the height of the wave made my head spin. The wave was monstrous. Not quite a breaker, but nowhere near a swell, our adversary was nearly vertical in its countenance. The sight of it was enough to stop any man's heart. But what I sensed even more, was something behind the wave. Something hidden and horrible, that was deadlier still.

The wave granted me a moment to ponder what that could be. Time to think long and hard about what monster it was that crouched down behind her. I stammered for a moment, wondering… before a horrifying realization rushed forth that made the wave itself seem nearly benign.

"OH GOD!" I cried, as the realization hit home. "IT'S THE TROUGH! The dark hollow behind the wave, that's going to swallow us whole!"

This new twist was almost too much to comprehend. The wave itself would surely kill us. But if for some twisted reason it didn't, the yawning chasm on the flip-side, was going to drag us straight down to Hell.

Death-mist phantoms fell from above, while time moved in clicks, like the staggered frames of an old foreign film. The wave pulsed like a black wall of cellophane, and as I listened to the "Tink, tink, tink," of Annie's hidden bell, a familiar form materialized, at the worst possible moment.

"Mind if I join you?" He said, as his shadow-form tore in the wind. "Mind if I join the party?"

I would have said something sarcastic, had his presence not foretold of darker things to come. Staring at Him as he floated above the deck, I asked point-blank if he was there to take my soul. But he said nothing, as he seemed to phase between shadow and substance. I stared at Him a moment, until after an overly dramatic pause, he asked, "How's it going?"

"HOW'S IT GOING?" I blurted out. "Did you swim all the way out here to ask me THAT?"

"Not entirely," he said with a grin. "And just for the record, I rarely swim. It's REALLY dangerous!"

"Oh, man," I muttered, as I shook my head. "You're a real piece of work!"

He seemed pleased with that. Then, as he slid closer to me, he asked, "Why do you think I'm really here? Go ahead… tell me."

"Because you're going to watch me cheat death one more time!" I told Him. "That's why!"

He nodded as if to say, "Touché." Then, just a second before he began to fade away, he said, "Show me."

There was a blur, as I was transported back to reality, where the softly clanging bell punctuated a strange, scuffing silence.

"Tink, tink, tink," went the bell, like the radium clock in an atomic bomb. It counted down a moment, until Annie revved her engines, before thrusting her bow into the giant like an enormous wedge. The wave shuddered, as she cut into its underbelly. Until it gripped her like a vise, lifting us skyward, as her props churned the water to foam.

It looked as if we were through. Or at least I thought we were through, save for a miracle sent by the gods. I grabbed hold of one of the steel rungs that were welded to the wheelhouse, and as I did, I looked up toward the sky. Higher and higher we climbed, clicking our way up the conveyor belt of death, where I expected we'd catch one last glimpse of the horizon, before plunging deep down to where we'd never, ever be found.

Up we climbed. How far I can't say, other than that eighty five feet of trawler nearly stood on its tail. As we carved up the wave's immense face, I looked down, to see my legs dangling in the air, while my feet scrambled for a foothold on a loop-rung below.

There was a plan I suppose. One that involved holding on with a death-grip, while I begged the sea gods for my life. I tried that for a moment, but then, as I dangled precariously between life and death, Plan-A didn't seem to have much chance of succeeding. I needed to do more than hang on and scream . . . But what could I do? So I hung there like a kid on the monkey bars, hoping desperately that Plan-B would fall from the sky, just in time to save the day.

Of course, diving into the water was always an option, although it was definitely the last on the list. It was, after all, just a wave. And as a big wave surfer, I knew that I could wim under her if push came to shove. But before I jumped free there were other things to consider. Such as the heavy clothes I was wearing, and the hundred ton fishing trawler that was sure to land on top of me.

Those fine points, plus the fact that I'd surely die of hypothermia, kept me from jumping into the drink. So I just clung to the bulkhead with a vise-like grip, as we rose up toward the sky.

Some of the others screamed for their lives, but quite frankly, I never expected to see any of them again. In that moment of clarity, their living or dying was none of my concern. For survival mode had taken over, and sadly, there in the hollow of death, it was every man for himself.

Besides, being the only crewman who was actually on deck, I was the only person who stood half a chance of being thrown clear if we capsized. That was in stark contrast to the situation below, where my comrades were about to be bludgeoned to death, when the ship rolled around like a giant rock tumbler.

I guess that's when I wrote them off, for there was no time for heroics, especially now that my own survival rating was down to one percent. It was all up to Annie now, and I knew that what she did in the following moments would forever determine the course of my life.

That's when I kicked her in the loins. Like a cowboy does, when there's something to be done that the horse isn't doing. It wasn't as if she needed a hint... it's just that she needed a bit of encouragement, from someone else on board who had a firm handle on things.

So I obliged as best I could, yelling, "COME ON GIRL! COME ON!" as we climbed up toward the sky.

Annie kicked with amazing torque, driving her hull skyward as if she was on a conveyor belt. For a glorious moment I believed we might actually survive, especially when we breached the wave's crest, carving a deep vee into the monster's shoulders. We teetered there a moment, half way between the wave's face and the bottomless trough, when suddenly, something happened, that I

264

never, ever expected.

Annie's propellers came out of the water. And when they did, all hell broke loose...

First there was a shudder, as the port prop rose out of the water. Its blades grinding with such ferocity, that they nearly tore the drive-shaft loose. Annie shook violently as the shaft nearly snapped, and as she did, I felt as if my teeth were being hammered out of my mouth.

There was a terrible grinding sound, along with a chopping, harmonic resonance that nearly burst my eardrums. "This is it!" I thought, as the prop strained to split from the shaft. "We're going to be chopped into a thousand pieces, just as soon as the prop weed-whacks its way through the hull!"

Closing my eyes, I cringed, as the starboard propeller joined its partner in a howling dance that sounded as if the gates of Hell had just opened. In retrospect, I hoped that Tom would do something valiant, such as throttle Annie's engines back. But from the way Annie screamed like she was on fire, I knew deep in my heart that no one was at the wheel. We were all going to die. And as we teetered atop the precipice, I took one last look toward the horizon.

Far in the distance, I could see a sliver of light, a parting in the clouds where the sun had broken through. It was so beautiful the way the rays of light beamed down, in a rainbow of color that seemed like it had been painted on the horizon. "Maybe I'll jump in and swim toward it," I thought. "Maybe I'll just swim over there, and look up toward the sky."

It was so peaceful on our perch above the sea where millions of gallons of jet-black water tumbled over the falls. The water pounded like a drum, beating faster and faster with each second. Then, as I looked to the horizon one last time, Annie dove nose-first into oblivion...

I locked in my grip as we plunged into the abyss, feeling weightless for a moment, as we fell like a stone. Annie pitched nose down, with her props flailing wildly. And as she did, I slid sideways, slamming against the lower bulkhead with a kidney-crushing blow.

We were falling toward certain death. Yet for some odd reason, I couldn't look away from the spectral mists that flew around like seagulls. I stared at them as they darted and danced, while in half-time, Annie screamed, as we plunged into the cavernous hollow.

I darted my head down as the wall of water enveloped me, washing away nearly everything but the rhythmic sound of drums. I couldn't feel a thing as the sea folded around us, save for the vice-like grip I had on a thin steel pipe. From her bow pulpit, to halfway up the wheelhouse, Annie was underwater. And now, for better or worse, I was down there with her.

She pirouetted on her nose, while her twin screws screamed at the sky. I could hear them through the water, as they strained to find a foothold. And I knew quite well, that once they did, we'd be propelled straight to the bottom.

There was a choice to make: either ride the A-Train to Hell, or push myself free, and swim toward the light. Both directions led to certain death, but for many reasons, chancing the swim seemed the right thing to do. I was about to swim free, just seconds from loosening my grip, when Annie twisted sharply, slamming her starboard side against the sea.

I remember the taste of blood, along with a weird state of confusion, as my body slapped the deck like a wet dish-rag. The impact stunned me, and as I lay there a moment with my feet to the heavens, icicles fell from the sky.

Annie had survived the wave, but her engines still revved to the red-line. I rolled to my side as her screws sought their mark, just a second before she lurched forward, sending a wave of deck-water my way that was at least two feet tall.

I ducked my head under the surge as the wave hit like a bull, blowing me across the deck like a leaf in the wind. I held my breath as the wave bludgeoned me, while a number of crates and boxes rudely made my acquaintance. One by one the crates slammed my side, until the surge subsided, leaving me numbed, but still quite alive.

The water was damn cold, but for some reason, I didn't feel a thing. Perhaps I'd been numbed to the point where I really didn't care. Or maybe, now that we'd survived the monstrous wave, all of the aftermath was just a fickle, harmless side-show.

There was shouting in the wheelhouse as I strained to right myself, just a moment before I heard a *whoosh!* as Tom throttled

Annie back to idle.

Crawling to the port gunnel, I looked to the East, where the wave sauntered off without a care in the world. I suppose you'd think the thing had no feeling at all. But that was far from the truth... for as it blotted out the horizon, the ghostly white imps, taunted me from afar.

Much had been lost that day, yet for all the chaos, no one had lost their life. In fact, despite several deep bruises, there wasn't a broken bone between us. We escaped death that day, and Annie did too, as she continues to ply the seas, to this very day.

We never did get to fish that fateful morning. Nor did I get to use the tricked-out leaders I'd set up earlier in the day. They, along with many other things, had washed off Annie's deck, deep into the abyss, where things are lost forever. Sadly, at first, I thought I'd lost the lures that my father had given me. But by some saving grace, we found the tackle box days later. Floating in the galley, where there was at least a foot of standing-water.

I've still got those rusted old lures. And every so often, I take them out of the box, and hold them one more time. I run my fingers over them, feeling the deep tooth marks that have been there for decades. They feel good in my hands, and as I hold them, I think back to the day when my father first showed them to me.

That was a long time ago. Back when I'd sit beside his workbench and play with the sawdust on the floor. He'd sit on his stool, with a faraway look in his eyes. And I'd often wonder what he was thinking, as he'd look down at me, without saying a word.

Maybe he knew a storm was coming. Or maybe he knew that somewhere down the line, those rusted old lures would end up at a garage sale somewhere. Perhaps they will. And perhaps, I hope, they'll find their way into the hands of someone who can decipher the marks of time.

But until then, they're mine.

And I'm keeping them, until my dying day.

The Ghost Ship

As a thousand tons of shipwreck cut past me like a razor, I could feel a life force pulsing deep within its hull. Side-slipping the bow as it thrust out of the darkness, I dodged to one side, as the rusted hulk slipped angrily by.

"Whoa girl…" I whispered to the ship. "It hasn't been that long since I've visited. Calm down, and let me come along side."

Approaching amid-ships, I held tight to the hull as I ran my hand along the starboard deck rail. At first she pretended not to notice, but as my hand slid down the curves of her spine, she reluctantly gave in, groaning loudly as her hull twisted in the sand.

With a glance over my shoulder, I could see my fellow divers, staring wide-eyed like deer in the headlights. "I bet they've never seen a wreck do THAT!" I thought, as they tucked in close behind. "She's definitely one of a kind!"

Neither of them could believe what they'd seen, which probably accounts for why they looked like the ship was about to cut their heads off. I motioned for them to follow, keeping close to the hull, where there were no surprises, and our path to the wheelhouse was clear of obstacles.

All around us was shadow, topped with a purplish blue that seemed most surreal. Looking up, I could see the ghostly silhouette of the ship's wheelhouse fading into the oily gloom. "Wow, we're deep," I thought, as I neared the stack-like structure. "The water feels like it's made out of lead."

I switched on my primary light as we neared our target, illuminating the ship with an eerie, orange glow. We moved methodically, swimming to the port side of the wheelhouse, where I grabbed the frame of an open water-tight door. Sweeping my light into the doorway, I did a quick scan of the interior before motioning that we'd found our mark.

The ship's deck sloped with a considerable list, and I tested the door with both hands before squeezing through the narrow gap. I pulled, once, twice, and maybe more, before I was reasonably confident that the door wouldn't close if she decided to roll.

"So far so good," I thought, as we wormed through the doorway without a creak or groan in rebuttal. "Give up your treasures, and I promise I'll visit you much more often!"

Pausing a moment, I rested on my fin tips, as I stared out an open porthole. I saw nothing but darkness, and I looked away, before I caught sight of something I'd rather not see. There was something out there shadowing us. Something large, whose imposing presence seemed to bleed through the water. It had the eyes of a predator, and ever since we'd entered its domain, I couldn't help but feel that I'd been locked onto by a radar gun.

"Maybe it's a shark," I thought. "Or maybe it's something else that I'd rather not acknowledge." Both those thoughts were disquieting, yet in the moment, the skulking presence seemed much less of a threat than the rusted ship was.

As I drew a labored breath from my regulator, the voice of reason chimed in loud and clear. "You barely got out last time," it said. "And here you are again, just ASKING for trouble."

"Yeah, yeah, yeah," I knew all about that. Especially since the last time around we barely escaped with our lives.

I knew far too well the danger of what we were doing. But somehow, the overwhelming sense of discovery seemed to blot out all reason.

After doing a systems check, I frog-kicked down the corridor, careful not to stir up any more silt than was absolutely necessary. Behind me, just inches from my fins, was Tim, followed by Brian, who brought-up the rear. We moved purposefully down the hall, to where I paused by the entrance to a deep, narrow stairwell.

Here too, was an open door, suspended in mid-swing when the ship went down. I leaned into the half open doorway, swallowing hard, as the ship began to groan.

The door hung open precariously, and I knew far too well that with a purposeful twist of her hull, our fickle hostess could imprison us forever. Not wanting to chance that, I grabbed the door's wheel mechanism with one hand, while holding the jamb with the other. I pulled hard, trying to actuate the cam-lock, but as suspected, the entire mechanism was rusted solidly in place. Passage seemed a safe bet, but knowing what she was capable of, I had my reservations.

Tim pulled against the door, and he too found it immovable. It seemed to be rusted in place, so, feeling reasonably assured that passage was given, I motioned to my friends for us to move forward.

I whispered, "Don't roll on me girl," as I wiggled through the slot. Then, after tying the bitter end of my safety line to a water pipe, I descended down the stairwell with the others close behind.

The thin, nylon cord rolled off my reel as I crested the stairwell's threshold. I fell like a balloon, gliding over the stairs as I descended below. At first I couldn't see the floor, but then, as the deck plates loomed out of the darkness, I folded to my knees, for the softest landing possible.

Hitting fins-first, I tucked against the floor with a soft touch. It took a moment for the others to follow, so I beamed my light down the twisted hallway as I waited on their company. The pathway was unobstructed, save for a few small items that were scattered around the floor. I was pleased that we weren't going to have to horn our way under any debris, and with the "Okay" sign, I conveyed that to my fellow divers.

We took a moment to monitor our gas-load, huddling closely as we compared gauges. Our air consumption was a bit faster than I'd hoped, but given our excessive depth, some fudging room was to be expected. A quick check of my team's consoles revealed they were within two hundred P.S.I. of my back-gas load. Then, quickly calculating our descent/ascent ratio, I realized we had only seven minutes of bottom time to find what we were looking for, if we wanted to get back alive.

We moved fast, heading deep into the ship, to where my team had aborted its dive months earlier. That drop had gone wrong for a variety of reasons. Not to mention the fact that the ship was alive... a curious little side-bar that took us all by surprise.

She'd been an enigma all along, just a blip on the sonar, deep within a dark, benthic canyon. Her silhouette could easily have been dismissed as artifact or clutter. But as I stared at the grainy report on the thin graph paper, I could see linear structure, dangling precipitously near the edge of the canyon.

That's how we found her. Hiding on the sea floor in a place

where nobody should have looked. She was safely hidden until I came along, and now that I'd found her, I just had to take a closer look.

Of course, we didn't have much choice, as she'd called out to us with her wailing, siren song. She buckled and rolled when she realized we'd found her, filling the water with a scream-like sound that stood my hair on end. That alone should have kept us away, but as she called out from below, we had no choice but to visit her, in a place that was haunted by more than just ghosts.

None of us cared to admit it, but when we first saw her dark silhouette, there was a sense that she might bite. It was a palpable feeling, as if the water itself was warning us to stay away. I wondered if I might have been losing my mind as I harbored such thoughts. But then, as she came alive before our eyes, I knew for certain that I'd gone mad.

We never should have gone into her that day, nor should we have made it out alive. But she wanted us back, perhaps with new meat, for a trip down to Hell, where she'd be our tour-guide. So there we were, back in line to ride the coaster two times in a row. I knew that at any second, the car could fly off the tracks. But as we stared down the hall, toward the place where we'd first seen the light, I couldn't imagine anywhere else I'd rather be.

The corridor beckoned with a hollow pull that tugged at my soul. I glanced at my gauges, seeing there was enough air to do the job, but hardly enough for error. "It'll have to do," I thought. "It's enough to get things done, as long as we don't get careless."

I should have laughed as I debated the parameters of carelessness knowing damn well that the point of carelessness had been breached when our fins hit the water. Now, as my friends followed me deeper into her hull, we swam toward an end... although to what end, I really didn't know.

Swimming single-file, we wound deep into the ship, careful to stay tight and ready. We clustered together at each descending stairwell, staring at one another, before dropping into an oily blackness that shimmered against our masks. Once we'd reached three decks deep, I looked to my left, where a jumble of desks and cabinets were strewn about the room. Some were lying on their sides, while a large file cabinet seemed to have been jammed in a doorway, as if it had been placed there on purpose.

Looking up, I could see recessed deck plates, heavily laden with marine overgrowth. Between the plates were quivering pockets of trapped air that had been formed when the ship went down. They reflected with an opalescent purity, glistening like bottomless pools that were suspended overhead. Someone once told me that those pockets of air were the trapped screams of sailors, who'd embraced the horror just before they pushed away from the steel. A chill came over me as I imagined doing that, and as I wondered if their voices could still be heard, I considered putting an ear to the hull.

I think we were all pondering the same thing as Brian pressed a finger into the void. And as he did, I half expected to hear a scream. But we heard nothing at all, nothing but the sound of our regulators, and the distant groan of the ship's restless hull.

Tim tugged on my fin, while giving me the "Do you have any idea where you're going?" look. I gave him the "Okay" signal, before looking down at my air gauge, just long enough to question myself.

Those questions were two-fold, the first being, what business did we have looking for something that nearly took our lives? And more importantly, what were we going to do if we found it again?

I needed a moment to figure that out. Especially given that the extreme depth had begun to cloud my decisions. I focused through the haze, wondering if searching for a ghost-light really was something we should have been doing. We were after all, at nearly one hundred and sixty feet deep. Three decks down, into a ship that was held captive by two gigantic boulders. The stone monoliths held her like a vise, grasping her amid-ships as if they were fearful of what might happen if she squirmed loose.

"Okay," I thought, "Maybe it's time to turn-tail and run, before we piss anything off, especially her!"

Giving the team the "All-stop" sign, I poked my head around the corner for a quick look down the hall. I stared into the darkness for far too long, half expecting to see The Devil looking back at me. I called him out, but he didn't appear. Nor did the glowing light that started the panic the last time we'd ventured into her hull.

I floated there, conscious of neither time nor circumstance, wondering if the light really had been The Devil, or if it had been something else entirely. I began to feel lost, confused in many ways, when I was shocked into my senses by a sound so loud, I slammed my tank into the ceiling.

Rust rained down as I turned in the direction of the sound, where I saw Brian smashing the blade of his utility knife against the latch mechanism of a rusted lock-box. He seemed possessed as he swung the knife, wildly smashing the box with a blade that was landing dangerously close to his fingers.

Something seemed to be controlling him, and I watched in horror, as he hacked away with zero reverence for the steel. I pulled him backward in an attempt to break his trance, but without so much as a glance in my direction, he forged on, nearly hacking his fingers off in the process.

This was madness in its purest form... Sure, the box was interesting. And I too, could feel its mysterious draw. But as we clustered together in the bowels of a ship that stretched like a cat on a fireplace, that familiar voice began to speak, telling me to swim fast and true, if I wanted to escape certain death.

It was time to go, and I knew that if there was to be any chance of saving Brian, Tim and I were going to have to work fast. I turned toward Tim, hoping to catch his eye, when I saw him groping for the box, while Brian's knife landed with shearing, slicing blows.

"What the hell?" I thought, as Tim grabbed for the box. "There's something inside that thing that's taken control of them!"

It seemed I'd lost them to madness, and now, as they fought for control of the blade, I feared that within seconds, the knife would be at Tim's throat.

It was pure insanity as they fought for the box, while silt rose up like a slow moving curtain of death. The cloud began to envelope them, but even as it wrapped around their bodies, neither seemed to care about anything other than breaking the box's latch, and freeing the demons inside. Both of them were crazed, and in the midst of the mayhem, I began to fear that only one of us would be returning to the surface. If I didn't do something fast they'd both be dead. Yet, as I pondered that and more, I couldn't imagine what to do.

I thought for a moment, until dragging them across the floorboards seemed the right thing to do. "That might just work," I thought. "It might knock some sense into them!" So, I swam toward my friends, while telling myself that no matter what madness poured from the box, it wasn't going to affect me. I was there to save my friends, and regardless of the box's demonic pull, somehow, I was going to shock them back to their senses.

As I swung in from behind, I placed one hand on a ceiling beam, while forcefully grabbing the horn of Tim's tank. I pulled hard, tearing his hands off the box just a second before his tank slammed against the floor.

He lay on his back like a cockroach, with his arms and legs curled up as if he was dead. I shined my light into his eyes, but he seemed to be locked into some kind of trance. I rolled forward, looking into his eyes, and as my light illuminated his faceplate, I saw one of the strangest things I've ever seen.

It wasn't Tim's face looking back at me. But rather, it was another face altogether… the face of a porcelain doll.

As I looked into Tim's dead, black eyes, I knew for certain that Elvis had left the building. Tim's body lay in front of me, but he himself was gone. As if the force in the box had taken his soul and nullified it somehow.

I began pulling him across the room, when You-know-who appeared out of nowhere. "GET OUT!" The Reaper said loudly. "GET OUT NOW!"

His voice echoed through the hull, in a metallic tone that was nearly deafening. "How 'bout giving an old friend a hand?" I thought back to Him. "You didn't come all the way down here just to say hello, did you?"

Of course he hadn't, nor had he swam down to the murky depths just to see the fish. He was there on business. Yet as his voice lay quiet, I felt strangely assured that he wasn't there for me.

Without hazarding a glance into the darkness, I grabbed the horn of Tim's tank, dragging his lifeless body across the floor. As I pulled, his tank bounced over the bulkhead, while his expressionless doll face stared at the ceiling. He lay there completely motionless, amid the non-stop *clack, clack, clack!* of

Brian's relentless hacking. Everything seemed so hopeless, and I began to feel a sense of desperation that was nearly overwhelming. Looking into Tim's lifeless eyes, I felt responsible for all this. And as I did, the ship's hull began to groan, as she tasted death in the water.

She cried softly at first, in a voice that was nearly indiscernible. But then, as the ship came to life, she wailed like an alley cat, so loudly it was nearly a scream.

I leaned against the bulkhead, as the ship's shrieking wail resonated into the sea. There was a whale-like tone to her voice, and as she cried her metallic cry, the sound rattled my soul as if she'd poked a bony finger right through me.

Trying my best to stay focused, I shook off the dizziness, while a silt cloud wrapped its shadowy arms around Tim's body. I closed my eyes, focusing on the sound of my breath, as the ship wailed with delight. She sang to me, with the song of a maiden long forgotten. And as I listened to her voice, I knew for certain that she wouldn't be letting us go.

Silt rose around me as I floated in the scream pool. While deep within myself, I pretended not to be there. The ship's voice began to fade, when suddenly, another voice chimed in that made everything seem quite clear.

"She's seduced them," He said. "You've got to leave them, if you want to save yourself."

"I know, I know… I KNOW!" I screamed through my regulator. "I KNOW QUITE WELL WHAT I'M GOING TO HAVE TO DO! Now just give me a moment to think this through, okay?"

I paused for a moment, how long I can't say, to reflect upon thoughts a man shouldn't have. Yes, I'd considered leaving them to their own devices. And yes, I'd considered what I was going to tell the authorities after rising to the surface. But that was only a contingency plan. For while I still had a bit of air to work with, I figured there had to be something I could do.

That's when I paused, to reflect upon the fact that I hadn't thought of anything but the mayhem, in a dangerously long time.

"How long had it been since Brian found the box?" I wondered. "And had I tried to save Tim once, or three times now?"

It was all a blur, yet in the oddest way, it seemed as if we'd been inside the ship for hours. How long we'd been there I didn't know. Nor did I hazard a glance at my gauges, which seemed so utterly irrelevant. Time had slowed somehow, compressing thought and action into a shapeless form that didn't really matter. Was I thinking, or acting, or thinking of acting? That I didn't know. All I knew was that Tim was rolling around, and that the sight of his movement had jerked me back to my senses.

Tim sat up, looking around as if he'd just been thrown from a horse. Relieved as hell that he was among the living, I flashed my light in his eyes, as he slowly broke from his trance.

"It's IN the box," I thought. "And by touching the box, it somehow gets under your skin." That made sense, especially in light of how quickly Tim had recovered since I'd pulled him free of the menace. Now all we had to do was free Brian, without either of us touching the box, or getting our throats slit in the process.

I glanced down at my gauges, where the numbers blurred behind a droplet of water. As I squinted in the dark, it all seemed so weirdly surreal. Tim's lifeless eyes…. the slowing of time… and the sound of Brian's frenetic banging, which for all I knew had already cost him his fingers. I couldn't begin to understand it all, nor did I even try to. But as the metallic taste of rust flowed from my tank, I pulled hard against the cord reel, swimming in Brian's direction, where hopefully, I could save him from himself.

As I swam, I was beginning to prepare the speech that I feared I'd be delivering to his mother. It escapes me now, exactly what I was going to say, other than "Something strange happened," seemed like it would do in a pinch.

I supposed that would have worked. That combined with my scuffing my feet, while making the obligatory scant eye contact that all bearers of bad news pull off so well. Yeah, that's what I was going to do. And it would have worked, while all along, what I really would have been thinking was, "The whole damn thing was all my fault."

With that in mind, I never expected to find Brian with all of his fingers intact. Nor did I expect that he'd actually live to miss them. Rather, I figured that his tank was a breath from bone dry, while for some unexplained reason, mine still had a bit of air left in it.

He was likely a goner, but being his friend, I swam into the silt cloud hoping for one last chance. The cloud reflected light in every direction, compounding my light's beam in a thousand different ways. I was nearly blinded by my own light's reflection, so I lowered the light cannon, blindly swimming toward the rhythmic sound of his chopping blade.

Brian wasn't far from me, and I bumped up against him as his knife delivered another chunking blow. I felt for his tank, positioning myself where the knife was less of a threat. He thrashed wildly as I grabbed his tank by the horn, but being that he had one hand on the box, it was easier to control him than I'd expected.

I pulled with all my might, until Brian flew backward against the rotting deck plates. He landed hard, dropping the knife, as his shoulder slammed against a small, steel desk.

We were at the edge of the silt cloud, where I could see Tim, just a few feet away. He swam toward me, grabbing Brian by the scruff. We pulled in unison, and within a second, Brian emerged from the cloud, holding the box to his chest like a teddy bear. He stared wide-eyed at the box, just a moment before I kicked it from his hands, sending it tumbling into the darkness.

The box landed with a "Clunk," while the ship cried as if someone had taken its lollypop. Brian lay there a moment, much like Tim had done, before he came to his senses with the strangest look on his face.

It was strange how he sat there, with his body hunched forward, and a billion sparkles of silica swirling all around him. He slowly turned his head, before looking at his hands, like a child who had just dropped an ice cream cone.

We looked at one another, and in that moment, time rushed forward in a chilling wave. We were in big trouble, not just from the nameless force that had mesmerized my friends, but from the onset of time, which had churned forward all along. The taste in my mouth told me everything, as each breath brought a tell-tale metallic sting to my teeth. I knew without question that our air supply was down to the wire, and from the taste of copper in my mouth, I knew we had just seconds to spare.

As I took a breath, I remembered my instructor saying it didn't matter what the gauge showed, as long as air kept coming out of the tank. I knew he was right, and I also knew that if I could clear the ship's hull with a couple of breaths in the tank, there was a very good chance I'd make it to the surface alive.

Swimming as fast as I dared, I reeled in the cord with the others close behind. "Just get to open water," I kept telling myself. "Get to one hundred feet, and free-ascend to the surface . . . You know you've done THAT before."

Yes I had. I'd done exactly that, maybe not from one hundred and fifty feet, but certainly from one hundred. In fact, the old-school, Navy Frogman that had done my check-out dives, had regularly pressed me to free-ascend from triple digit depths. That's just the way we did it back then. So, I figured with any luck, milking one deep breath should be a piece of cake, as long as I didn't die from the bends.

Now all we needed to do was break free of the wheelhouse while there was still a breath or two in our tanks. Then, if we could sneak away from the ship without her noticing, all that stood between ourselves and the surface, were a few million gallons of water.

It all sounded easy enough. Easy enough in theory, until a light appeared in the hallway, that had no earthly reason being there.

I shielded my eyes as the corridor lit aglow, awash in the surreal light of something that floated just out of reach. It was a ball of light, crystalline sharp, and brilliantly beautiful, floating above the deck-plates, as if it was beckoning us to follow.

"It's the same orb we saw months ago," I thought, "the very same one that nearly led us to our deaths!"

"Why don't you follow it?" the ship whispered. "Isn't that why you came down here in the first place?"

It was, and she knew it. For ever since the first time we'd seen it, I'd been obsessed with seeing it again. But this time something felt different. And as I stared into the crystal clear light, it began to pulse like a candle, as if The Devil himself was holding it.

"What the hell is this thing?" I thought. "Has the ship's life come to light, or is it something else entirely?" I knew neither answer, but I did know that following the light would bring only darkness. With a glance, I could see my friends staring at the light, but by the grace of God, neither had taken the bait. Maybe one supernatural, time-altering session had been enough for them, for as the glowing orb moved farther down the hall, we headed for the gangway, as we made a break for it.

We moved quickly, heading toward the wheelhouse deck, where the black water turned to violet, and the promise of life rained down from above. As we neared the final bulkhead, I turned sideways to slip past the watertight door. Carefully, I motioned toward the surface, when Brian pushed me out of the doorway like we were jumping from an airplane. I tumbled forward, rasping against barnacles as the ship's deck-rail sliced out of the darkness. Had I tumbled farther, I'd surely have plunged into the abyss. But as luck would have it, my gloved hand grabbed the rail just a second before I flew overboard.

That wasn't a place you wanted to be, not next to the ship, nor beneath her… where things reached up from the purplish depths that have never seen the light of day. Had I fallen below, I'd never have returned. But now, as I clung to the rail with a straight shot to the surface, I couldn't help but think she'd let us go too easily.

"This is way too easy," I thought, as Tim sprang from the doorway. "She's letting us go WAY too easily."

But she really hadn't. For instead of crushing us under a two-ton deck plate, or locking us into a watery tomb, she'd done something far worse. She'd released us back to reality, where the air in scuba tanks doesn't last forever, and her other-worldly command over time and space was no longer applicable.

Sure, we'd cleared her hull, but we'd been left to die none-the-less. For as my lungs drew heavily against a vacuum filled with rust, I knew for certain that I'd taken my last breath.

She'd tricked us, or tricked me, at least, into believing that there might actually have been a few precious breaths to work with. The truth, however, is that there was nothing. Not a breath to be had, other than the air in my mouth, and the rust laden gas in my regulator hose.

It was nearly comical the way I spun in place, as I half expected The Grim Reaper to swoop in and save the day. But for a reason I didn't yet understand, He watched and waited. Wondering once again, if I had what it took to master the challenge.

"Alright, fine. It's all up to me," I thought. "It's up to me to make this work, and prove once and for all that I'm no longer his student."

In an act of defiance, I pushed clear of the ship, while staring into the abyss. The darkness rose up from below, its shadowy curtain disguising shadows that moved like waves, as something monstrous rolled its heavy back below.

"Oh God," I thought, as I stared into the darkness. "Which way do I go? And which way is really home?"

I looked away, fixing my gaze on the Ghost Ship's profile as my lungs burned with fire. Sparkles filled the water as I hung there motionless, and as I thought of a thousand things all at once . . . Only one of them seemed to matter.

It was just a memory. A stitch in time where my scuba instructor had told me something I'd almost forgotten.

"Don't waste your last breath," he'd said. "Blow it back into your buoyancy vest and re-breathe it a few times!"

The idea was unconventional, but breathing air with a depleted oxygen content was a hell of a lot better than filling my lungs with water.

There wasn't time to do the math, nor was there time to care about carbon dioxide build up. I knew that metabolically, the same breath of air was good for at least three more blows. So, trusting myself, and my uncanny ability to worm my way out of trouble, I inhaled hard, sucking air out of places I didn't know existed.

Where it came from I don't know, but somehow, between the hose, and my mouth, and the air in my face-plate, I managed to suck in half a breath. That did the trick, just enough to fuel a few fin strokes that propelled me toward the surface. I kicked a few times, not nearly enough, before the need to inhale nearly overwhelmed me. "BLOW IT INTO THE VEST AND BREATHE IT AGAIN!" yelled the voice in my head. "DO IT NOW!"

I blew into the vest, expanding the bladder just enough to gain positive buoyancy. Up I rose, away from the ship as it let out a sickening cry. I'd gained thirty feet, perhaps a bit more, before the fire in my lungs became crippling. There was no time to lose. I needed to breath or I needed to die. So I sucked against the vest's inflator valve, taking in a breath that was surprisingly satisfying.

The stale air felt wonderful, although now that I'd sucked the vest dry, I began to sink like a stone, in a cruelly, fickle way.

"KICK, KICK, KICK!" I thought, as I fought to maintain neutrality. "You've got to kick when you exhale, unless you want to join that thing in the abyss!"

I had no idea where my friends were, or if they were still alive. All I did was kick toward the surface, while breathing the same breath, over and over again. Up I rose, to one hundred, eighty, and sixty feet... until somewhere along the line, I think I began to die.

That was the strangest moment... where it actually seemed okay to give death a chance. What was once so terribly frightening, had suddenly become so natural. It seemed the right thing to do, so I decided to close my eyes, and kick until I was dead.

Why I opened my eyes I'll never know. But as I did, lightning flashed, while millions of rain drops danced on the water.

I broke the surface with a second to live, gasping for air as rain fell upon me. It was amazing to be alive, and as I looked up toward a crazily stormy sky, I didn't care if the sun ever shined again.

Seconds passed as the rain fell, before both Tim and Brian boiled to the surface. Brian gasped for air as if he'd been reborn, while Tim looked at me with the fear of God in his eyes.

No one said a word as we bobbed in the chop, while rain poured down all around us. Brian pulled his mask to his forehead, as a stream of bloody mucous dripped from his nose. He looked up a moment, gazing at the sky, before turning toward me with a wild look in his eyes.

"MAN, THAT WAS A GREAT DIVE!" he shouted. "BUT CAN YOU BELIEVE THIS RAIN?"

I just looked at him with a smile, as lightning struck the water a quarter mile away.

"It sure is raining," I said. "It sure as hell is."

The Cottage

My first year as a whitewater guide was one of the most exciting times of my life. I partied, played, and saved a few lives, all while learning the true meaning of friendship.

We were a tight group of souls, each of us willing to risk our life for one another. That's what you did on the river back then. You watched each other's back, until you heard the call to action. Then, you'd jump into the rapids, without hesitation, fear, or falter.

I learned many things that summer, life lessons taught in the blink of an eye that changed my life forever. It was the best time of my life. And each and every time I look back upon those days, I can't help but smile.

My rookie year had been challenging, but thanks to the tutelage of my river brethren, I'd secured a staff position with a leading outfitter. Now all I had to do was wait out the Winter, until the tourists came back, looking for the ride of their lives.

Fall was fast approaching, and several of my fellow guides were readying themselves for the annual migration to the rivers of Central and South America. It was a rite-of-passage for many, who chased the sun during the long winter months. I'd been invited to tag along, but being a first-year guide, I decided to stay behind, and hone my skills on some of the treacherous high-water rivers that Northern California had to offer.

So I stayed at the river campground, where over the next few weeks, I watched the tents come down one by one. I didn't want to pull up stakes and leave the river grotto. But with winter fast approaching, my cabin-like expedition tent wouldn't be a suitable shelter. I needed to do something before the first freeze of Fall. So, while there were still a few warm days left on the calendar, I did the sensible thing, and began to look for a place to live where I could weather the oncoming storm.

My search began in Coloma, the micro-sized, western town that was ground-zero for The Great Gold-Rush of 1849. It was a beautiful place, both scenic and peaceful, but with no rental opportunities available, I needed to set my sights elsewhere.

The next stop was the town of Placerville, where I worked part time at a local hospital. It was a few miles down the road, so I hopped in my trusty pickup truck, before driving down the highway with my shoulder-length hair in the wind. The area was amazingly picturesque, its winding roads punctuated with barns and buildings fit for a Norman Rockwell painting. It was an amazing place to be, and as I drove along, the scent of orange blossoms filled the cab with a welcoming presence.

When I reached the historic town, I drove down Main Street, before stopping at a mom-and-pop grocery store at road's-end. Beside the store's entrance was a cork faced bulletin board, covered with hand written want-ads that looked like they'd been there for years. Sipping a soda that I bought from an old Coke machine, I perused the rows of ads, until I spied an index card that immediately piqued my interest. I don't know what it was about that old, dog-eared card, other than it felt magical somehow… as if the words written upon it, had been meant just for me.

I read the handwritten header over and over again. "Adorable cottage for rent," it said. "Out in the woods." The place sounded perfect. Now all I had to do was call the number, and hopefully, with any luck, the place would still be available.

To my right, was a long, wooden porch that ran the length of the country market. While beyond its wobbly planks, was an old phone booth that was completely covered in road dust. I walked toward the booth with the index card in hand, sliding past the accordion door as its wheels groaned in the slider. Looking down at the card, I could have sworn that Old Mother Hubbard had written on it herself. The penmanship was perfect, and for all I knew, while she'd written on it, elves had crouched beside her, skillfully shining her shoes.

The phone rang many times, then, just as I was beginning to feel dejected, a woman answered the phone in a manner that made me smile.

"Helloooo," she said, in a thick Bavarian accent. "Helloooo… who is this?" I introduced myself, and to my delight, I learned that the cottage was still available. The woman went on and on about the home, and as she did, it sounded like the perfect place to live. I wrote down directions to the property, then, after saying goodbye, I felt an unexpected rush of butterflies in my stomach.

Returning to my truck, I pulled my hair back in a respectable looking pony-tail. The drive up the mountain was a bit long, but with the scent of cedar in the air, and an incredible view of the Eastern Sierras, the length of the journey didn't bother me at all.

Soon I'd climbed to nearly four thousand feet. "It's above the snow-line," I thought. "This place will definitely freeze over in the winter." That was for sure, but I didn't care, as something about the high mountain pass made me feel like I was coming home.

Barely ten minutes passed before my exit loomed on the left, where I pulled onto a mid-highway turn-out. A line of logging trucks thundered past, some coming so close they shook the cab of my small pickup. I was beginning to get antsy, when I saw a small break in the traffic just up ahead.

Side stepping the clutch, I zipped across the gap as a logger hit his high-beams. He'd come a bit close, and as I rolled onto the service road, I knew I'd need to find a safer way up the mountain if I was to survive living there. "I'll figure that out later," I told myself, as I rolled through the quaint logging town. "This place is just amazing!"

It was amazing, especially in the way a reddish cloud of sawdust hung heavily in the air. The cloud was huge, tinting the sunlight in such a way, that it seemed like I'd traveled to Mars. I'd never seen anything like it, and I knew right then that I was there to stay.

Soon, I passed a tavern that looked like a great place to get into a fight. "Loggers and river-guides," I thought. "Now THAT'S a volatile mix!"

I chuckled as I rolled down the street, heading toward a totem pole of lost-cat and garage sale signs. "Bear left at the signs," I'd been told. "Then drive a while until you see a big white rock." That sounded easy enough, and before too long, a large, white boulder loomed in the distance.

The thing was big. Set there no doubt, as a marker-stone to a small service road that was barely noticeable. I turned onto the narrow dirt road, following a dog-legged left that led to the base of an enormous hill. "Wow!" I thought, as I looked up the hill, "That thing is steep!"

I paused a moment, as I lined up my tires with two deep grooves in the road. The grooves were well worn, while the rest of the hill was covered in sun bleached grass. "Here goes!" I said, as I dumped the clutch. "Time to eat this hill alive!"

My tires dug in hard, as a hand-full of guinea hens ran for their lives. I laughed as the yard-birds bolted from the brush, being careful not to flatten too many of them. They scattered like rats as I crested the ridge, rolling to a stop amid a hard-packed, dirt plateau. I gazed in awe at my surroundings, while cedar trees rustled in the High-Sierra breeze. It was a beautiful place, where the sun twinkled like diamonds through the pine needle canopy. I felt at home the moment I arrived, touched by a magic that softly stirred my soul.

After parking in a gravel turn-out, I walked through the most meticulously manicured yard I'd ever seen. Everywhere I looked there were ornate flower boxes, adorned with orchids, tulips, and lilies, the likes of which you'd see in a botanical garden. There was a path that led through the planters, and toward the rear of the property was a beautifully maintained home that looked like someone had put a great deal of time and effort into keeping it that way.

As I approached the home, I was mesmerized by the dream-like nature of my surroundings. I felt like I'd wandered into a fairy tale, where seven dwarfs might actually have been waiting just around the corner.

Since the woman had told me to meet her in the garden, I figured she'd be waiting for me. But when I called out to her, all I could hear was the river-like sound of rustling pine needles. After mulling around a bit, I figured she may have been in the backyard. So, rather than wasting my time, I walked toward the rear of the home in the hope of finding her there.

My ninja skills must have been lacking, for as I walked down the narrow pathway, something sinister shadowed me step by step. I had no idea the beast was there, until it let out a loud "HONK!" that nearly gave me a heart attack.

I ran for my life as a huge goose took chase, narrowly dodging its beak as it snapped at my calves. "DAMN!" I yelled, as I dodged behind a planter box. "DON'T SNEAK UP ON ME LIKE THAT!"

The beast was indignant, preferring to give me the "Don't EVEN try to come around here," look. I had to laugh as it shook its silly butt, not only at its ferocity, but at how easily it had gotten the best of me.

With one eye on the militant goose, I walked past the main house, to where I heard someone call out from across the way. Turning toward the sound of the voice, I saw a white haired woman with a spade shovel in her hand. She was a stout looking woman, at least eighty years of age, who carried herself with confidence. With a powerful handshake, and sparkling eyes, she introduced herself as Frances. And from the moment we met, I knew I'd be renting the cottage, regardless of its condition.

"You can call me Mrs. Z," Frances said, in a thick German accent. "Everyone else does, because my real last name is a quite a tongue-twister!" I smiled when she said that, telling her that I too had a surname that everyone tied into a knot. We laughed a moment, before I changed the subject, mentioning how beautiful her garden was. "Why thank you!" she said. "It's my pride and joy. I work on it every day!"

We chatted a moment, before Frances led me toward what she called "The Summer Cottage." As we walked, we passed a large shop-like building that stood beside a gravel driveway. Frances mentioned that use of the shop was included if I decided to become her tenant. I was thrilled to hear that, because the thought of having my own shop, meant I could build some rustic birdhouses that would sell well at local consignment stores.

I was growing happier by the minute, then, as we rounded the corner, my new home came into view. "Wow!" I thought. "It's kind of big for a cottage... It's more like a dinky little house!" That it was. For what Frances called a "Cottage," was actually a one bedroom version of a relatively modern home.

"I like it!" I said with a smile. "It's really, really cute!" She was happy with my assessment, and as she showed me around the small, finished home, I found it hard to contain my enthusiasm.

"Here's the patio door," she said. "You get to use the whole patio too. It's even got a place for a barbecue!"

That was great, but frankly, I was sold on the place the moment

I stepped out of the truck. Frances gave me the grand tour, then, after she went on about "No wild parties, or loud music after nine o'clock," she paused, wondering what I thought about the place.

"I love it!" I told her. "It's absolutely perfect!" Then, as I pointed to the EMS sticker on my truck's rear window, I said, "I'm very trustworthy, I wouldn't work at the hospital if I was some kind of idiot!" She smiled as if she'd known that all along, before sheepishly mentioning that we needed to talk about the rent.

"You seem like you'll make a good tenant," Frances said. "I just hope that the rent isn't too high." I asked how much the rent was, then, after learning that it was surprisingly low, I said, "I'll take it!" with a warm hand-clasp.

Everything had gone as planned, and within thirty minutes the deal was done. Once the money part was out of the way, Frances showed me around the property, familiarizing me with everything I needed to know. She showed me the large, submarine-shaped propane tank that supplied fuel for the cottage's stove. As well as the ramshackle pump-house that needed tending-to now and again. All this rural living stuff felt so fresh and new, and from the row of country mailboxes, to the double-sided axe in the wood-pile, I knew I was in for quite an adventure.

As we walked back to my truck, Frances mentioned one last thing. "Watch out for the geese," she said. "They are VERY protective of the garden!" I pretended to be surprised, before asking, "Are you telling me that there are MORE THAN ONE of those things on the loose?"

Frances smiled as I drove away, waving goodbye till I was well out of sight.

Within weeks fall was upon us, and the playful Summer river began to morph into something unrecognizable. I'd never seen the river look that way, nor had I ever felt the malevolence that churned below. It used to welcome me, but now, as I stood on the rocks beside an empty campsite, it reached up behind me, slapping an icy finger down my spine. It was definitely time to leave. Time to leave the low-lands until the water warmed again. Sure, I'd still guide the river, but as far as living beside it, that would have to wait until at least early June.

Before long, the local country roads were lined with pumpkin patches and overstuffed scarecrows. Everything began to change, and soon enough, the wind began to blow, ushering in a hint of frost, that seemed a fitting touch to my quaint mountain retreat.

One day, a couple of weeks after I'd settled in, I cleared an area that was the ideal place to store my boat and trailer. Frances had given me permission to park the rig anywhere. So, after weed-whacking the grass to a nub, I backed up the trailer beside the old propane tank. The trailer fit perfectly on the small, square pad. Then, after I raised the tongue a bit, I blocked the wheels with a pair of sturdy, wooden chocks.

All had gone well, and now, all I had to do was secure a tarp over the skiff with a few bungee cords. The tarp fit snugly, but I knew that if it rained or snowed, it wouldn't be long until it sagged into the hull. I needed to prop up the center with some kind of pole, so I looked around the yard, in the hope of finding something that did the trick. There were a few scraps of wood lying around, but most of them looked like they'd poke a hole in the tarp. I needed to use something else, and just as I was about to cut the handle off an old post-hole digger, I remembered that I had a few lengths of PVC pipe in the bed of my pickup.

The one-inch pipe worked perfectly, and within minutes I'd fashioned two stake poles that were sure to fit just right. I sanded their rough edges, then, after capping them both with rounded ends, I wormed under the tarp to prop up the tent.

I felt like a kid as I slipped under the tarp, with my legs sticking out, and my upper body draped across the boat's folding seats. It was like a little tent in there, just like the blanket forts I used to make as a child. I smiled as I set up the poles, until someone grabbed hold of my leg with a surprisingly powerful grip.

At first I fought to break free, before realizing it was probably just one of my river guide buddies playing a trick on me.

"YOU'D BETTER LET GO!" I yelled. "YOU'D BETTER LET GO, BEFORE I KICK YOU IN THE HEAD!"

That was fair warning, especially since I was wearing work boots. But the unseen hands didn't falter, nor did I hear the mindless giggles of my river guide brethren.

"All right!" I said, as I wormed my way backward. "I'm coming out now, and I'm kind of' getting pissed!"

Whoever it was, they must have known I was serious, for as I pushed hard against a folding seat, my leg pulled free as I popped into the sunlight.

I spun around, ready to fight, but all I could see was the propane tank, and a pile of logs that didn't amount to anything. At first I looked under the boat, but then, after realizing no one was there, I sat on my truck's tailgate with a serious case of the creeps.

There wasn't a soul to be seen, nor could anyone have moved quickly enough to find a hiding place. There was just no way a person could have vanished like that. And as I sat there, I began to wonder if things from the past had finally caught up to me.

I shook my head, wondering if I might have experienced a weird cramp or something. My calf was a bit red, but aside from that, there really wasn't any indication that I'd been grabbed by anyone. "Whatever!" I thought. "That was just some kind of a quirk. Something to forget about before you give yourself a case of the Heebie-Jeebies!"

That made good sense, until I walked past the propane tank, where an icy blast of air blew down my back.

"WHOOOOAH!" I yelled, as I jumped back. "This is getting weird, WAY too quickly!"

I didn't know what to think. Other than that I'd just been sprayed with a shot of propane from the tank's relief valve. That would have made sense, seeing that the tank had been warmed by the sunlight. But knowing that I'd been grabbed . . . I wasn't too sure.

It seemed like the tank had vented itself, but as I backed away, there wasn't a sign that anything had leaked at all. In fact, there wasn't a whiff of propane in the air, or on my clothes. "What the hell was that?" I wondered, as I slowly approached the tank. "Is there some kind of leak? Or did something else reach out for me?" I wasn't a fan of the second thought, so, moving fast, I fastened the remaining bungees to the tarp's grommets, buttoning her down as best I could.

I looked to the sky, where the high clouds of winter soared in the jet stream. "Sleep well," I said to the little boat. "Sleep until Spring, when we'll have ourselves a whole lot of fun!"

Days passed, and soon enough, the propane tank episode was just a distant memory. I chose not to think about it, opting for other points of interest that had nothing at all to do with things that went bump in the light.

One such thing was the barn, a place that beckoned with unyielding ferocity. I was drawn to that building like a moth to a flame, but much to my chagrin, Mrs. Z didn't seem thrilled with the idea of my rummaging around. She was oddly hesitant at first, almost as if my poking through the place was going to unearth something she didn't want me to find. Every time I mentioned the barn, she tried to change the subject. And the more secretive she became, the more tantalized I was at the prospect of getting my foot in the door.

There was something good in there, and I knew that with a bit of wit and charm, I'd eventually worm my way in. But first I'd have to wait, until just the right moment when the barn's inner secrets would be fully disclosed. Luckily, it didn't take long. For after I fixed a few things around the yard, Mrs. Z really began to soften up. She trusted me more with each passing day, and within a few short weeks, she began to treat me like family.

Early one evening, there was a knock at my door, and as I opened it, I was delighted to see Mrs. Z standing there with a plate full of homemade cookies. She'd baked just for me, and I smiled a huge smile as I thanked her three times over. I stood in the doorway as we talked a while, then, she offered to take me on a tour of the barn, "If I was still interested," that is.

"Heck yeah!" I said, as I placed the cookies on the kitchen counter. "I'm ready now!"

I followed her to the barn, where she slid open the door for the very first time. The
barn was dimly lit, but I could immediately tell that it was filled with valuable treasures. She seemed to have one of everything, from an old, steam powered punch press, to an eight foot ox-brace, that hung from the rope of a six-wheeled pulley.

"Oh, my God," I muttered, as I tried to take it all in. "This place crawls with history."

It sure as hell did. For the barn was filled with hundreds of objects, each with a story to tell. I was mesmerized by the collection of oddities, to the point where I nearly walked into a vehicle that was partially covered by a ragged old tarp. At first I thought it was a modified Jeep, but then, as I lifted the tarp from the high-browed grill, I saw for the first time what the thing really was.

"Wow!" I whispered, as the narrow-set headlights came into view. "It's an old Chevy truck, one of the old Forest-Service models!"

That it was. And as I stared at its grill with the grin of the Grinch, I knew it had to be mine. But that wasn't going to be easy. For just as I began poking around the truck, Mrs. Z curtly barked out, "THE TRUCK IS NOT FOR SALE, AND I DON'T WANT TO TALK ABOUT IT!"

"That's weird," I thought, as she shot me down cold. "There's something about the rusty old thing that's really got her on edge."

"It can wait," I told myself. And besides, by the look of its deflated tires, it definitely wasn't going anywhere. So, I dropped the subject, in favor of a quick look inside the cab, where I could have sworn that someone whispered to me.

Before long, fall had turned to winter. And just about the time the leaves had fallen from the trees, Mrs. Z informed me that she was going to be "Wintering" with her family in Los Angeles. That caught me off-guard, because prior to that moment, I hadn't considered that the kindly old woman would be gone all winter long.

I suppose she'd planned in advance, for no sooner had she mentioned her hiatus, was she all packed up and ready to go. It was scary how quickly she got her things together. Then, as the first flakes of snow painted the dogwoods, she drove off in her ancient Volvo, toward warmer and greener pastures.

In retrospect, I should have seen it coming, given that she'd broken-out the battery charger and all. But I just figured that she was getting ready for the snow season, prepping the car for the oncoming chill before everything locked-up solid. Boy, was I wrong about that. For as I watched her drive past the chickens, and the geese, and the big white rock, I felt for the very first time, that I was truly alone.

It felt strange having the run of the property. And stranger still that I was the only living person on the entire mountain ridge. I suppose there had been comfort in knowing that Mrs. Z was just a quick shout away. But now that she was gone, it was just me and the geese... or so I thought, anyway.

A few weeks later, a powerful storm rolled down the mountain, covering everything in sight with a blanket of snow. At first the whole blizzard thing was a bit of a novelty, but then, as I learned there wasn't any snow plow service in my area, it began to look like I'd signed on for one hell of a winter. I took it all in stride, telling myself that I was a real mountain-man. But the truth is, that was a bunch of crap, because, to me, living in a place where you had to burn firewood, was nothing short of barbaric.

I suppose there was a rustic charm to the wood burning stove. But that was quickly quelled when I realized the wood pile was infested with Wolf Spiders. Those bastards were big, and they'd hide in the logs as I brought them inside. I hated that. Almost as much as the way they'd run across the floor after leaping from the log-rack.

That wasn't going to fly. For living with giant arachnids wasn't something I cared to do. So I killed what I could, before evicting the rest, amid the stark realization that my days on the mountain were numbered.

Winter wore on, and late one night, I was headed up the mountain after an especially long shift in the Emergency Room. The snow was deep, and mandatory chain-ups were in order. So I'd rigged-up at three thousand feet, hoping to make it up the hill before I drove into a snowbank.

My truck fish-tailed in the turns, but thanks to a new, used set of snow tires, I managed to reach my road before plowing head-first into a snow drift. "Whatever," I told myself. "I'll just leave the truck here and hoof it the rest of the way." That was a sound choice, I suppose, given that staying put and freezing to death wasn't a viable option. Now all I had to do was watch out for bears, especially now that the scarcity of food had made them much more aggressive.

Walking through the forest was a bit of a gamble, but with less than a half mile's hike, I decided to roll the dice. Needing to get moving fast, I reached across the truck's bench seat, to where a tight leather flap concealed a large bowie knife. Loosening the straps that set the scabbard to the blade, I slid the knife into my parka, before heading off on my way.

The forest was dead silent, save for the *crunch, crunch, crunch* sound of my waffle-stomper soles. "So much for the ninja approach," I thought, as I trudged through the snow. "If the bears didn't already know I was here, they sure do now!"

A bit of humor helped as I walked the moon-lit road, where after a minute or two, the trees and the snow all began to look the same. Had the road not curved in an arc, I'd surely have walked into the forest. But thanks to my internal compass, I trudged along, fairly confident in my course. Occasionally I'd stop and turn around, hoping there wasn't something trailing me with drool dripping from its lip. But thankfully, all I saw were footprints in the deep, powdery snow. "There's nothing out here that you can't handle," I paused to tell myself. "Leave your six to your senses, and get home fast, before you start to freeze up."

"Roger that," I replied, as I pulled on my parka's hood strings. "Stay on track and rely on your senses."

Trusting my gut, I moved forward, while tracing the lay of the land. How I found my way I'll never know. But just as I was beginning to wonder if I'd taken a misstep, a familiar ridge-line appeared to the North.

"Thank God," I thought, as blue streaks of moonlight beamed through the trees. "Now it's just a short trudge up the hill, and I'll be as good as home."

I began the final pitch, under a crystalline sky, and the fullest moon I'd ever seen. With each footfall I climbed, huffing into my parka's collar like a steam locomotive. The road was steep, and I stared straight ahead as my boots cut stair steps into the foot deep snow. Higher and higher I climbed, until for some odd reason, I felt compelled to look up, toward the leading edge of the anvil-shaped ridge.

At first I saw only shadows, spaces between the trees that faded into the distance. But then, as my eyes focused to depth, something stood out among the rows that made my blood run cold.

It was a man... or at least the silhouette of a man, standing just beyond the hill's apex. "What the hell?" I whispered, as he stood there like a statue. "Who the hell is THAT?"

At first glance, you'd have thought he was human. But as we stared at each other on that still, moonlit night, I knew for certain he was anything but. There was something strange about him. Strange in his countenance, and stranger still, in the way he seemed to be propped up, like a disjointed, lifeless scarecrow. I was compelled to come closer… drawn to him, in fact. Only not in the way you'd greet a passing neighbor. There was a seething sense of intrusion bleeding from his form. And as I slowly climbed the hill, the knife found its way into my hand.

I approached like a cat, keenly aware that at any moment he could bolt off into the night. Sure, I could have followed his tracks through the snow. But to where? And to what end? Especially now that his presence had awakened the part of me that's better off laid to rest. He was all predator, and I knew that once I crested the hill, what was destined to happen was every bit as twisted as the man's tortured frame.

Gone was the thought that this was a man, especially now that we stood on even ground. I paused, thirty feet from him, staring at a shadow that had no business walking this earth. This thing was far from human, and as it stared me down with a crook in its neck, I drew the knife from its sheath…

It leaned a moment, sort of the way The Reaper leans before he delivers a one-liner. But this thing wasn't The Reaper. It was something else entirely, something that had crawled under the fence, way back yonder, where no one has been in a very long time.

I was about to close the gap, and see if shadow cut as easily as flesh, when the thing moved across the yard, as if it had been carried by the wind. "HELL NO!" I yelled, as he blurred off toward the North. "You're not going to get away that easily!" But it seemed as if he had… for in a blink of an eye he was gone, as if he'd never been there at all.

Snow fell as I stared into the darkness. "That wasn't right," I thought. He moved way too fast for a man, almost as if he'd phased across the yard, in a strange, ripping blur. He was long gone. And now, as I stood where he once had, there wasn't a hint of a footfall, nor the slightest sign that he'd been there at all.

"What the hell was that?" I wondered, as I crouched down in the moonlight. It wasn't like any other shadow-form that I'd previously seen. And it certainly wasn't Him, for if it was, he'd definitely have stood his ground.

This thing was completely different. Nothing at all like the countless others I'd elbowed aside in the past. This one was seething with intent, and as the hair stood up on my neck, I needed to get some answers.

"What if it wasn't a shadow-form at all?" came the voice of reason. "What if it was a man, who was very fast on his feet?"

"That's crap!" I said aloud. "You know what you saw, and it was ANYTHING but human." I knew that was true. But in the moment, the thought of hunting down a real live human was much more palatable than chasing a nightmarish scarecrow.

"You can't let this go," said the voice in my head. "That thing will be back, and you can't have that."

No, I couldn't have that. I couldn't possibly allow that shadow thing to tip-toe around my property with a pitchfork in its hand. I'd rather hunt the thing down, than play a game where it comes and goes on its own terms. It had pissed in my yard, and now, like an alpha wolf, I was going to kill it.

That thought was cause for concern, for if I was seriously considering a moonlight hunt, I'd need some heavy artillery. The knife wasn't going to be enough. And even though it would have worked in a pinch, I needed a more powerful weapon, one with an edge that would put him down for good.

Seeing how he'd gone left, I crept along the ridge that led to the southernmost end of the property. From there it was a quick dash to the main house, where I dropped to one knee, beside a tarp covered wood-pile. There was a large, double-ended axe under the tarp, and I reached under the flap despite my spider-filled reservations. At first I felt nothing but rough-cut logs, until a rosin covered handle fit firmly in my hand.

I threw back the tarp, lifting the axe to the sky as its blade gleamed in the moonlight. Its weight felt good in my hands, and I smiled a wicked grin, as I'd just become the executioner.

Yeah, maybe I'd gone a bit crazy. But as I stood there like The Headless Horseman, I sensed a power rushing through me that was nothing short of incredible. If he'd come to the party looking for a fight, he'd definitely found one. And it was best advised that he go home.

With axe in hand, I stepped into the garden, as the blade swung like a pendulum. The snow covered field glowed a teal blue, the type of light that leaves no shadow, nor any place to hide. He was out there, that I knew. And it was just a matter of time before he stepped into the light, where I'd cleave his shadow in two.

I could have walked to the cottage to get my gun, but bullets alone would have done nothing to affect this adversary. It feared copper, iron, and steel... things forged from fire, in the very same ground that it came from. I knew that, and it did too, much to its chagrin.

So began the search, beginning with the barn, where shadows ran for cover as I switched on the light. He wasn't in there, although a few of his brethren were, just some weary, forlorn ghosts who had no place else to go. They shuffled and slid from place to place as I moved throughout the barn, wondering who the axe was for, as I swung it high and low.

"Come out, come out, wherever you are," I called out to the shadow. But no matter where I searched, or how many times I felt its eyes upon me, it knew enough to remain hidden... for the time being anyway.

After searching the property two times over, there was nothing more I could do. The shadow man was nowhere to be found, and as the biting cold began to displace my adrenaline fueled bravado, I checked both locks on the barn, before heading back to the cottage.

After locking the door behind me, I sat on my futon with the axe on my lap. "Why is there a shadow-form in my yard?" I wondered. "And why did it stand at the property's edge as if it belonged there?"

I pondered that, before walking toward my gun cabinet. My shotgun was at the ready, and I ran my thumb over the gun's release, ejecting a shell from the magazine. As the breach opened, the shell fell to the floor with a dull, muted *flop*. I picked up the shell, holding its brass end-case to the light. "Three inch magnum," the inscription read, plenty enough to do the job, just in case it was a man…

So began the Winter-long vigil where I reluctantly slept with one eye open. Something dark had its eyes on me. And while that was nothing new, there was something about this particular prowler that felt most unsettling. I knew it was out there, and I wouldn't let it win. But for the sake of my own sanity, I wished it into the wood-pile, along with all the other monsters.

Over time I put the incident behind me, choosing to concentrate on my burgeoning wood-working business. Night after night, I worked in my shop, and before long, I had dozens of birdhouses consigned in several local gift-shops. That was a very good thing, as it kept my mind occupied, while the extra money I earned, went a long way toward making the winter a heck of a lot more tolerable.

Late one night, sometime after I'd switched to the lighter, springtime blankets, I was awakened by a dull, thumping sound. At first, the sound was distant, as if I'd heard it in a dream. But then, as the sound resonated through the wall, I leaped from my bed in a head-spinning daze.

My heart raced, and my head swirled, as I leaned against the wall, shaking off a head-rush that was nearly incapacitating. I stood there a moment as my head cleared, before grabbing the shotgun I kept at my bedside. "What the hell?" I thought, as blood returned to my brain. "That sounded like the Thumping Man… but it couldn't possibly be."

Not wanting to consider that option, I slid into the hallway, where I had a direct view of the living room area. There wasn't a thing out of place, nor was there a grinning, fence post demon staring in my direction. Whatever this thing was, it had to be outside, and I began to consider that the thumping sound may have been someone breaking into my workshop.

I crouched down low as I headed toward the door, pausing in the entryway with my ear to the wall. The sound was much louder now, vibrating through the cottage as if someone was kicking his boots against the porch. I didn't know who or what it was, other than that it sounded like a man, with considerable weight to his foot falls.

It was really dark out, and as I peeked through a slit in the mini blinds, I couldn't see a thing. Judging by the sound and vibrations, the unseen visitor was just a few feet from the front door. I listened intensely, and the more the person kicked, the more it sounded like he was trying to knock snow off his boots.

That would have made sense, had it snowed recently. But seeing how it was nearly summertime, I didn't know what to think. All I could do was listen with my back to the wall and the shotgun in my hand.

"This is freaking bizarre," I thought. "If this is a burglar, why is he making so much noise? And if he isn't a burglar, what the hell could he be doing?" I needed an answer, so, as stealthily as I could, I reached for the light switch, ready to fall back in case he went ballistic.

I was about to flip the porch light on, when he stomped down so loudly, it shook the floorboards. "This isn't funny," I thought, as I stepped away from the door. "If he keeps screwing with me, he's likely to get his head blown off!"

I was done lying in the shadows. This guy was pissing me off and he knew it. Fully ready to rock, I flipped on the porch light as I pointed the shotgun at the door. "WHO'S OUT THERE?" I yelled to the man. But as I'd expected, there was no reply, nor was there any indication that he'd left the premises.

Holding my foot against the door, I moved the mini-blinds aside with my free hand. The porch light was on, and in its glow, all I could see was a whole bunch of nothing. There wasn't a thing out there, except for the wooden porch rail, and a muddy old doormat. Leading with the gun, I slowly stepped onto the dew soaked porch, where the reddish-brown deck boards glistened in the glow of the porch light.

There wasn't a footprint to be seen, other than those I'd made with my own bare feet.

As I dropped to a knee to feel the deck, the smell of sulfur blew past on an unsettling wind. I couldn't imagine where the strange scent had come from, other than the old propane tank may have spouted off again.

"This is WAY too weird," I thought. "First the footsteps, and now that smell... what the hell is going on?"

I leaned against the wall as I pointed the shotgun toward the trees. Things were growing creepier by the minute, and I have to admit that I was getting a bit spooked. Whoever this man-thing was, he was taunting me. Yet for all his hubris, he knew better than to face me head-on. That scared me the most. Because not only was he brazen, but he was methodical as well. To what end I didn't know.

A few minutes passed as I scanned the forest. Then, after I was reasonably sure the prowler was gone, I stepped back into the cottage, before bolting the door.

There was a beer in the fridge, and I cracked it open before plopping down on a beanbag chair beside my fish tank. My fish swam back and forth, casting weird shadows on the living room wall. "Who do you think that was?" I asked them. "Do you think it was a ghost? Or was it something else?"

They didn't reply, but I didn't need their input to know that the unwanted visitor hadn't been a ghost. "It was way too corporeal," I thought. "And it had way too much strength. Whatever this thing is, it's crept in from the dark side, and it's definitely trouble."

I could have mulled over the laundry list of hellish creatures that poke around in the night. But rather than stare at the wall all night long, I stumbled off to bed, with my shotgun at the ready. "The deadbolts will keep him out," I thought. "Even if he tries to kick the door in, I'll be ready."

As always, life moved on. And soon enough, Mrs. Z returned to the mountain. It was good to have her back, and as the days grew longer, the thoughts of shadow-men and other uninvited guests slipped to the back of my mind.

One spring evening, my girlfriend Lisa arrived at my house, just prior to our heading out on a dinner date. I could hear her car's engine as she motored up the hill, and as she rounded the bend, I stepped onto the front porch to greet her. Lisa parked beside my boat trailer, and I waved to her as she stepped out of the car. I expected her to wave back, but much to my surprise, she quickly spun around, staring into the woods as if something had suddenly spooked her.

Whatever she'd seen, it had frightened her, and I rushed to her side within seconds. Placing my hand on her shoulder, I asked "Hey, what's up? What's got you spooked?" She didn't say much, other than that "Something had been standing beside the propane tank that totally gave her the creeps."

"What do you mean by "Something?" I asked. "Was it some kind of animal?"

"No," she said. "It was like a shadow or something."

"That's weird," I told her. "The forest does play tricks on the eyes. I've seen a few strange things myself lately."

Taking her hand, I assured her that the only creepy things on my property were the militant, ninja geese. She laughed, before joining me in the cottage for a pre-dinner cocktail. Once we'd unwound a bit, we hopped in my truck, before heading out to a local Italian place. While we were at dinner, Lisa brought up the propane tank incident, mentioning that she'd sensed something strange on my property for some time now. I wholeheartedly agreed, before saying, "I can totally relate, there's something about the property that's just not right."

I then went on about this and that, before asking, "Would you please tell me everything you've experienced on the property? The creepy stuff that is."

"Are you sure you want to know?" She said with a smile. "I don't want to scare you!"

"I'm a big boy," I told her. "I ain't afraid of no ghost!"

We laughed, before Lisa went on with a surprisingly long list of things she'd felt and experienced. I was floored by what she told me. Then, as she began to expound further, I asked, "Why the hell didn't you tell me about this before?" She paused, stirring her drink with a teasing sparkle in her eye. "It's because I didn't want to scare you, silly! I didn't want you to have to cover your head at night!"

Boy, did that open the flood gates, because now that the cat was out of the bag, we talked about the ghostly happenings half that night. Curiously, one of the things she mentioned was that whatever the thing was, it didn't have the vibe of a typical ghost. She felt it was angry and bitter, and its overall tone didn't mesh with the happy, sunny property. I didn't know what to make of it all, other than I'd felt the anger too, and that Lisa's assessment was dead-on.

"You're right," I told her. "It's a VERY scary ghost. That's why you're going have to stay with me tonight!"

After dinner, we returned to the cottage, where some hot cinnamon oil washed away all thoughts of the dark, scary forest. It was a beautiful night, and sometime in the early morning hours, we drifted off to sleep, safe and secure, in our own little world.

It was roughly three A.M. when Lisa rolled out of my waterbed, setting the mattress in motion as if I was floating on a life-raft. "I'll be right back," she whispered, as she walked toward the bathroom, "Back in just a sec."

"Don't get lost!" I called out, as she cat-walked away from me. "I might get scared!"

She paused a moment, while turning to face me. "You'd better not go anywhere," she said, as she swayed her ample breasts, "I'll be right back..."

I wasn't going anywhere. So I just lay there, hoping she'd spin and tease me one more time. She made it half way down the hall, before stopping dead in her tracks, as she stared into the living room. I wasn't sure what she was doing, until she broke into a run as if someone was chasing her. "THERE'S SOMEONE HERE!" She yelled, as she ran toward me. "HE'S IN THE LIVING ROOM!"

I reacted fast, rolling off the bed as Lisa leaped over me. Beside the bed was the shotgun, and I pumped one into the chamber before jumping to my feet.

Lisa hopped on the bed like a trampoline, babbling something about a man, and the way he was "Floating" in the living room. That didn't make any sense at all, but from the way she was acting, I had a gut feeling that the Shadow Man had come to call.

"STOP BABBLING!" I yelled, as I pointed the gun down the hall. "IS THERE A PERSON IN THE HOUSE, OR NOT?"

"It's not a person," she said, with a trembling voice. "IT'S SOMETHING ELSE!"

"Oh great!" I thought. "It's a 'Something else,' Now THAT'S reassuring!"

I yelled out to the thing, leading with the shotgun as I crept down the hall. There wasn't a sound to be heard, and as I turned on the kitchen lights, all I could see were shards of broken glass, scattered all over the kitchen floor.

As I surveyed the unexplained damage, Lisa called out from my room. "DO YOU SEE IT?" she asked. "IS IT STILL THERE?"

I wished I had an answer for her, but as I stood there with the gun by my side, I really didn't know what to say.

"THERE'S NO ONE HERE!" I yelled back. "THERE'S NOTHING BUT A BUNCH OF BROKEN GLASS!"

Lisa was pretty freaked out, but after seeing we were alone, she sat on the futon with a blanket wrapped around her. "What the hell was that thing?" she asked. "And where did all the glass come from?"

I couldn't tell at first, until I saw a tell-tale smudge of lipstick on one of the larger shards. "It's your wine glass," I told her. "It fell to the ground somehow… And what's weird as hell, is that I put both of our glasses in the sink right before we went to bed."

Lisa was terrified, and I sat down beside her with arms outstretched. "Come here," I said, as I put my arms around her. "Tell me exactly what you saw."

"It kinda looked like a person," she said, as she nuzzled close to me. "It looked like a person that was cut in half, or something. I can't quite explain it, but it seemed like it was floating in the room, while it waved its arms around like giant wings!"

When she said that, it really gave me the creeps. Because I knew damn well, exactly what the thing was. It was much more than a shadow-form, and now that it had entered the inner-sanctum of my home, the game had changed considerably.

"I think it might have been that creepy scarecrow guy," Lisa said. "Maybe he's gonna start coming into the house, now that he's done it once already."

"Are you trying to give me the creeps?" I asked. "Because, if you are, I might just end up at your place!" Lisa gave me a soft, warm kiss, before saying, "Let's go back to bed now baby, I'll make all your worries go away."

Before long, summer was in full-swing, and Mrs. Z was buzzing around the garden like a giant worker bee. I considered mentioning the creepy goings-on, but it didn't seem proper to trouble an elderly woman. Besides, given that it was the busiest rafting season on record, I found myself spending so much time at the river camp that the cottage often seemed like a memory.

It was the Fourth of July weekend, and I hadn't been home in days. We'd been running rapids non-stop, and between the fun, and the girls, and the bottomless margaritas, I was ready for some serious down-time. The week had been a blast, but now that the tour buses were gone, it was time to head home for a deep, restful sleep.

It had reached 108 degrees in the river-gorge that day, and I was tanned so deeply I hardly recognized myself. A few days on the mountain would do me good, so I loaded up some laundry and zipped up my tent, before heading up the highway, toward the magical, whispering woods.

I rolled down the windows with the stereo on, driving beside the river till it veered into the gorge. The drive cleared my head, and before I reached the old mill, I felt like I'd been reborn. It had been a glorious weekend, and as the sun began to set, I realized it was much later in the day than I thought it was. "Jeez, it's nearly nine," I thought, "just enough time for a cold beer before lights-out."

That sounded good. An ice-cold beer, and a two day sleep. Or maybe a one day sleep, and a day up the mountain with my new fly rod. Whichever it was I didn't care, as long as I could lay motionless a while, on my soft, comfy waterbed.

I took the long way home, weaving up roads with the scent of jasmine in the air. I didn't have a care in the world, driving along with the wind in my hair, grateful for my life and the opportunity to live it my way.

Soon I pulled onto the property, weaving around a couple of whitewater rafts that I'd purchased that summer. I parked beside the barn, before walking around to the passenger's side, where I retrieved my laundry bin. It was piled high with swim shorts and beach towels, and as I held it close to my waist, I could barely see over the top of the heap.

I stumbled toward the front porch, certain that at any moment the geese would attack. "This is exactly the moment they've been waiting for," I thought. "I'm at my most vulnerable, and they damn well know it!" I would have laughed, had I not caught sight of something that froze me dead in my tracks.

It was the front door of the cottage... swung wide open, as if someone had run from the building just moments before I arrived.

I stared at the doorway, and the dark patch of shadow just behind the threshold. "What the hell?" I whispered. "That door was locked. I know it was."

Something was wrong… eerily wrong. Because Mrs. Z was away on vacation, and there was no chance in Hell that I'd left the door open.

I would have walked right in, had the cottage not crawled with a menacing sense of danger. Something about the home felt different, changed somehow… as if in the oddest way, I'd stumbled across a place I hardly knew.

What had happened, I didn't know, other than it felt like the cottage was warning me to stay away. I stammered a bit as I stared into the darkness, and as I did, an eggy wisp of sulfur wafted up beside me.

"What the hell?" I muttered, as the vapor wisped around me. "Has the stove's pilot light blown out, or is it that damned propane tank again?"

I didn't know what to think, as it was beginning to look like my peaceful night in the woods had taken a serious turn for the worst. At first I was hesitant to enter, but as the sulfurous scent faded, I set the laundry bin on the porch, before stepping into the living room.

Looking left, and then right, I listened for the faintest sign of a presence. There was no one there, in spirit or otherwise. So, I turned on the kitchen lights, which responded with a welcome, glowing hum.

After a quick search of the home, everything seemed to be in its place. I wasn't sure what had happened, other than that Mrs. Z may have needed to get into the house for some unexplained reason. "Maybe she checked the batteries in the smoke alarms before she went away," I surmised, although that notion did nothing to explain why the door had been left wide open.

"Whatever!" I said to myself. "She probably got distracted, and forgot to close the door."

Besides, there was nothing I could do about it, other than close the door, and hope it stayed that way. That worked for me, so I brought in the laundry basket, and started a load, before grabbing myself a beer.

Something was on television, but after about ten minutes, all I wanted to do was sleep. I was beat, and by the time I'd stumbled to my room, I fell asleep so quickly that I didn't even take off my shoes. I slept deeply, lulled by the sound of the clothes washer, and the endless chirp of crickets, that sounded like a symphony.

It was three A.M., where as if on cue, an odd, scuffing sound rustled through the cottage. At first it was just like before, where I could have sworn I was listening in a dream. But then, as a red warning light came on, something deep down inside told me to wake my ass up.

The sound was coming from the living room, where it seemed like something was trying to scratch its way through the screen door. As I tip-toed toward the kitchen, I rounded the corner, to where the sound was the loudest. Whatever this thing was, it certainly wasn't a man, and it definitely wasn't a ghost. It was some kind of animal, doing it' best to claw its way into my home.

It was right outside the door, scratching the screen as it clunked in the door jamb. It didn't smell like a skunk, nor was it any of the other furry, forest creatures that visited me from time to time. This thing was different, and purposeful in its own individual way. I knew it had to be small, and that it couldn't pose much of a threat. So I flung open the door, as I switched on the light, laying eyes upon one of the strangest looking creatures I'd ever seen.

It was a cat, with a head so large, it seemed to have come from an entirely different animal. It was deformed I suppose, but not in a bad way. Rather, it looked like its head had grown out of proportion to his otherwise cat-like body. Its head was huge, and for some unexplained reason, it had grown to three times normal size.

The cat looked at me, with its head resting on a furry frill that made it look like a full grown lion. He was regal looking in a super strange way, and I've got to say that his fuzzy, lion frill suited his big-headedness quite well.

Leaning against the doorjamb, I asked the silly cat, "Would you like to come in?" He looked up at me with his big, frilly head, before letting out a "Braaaap!" that I figured meant "Yes I do!" in big-headed cat language. He looked harmless enough, so I stepped aside, while he strolled in like he owned the place.

I wasn't sure if I should have let him in, but like the kids in The Cat in The Hat, I really had no choice. He stared at me as we sized each other up, then, as he playfully flicked his tail, I had the feeling he wasn't too ferocious.

Walking toward the fridge, I opened the door before looking down at him again. He was the strangest looking cat I'd ever seen, with a normal house-cat's body and the head of a full grown bobcat. He was definitely one of a kind, and despite his having suffered a genetic misadventure, I thought the little lion was really, really cool.

"Do you want something to eat?" I asked, as I held the refrigerator door open. "I've got gourmet Top Ramen!" He didn't get the joke. Rather, he looked around as if to say, "I like what you've done to the place!"

Smiling down at him, I grabbed a bag of sliced turkey breasts from the cold-cuts drawer. He could smell the meat right through the bag, and before I could pull a slice from the package, he nearly climbed up my leg to get at it.

"WHOA!" I said, as I pushed him off my knee. "You can't go all jungle-kitty on me if you want something to eat!"

"Braaap!" was all he said. So, I tossed him a turkey slice, that he scarfed down so quickly he couldn't possibly have tasted it.

"Was that good?" I asked, as I threw him another slice. "Are you a happy little lion?"

He seemed fairly content, but just to be sure, I grabbed a carton of milk from the back of the refrigerator. I was about to pour him a bowl, when the wild beast turned, and bolted straight for my room.

"OH CRAP!" I yelled, as I took chase. "MY WATERBED!"

He had the jump on me, but I was right behind him. He was pretty fast for a big-headed cat, and with one gravity defying leap, he bounded straight onto my bed covers.

The beast stood on my comforter, with his burr filled coat, and his furry lion paws, making kitty bread as if he was a baker. I cringed at the thought of his claws on the mattress, and I needed to do something fast, before he caused a major catastrophe.

I ran to the kitchen, where I'd stashed the turkey slices. "HERE KITTY, KITTY!" I yelled, as I shook the open bag. "HERE'S

SOME FOOD FOR YOU!"

The thing had a keen sense of smell, and within seconds, he came barreling around the corner like a freight train. I threw a piece of turkey into the living room, and as he ran for it, I bolted toward my bedroom, where the door was closed in a flash.

With tragedy averted, I sat on my futon as he pranced around the room. "I've got a hunch you've been here before," I told him. "You act like you've been here a hundred times."

That seemed true, and I began to wonder if he'd been associated with one of the previous tenants. He was a wild kitty, that's for sure. But there was a hint of domestication about him that suggested something more.

It was nearly morning, and while the whole jungle-cat thing had been novel, it was definitely time for bed. So I gave him some milk, and showed him the door, before bidding him adieu. "Goodnight Cat with the Big Head," I said, as I shut off the porch light. "I've got to get some sleep, and you do too!"

He howled on the porch a bit, until something bigger came along, that ran him into the woods. "He'll be back," I told myself. "Now that I've fed him, he'll definitely be back." That thought was nice, because he was kind of cool, and I did like having him around. So I locked up the house thinking happy-cat thoughts, as I slipped into bed, where my dream world began.

A couple of weeks passed, and as suspected, The Cat with the Big Head had become a regular. At first he was fairly wild, but over time, I won him over with cold-cuts and a bunch of kitty treats. Hand-feeding was the key, and soon enough, he allowed me to run a brush over his burr-filled coat. His little lion frill looked so regal after I brushed him, and I joked with him constantly about how he must have escaped from the circus.

I suppose he'd become my kitty, and after a month or so, he officially moved into the cottage. Sure, he still lived outside, but on cold nights, and during scary storms, he curled up on my bed, atop three layers of comforters.

He was a mellow cat for the most part. But over time, I began to notice subtle changes in his behavior that were somewhat disconcerting. It wasn't so much about him, as it was what he saw. It's kind of hard to explain, other than that occasionally, there would be a look in his eye that said so much more.

He'd look up, as if he'd seen something, then, he'd glance my way, while seeking validation. "What do you see boy?" I'd ask. "What is it?"

He didn't need to answer, as his body language said it all. Sometimes he'd just sit there, staring at the wall. While other times he'd track an object, as it moved from room to room. I didn't place much concern upon his actions, until the day he reared up like a Halloween cat, showing his fangs to an unseen intruder.

That was enough to give me the creeps, especially when he started to howl. Yet for all his silly quirks, I respected his intuition. We were kindred I suppose. For there on the mountain, with no one around, you needed to trust your gut, if you wanted to survive.

I suppose that survival was the farthest thing from my mind, as I worked in the barn one day, repairing a river raft that had a foot long tear in its side. I was humming away, cutting patches out of PVC material, when the cat began howling as if something really had him spooked.

Hearing his cry, I looked up, half expecting him to be squared-off with one of the geese. That wasn't the case however, as I saw him standing atop an old band saw that was adjacent to the forest truck's side window. He was puffed up like a porcupine, while staring directly into the cab of the derelict pick-up.

"What's the matter boy?" I asked, as I approached from the side. "What's got you spooked?"

Wondering if he'd found a rattlesnake, I slowly approached the truck, before peering into the cab. The window was rolled down, and all I could see was the rotting seat, and some rusted springs that had protruded through the yellowish foam. There wasn't a snake to be seen, nor was there anything else inside the cab to explain his odd behavior. He seemed to be howling for no earthly reason, yet as I stood there staring at nothing, I knew we weren't alone.

"Can you feel it?" I asked the frazzled beast. "Are you feeling what I've felt for months now?"

Of course he didn't answer. But then again he didn't have to, because I knew damn well there was something about the old truck that Mrs. Z wasn't disclosing. I wasn't sure what that was, other than some of the things she'd told me didn't seem to add up. I had so many questions, such as, who was the truck's owner? Why had it been left there? And most of all, why was it all such a deep, dark secret?

It was high time for some answers, especially in regard to the ever present ghost. So I decided to approach Mrs. Z the very next time I saw her. But before I did that, there was work to be done, such as surviving the Labor Day weekend, where we expected over two hundred rafters in our camp alone. It promised to be a weekend for the record books, and I figured that once it was finally over, there would be plenty of time to address the ghost issue.

Returning to the river camp, I could hardly believe what I saw. There were small tents staked out everywhere, so many, that I couldn't find a place to park. As I drove up the road, a couple of river guides walked past, giving me the thumbs-up sign. They had beers in their hands, and right then and there, I knew I was in for one hell of a weekend.

It was hot and dry, and the high-water rapids were steep and powerful. I'd never seen so many boats flip over, and when it was all said and done, I must have swam half a dozen swift-water rescues. We needed to be sharp and tight that long Summer weekend, balancing the fun and the laughs, and the epic water fights, with the constant notion that at any moment, one of us could go down.

Somehow we all made it through, without one broken bone among hundreds of rafters. Sure, there had been a few moments . . . Mostly involving hangovers, and a few drunken souls who couldn't find their way back to their tents. But aside from that, everyone went home with a smile, and an eight by ten photo of their river raft, as it splashed through Troublemaker Rapid.

Once again, I headed home, where I was greeted by the most burr-laden cat on the planet. He must have rolled in the things, and from the way his fur was matted into knots, I knew I'd be grooming him for hours.

I sat on the futon with a beer by my side, while the cat purred with each stroke of the brush. He was a real piece of work, fluffing out his silly, lion frill as if he knew he was special. I brushed him for quite a while, then, as we both grew tired, he curled up beside me as I watched some late night television.

It was another hot night, nearly triple digits at the stroke of midnight. Having no central air conditioning, the best I could do to cool the place down, was open the front and rear doors for some flow-through ventilation. That worked fairly well, especially with the addition of two large floor fans, that were strategically placed in the doorways.

The fans were powerful and heavy, and their two foot wide blades circulated a considerable amount of air through the thin screen doors. They were loud too, providing an excellent source of white noise that drowned out the constant din of crickets and cicadas.

Cool air moved through the kitchen, flapping the dog-eared sticky notes on the front of my refrigerator. "You stay here," I told the cat, as I fluffed up his bedtime blanket. "You'll be safe here, in your happy little place!"

He let out a, "Braaaap!" of contentment as his fur blew in the breeze. Then, as he curled up on his blanket, I headed off to my room for some much needed shut-eye. I was dead-tired, and within seconds of hitting the hay, I was out like a light, amid the soothing drone of the twin floor fans.

I can't say for sure what really happened next, other than I was lost in a dream world where waters run deep, and fish grow to gigantic proportions. I remember staring a fish in the eye, a saucer-shaped eye as large as a dinner plate. The fish stared back, emotionless and cold, before banking away, as if something large was approaching. "Where did he go?" I wondered. "And what chased him off like that?"

Such were my thoughts, as a floor fan flew across the room, its thick metal frame imploding the wall just inches from my head. I didn't know what to think as I was pulled from my dream, other than I was under attack at the worst possible moment.

First there was an explosion, as the wall caved in. Then, as gravity took hold, the fan slammed down on my head, amid a cloud of acrid gypsum.

I was shocked beyond belief, not having a clue as to what happened, other than that something large had fallen on top of me. The object was heavy and solid, and as my mind raced, it felt like someone was trying to smother me. That wasn't going to fly, so I threw the fan to one side, while rolling to the floor with a dull, slapping "Thud!"

As I lay on my back, I couldn't see a soul. There was no one in the room, nor could I see anything to suggest who my attacker was. All I could see was my dresser, and the area near the door where the floor fan used to be.

"What the hell?" I thought. "WHERE THE HELL IS THE FAN?"

It didn't take long to answer that question, for as I quickly jumped to my feet, I could see the fan, lying beside my pillow, atop a pile of crumpled wall-board.

Chills ran down my spine as I digested what had just happened. Somehow, the fan had been thrown across the room, carving out a chunk of wall-board, just inches from my head

"SOMEONE'S IN THE COTTAGE!" was all I could think, as I scrambled for my shotgun. "How else could the fan have been thrown across the room?"

I chambered a round, before walking toward the screen door, where the lock was latched and secure. "They didn't get in this way," I thought. "The door is locked from the inside, and the chain is still in the groove." That left just one other entry point, in the living room, where I expected to find the door wide open.

That would have made some sense, but rather than finding answers, I saw that the door was latched shut, while the second floor fan was happily humming away.

The cat looked like he'd seen a ghost, and as I approached the screen door, I was sure he probably had. The front door was locked as well, meaning that either the intruder had vanished into thin air, or, I had one hell of a problem on my hands. I didn't want to believe that a ghost could have thrown the fan that way. But something had thrown it . . . Something with enough strength to pick it up, and hurl it across the room.

Returning to my bedroom, I stared at my pillow and the deep, oval groove where my head had once been. The pillow was covered in gypsum dust and wall-board shards while beside it was the fan, with its rat-tailed power cord lying on the sheets.

"I KNOW YOU'RE HERE!" I yelled out to the thing. "SHOW

315

YOURSELF, AND STOP BEING A COWARD!"

It mustn't have liked that, for as I called it out, the screen door rattled loudly.

"GET OUT!" I yelled. "OR CHALLENGE ME NOW!

I half expected it to materialize. But rather than chance a head-on conflict, it slipped into the night, on a faint wisp of vapor. I suppose I could have followed it, but there was no sense in looking for something that ran with the wind. It had come and gone, leaving nothing more than a trail of essence that lingered beside the screen door.

Since it was gone, I set off toward the bathroom to rinse the wall-board from my hair. Turning on the light, I looked into the mirror, before dipping my head deep into the wash basin. The High Sierra water was delightfully cool, and I let out a sigh as it ran over my head and neck, washing my fear away.

As I reached for a towel, The Cat with the Big Head entered the room, loudly announcing his presence.

"Braaap!" The silly thing said, as it jumped onto the toilet lid, "Braaaap!"

I looked at my friend and his little lion frill, wondering how my life had become so surreal. "There's no use looking for this thing, is there?" I asked the silly cat. "It hits and runs. Then it disappears without a trace."

He gave me a look that felt most unsettling, and right then, I knew I was out-gunned…

I couldn't fight what I couldn't see, especially something that had the ability to cross solid barriers. That was a real game-changer for not only did this thing have the strength of a man, but it also had a taste for blood. And as long as it was around, I'd have to sleep with one eye opened.

None of this was good. Not one bit at all. This turn of events changed everything. And now, more than ever, I needed to talk with Mrs. Z, just as soon as the rooster crowed.

I waited until nine, before walking toward the main house with closure on my mind. There was no way that Frances was going to worm her way out of an explanation. She'd lived there way too long, and she knew way too much. And besides, there was no possible way she hadn't experienced at least a few ghostly run-ins of her own.

Heading down the path, I side-stepped the geese on my way toward the front door. One of the bastards was awake, giving me the evil-eye as I slipped by. I knocked softly on the door, then, after a minute had passed, I heard footsteps within the home.

"Who is it?" Frances called out. "Who's there?"

After hearing it was me, she opened the door, greeting me with a smile. "Gootmorning! How are yoo?" she said, in her wonderfully crazy accent. "How are yoo today?

I smiled back, saying I was fine. Before pointing to the cottage, as if there was something she needed to see.

"Something really strange happened last night," I told her, "something that makes absolutely no sense at all."

She knew something was wrong, for no sooner had I uttered those words, did she take on a look of grandmotherly concern. She closed the door behind her. Then, after slipping on her gardening shoes, she said, "Show me."

As we walked single-file down the rough stone pathway, I turned around, saying, "Frances, I'm going to show you something, then, after you've seen it, I need YOU to tell me what did it... Okay?"

She said "Sure," as we neared the cottage. Then, after pausing on the porch for a moment, she waved me aside, before opening the door. I walked up behind her, pointing toward the bedroom, where the light seemed strangely diffuse. "It's in there," I told her. "You tell me what did it."

Frances looked puzzled, until she saw the hole in the wall, and the fan lying next to my pillow.

"I was asleep when that happened," I told her. "I was asleep when SOMETHING threw it across the room!"

She was about to speak, when I put my finger to my lips, saying, "Shush... don't say anything. Let me show you." She nodded in agreement, before following me outside toward the next piece of the puzzle.

We walked past the old barn, to where the propane tank stood. Turning toward her, I asked point-blank, "Frances, what happened here? And what is it that walks this property at night? I really need to know, because it tried to kill me last night!"

Frances covered her mouth, as if she was holding back a cry, before looking at me with the most apologetic look in her eyes.

"There's something I was supposed to tell you," she said sheepishly. "But I kept it to myself because I didn't want to scare you away."

"What the heck is it?" I asked. "It's become frighteningly aggressive!"

"It's a man," she said, "the ghost of the man who lived here before you."

I put my hand on her shoulder, saying, "Frances, tell me everything you know. It's okay to tell me everything." She let out a sigh as we walked down the path, then, as we sat side by side on the rim of a planter box, she finally came clean with what she'd known all along.

According to Frances, the man who had previously rented the cottage was named George. He had recently become a widower, and because his life had been turned upside-down, he had lost almost everything. The small cottage was the perfect fit for George, and he moved in just a few months after his wife's passing.

Shortly afterward, George asked Frances if he could store his truck in the barn, along with a few odds and ends that he'd had all along. Feeling for the man, Frances obliged, telling him that he could keep his things there as long as he wanted.

George lived in the cottage for several years, serving not only as tenant, but as handyman, to both Frances and neighboring residents. During the colder months, George sequestered himself to the barn and workshop, weathering the harsh winters much the same way I had. He worked tirelessly in the shop, constructing all of the ornate, wooden planter boxes that now adorned the garden. In fact, according to Frances, had it not been for George, the idyllic, magical wonderland, never would have existed.

Frances told me everything about the kindly, old man. And one thing that struck a note was the way he'd walk the property daily, often stopping to pace back and forth at the top of the driveway hill.

Roughly a year before I came along, George was diagnosed with a rare form of oral cancer that began to erode a large portion of his face and mouth. Tragically, without health insurance or proper treatment, the cancer ran wild, disfiguring George till he was almost unrecognizable.

When Frances last saw George, it was on the eve of her winter commute. They spoke briefly, and even though he had taken to wearing a bandana over his face, the hollow of his eyes told the entire story. She wished him well, not knowing what to say. Then, as she headed down the drive, he stood at the crest of the hill, waving goodbye.

It was time for George to move on. And in a letter to Frances, which she'd find some time later, George thanked her for everything she'd done, while apologizing over and over for what he was about to do.

No one knows exactly when he did it. But sometime after he wrote the letter, George walked outside with a shotgun, before painting the propane tank red, with what was left of his rotting face.

When Frances returned in the springtime, she found the door to the cottage wide open, and the letter tacked to the doorway, in a folded, plastic bag. A few yards away lay the shotgun, beside the propane tank, which was now covered with blood. They never did find George's body. For by the time the animals were done with him, all that was left were some clothes, and a few sun-dried bones here and there.

I wanted to know all the gory details, but as Frances began to tear up, I didn't have the heart to trouble her anymore. She felt guilty about it all, blaming herself for leaving him all alone. "Oh stop it!" I told her, as she painted herself the villain. "You had nothing to do with his demise. In fact, you gave him a new lease on life that he otherwise wouldn't have had."

With my hand on her shoulder, I told her that everything was going to be alright. And that no ghost, George's or otherwise, would ever scare me away.

Frances gave me a hug, as she stared into the garden. "Everything's going to be just fine," I told her. "This is my home now, and I love it here!"

She smiled a grandmotherly smile, before heading toward her home. I watched her as she walked down the path, then, as she was close to rounding the corner, I shouted out to her . . .

"Frances," I said. "I've got one last question for you!"

"What's that? She asked. "What is it?"

I just smiled, before asking . . . "Have you got any paperwork on that truck?"

Two years passed, and in that time George and I got to know one another. I never did see him again, but he made his presence known as often as he could. It makes me smile when I think about all the things I did for him. Like resurrecting his band-saw, and partially restoring the truck, which needed a hell of a lot of work. He was there every day, especially in the barn, and if I failed to greet him at the door, I was sure to hear about it.

Curiously, once I began calling him by name, his restless soul seemed much more at ease. He was finally at rest I suppose, and a little recognition kept the violent episodes at bay, at least for the time being.

As the seasons passed, my bond with Mrs. Z, and my little lion friend grew stronger every day. I loved living on the mountain, and there wasn't a day where I didn't feel as if miracles could really happen.

One night, as my days on the mountain were drawing to a close, my furry friend wandered off, and never returned. I worried about him for days, until a strange whim compelled me to walk to the part of the forest where the trees grow thin, and a carpet of pine needles covers the ground. I stood there as a warm breeze swirled around me, and in that moment, I knew for sure he'd passed on to Heaven. I never did learn where he came from, and I don't know where he went. But I do know he's safe, and that I'll never forget him, as long as I live.

Shortly after his passing, my life changed dramatically. I met a girl, fell in love, and soon the need to create a family of my own called out from down the mountain.

Holding out as long as I could, the day finally came where I bid Frances farewell. She was very special to me, and with a hug and a kiss, I told her I'd be back, to check in from time to time.

Four years later

As I closed the latch on the moving van, my little girl rushed to my side. "Are we going to Fordila now?" she asked. "Are we all ready to go?"

"Yes baby," I said as I held her hand. "We're ready to move to Florida, just as soon as Daddy does one more thing."

Walking into the empty house, I found my wife standing on our deck, as she looked out over the forest. "I'll miss this house," she said. "It was a good house, but I'm ready to move on... It's time."

"It will be time," I told her, "just as soon as I do one last thing."

She looked at me with a furrowed brow, knowing that whatever it was I'd be doing, I'd definitely be doing it alone.

"Just come back to us," she said, as she placed her hand on my shoulder. "We'll be waiting for you at my parent's house."

I kissed them both goodbye, before heading east, past dormant rows of grape vines that seemed to stretch for miles. The last of the waning sunlight filtered through the trees, while roads, once familiar, seemed strangely foreign to me. It was as if I'd never traveled them before, and as I passed the old lumber mill, I knew for certain that it had been far too long since I'd last come home.

Mailboxes with whirly-gigs lined the road, their shadows drawn long by the last light of day. I drove as quickly as I dared, darting from shadow to shadow on tree-lined curves. There were butterflies. Butterflies in my stomach over something I should have done long ago. Why I waited so long, I still don't know. Other than life seemed to have pulled me in a direction that was too far from home.

I was excited, almost giddy, at the thought of what was to come. It was going to be such a treat, to knock on Mrs. Z's door, and surprise her with a hello after four long years. I imagined the look on her face when she opened the door, and I knew that she'd be smiling, just the way she had, many times before.

Lost in thought, I nearly missed the turn-off as it loomed on the left. I hit the brakes hard, sending a cloud of road dust twenty feet into the air. As the cloud moved across the road, I could see a tattered row of mailboxes, sun-bleached and parched, set atop a twisted, sideways fence-post.

Mine was the third from the end, tilted to one side, just as it always had been. I stared at the box, and as I did it beckoned, as if there was a piece of mail inside, left there just for me. I rolled up to the box. Then, after looking over my shoulder, I peeked inside, seeing nothing but dust.

"GO HOME," a voice called out. "You don't belong here anymore."

I heard the voice, but I didn't listen, for sometimes opinions need to be set beside the road, like a well-worn couch, that you don't need anymore.

Throwing the rig in four-wheel low, I thundered up the bumpy road one last time. It was as rutty as it had ever been, more-so in fact, which is probably why I failed to notice that the big white rock was completely overgrown with berry bushes.

I should have noticed that and more . . . But as memories swarmed like fire-flies, the overgrown address marker went unnoticed, as it had for many years.

Cresting the ridge, I slowed, before turning onto the driveway that led to the old barn.

I'd planned on parking near the cottage, before walking to the main house with the biggest smile on my face. But that never happened, for as I gazed upon a place I once knew, all I could see was destruction.

"WHAT THE HELL?" I said aloud, as a pit bull strained against a chain. "WHAT THE HELL HAPPENED HERE?"

Something was dead-wrong. Something that became glaringly obvious the second I crested the hill. Gone were the ornate planter boxes that George had once built, as were the beautiful flowers that Frances had cared for with trembling, loving hands.

In their place were the crushed remains of what had been, seemingly over-run by the wheels of pickup trucks, during some makeshift monster truck rally. I could see tire tracks running over the crushed wooden planters, leading to a large, ashen burn-pile, amid the center of what was once the home's front lawn.

There were beer cartons everywhere, fire singed and torn, piled high beside a back drop of shattered beer bottles. Some of the bottles stood in rows, while spent shotgun shell casings were sprinkled throughout the yard. I couldn't believe what had happened. The once idyllic homestead had been turned into a white-trash shooting gallery. And now, in the saddest way, it was almost unrecognizable.

God knows what I was thinking, as I backed into the turn-out. Other than that I was compelled to know what I didn't dare consider. I stepped from the Four-Runner, before walking toward the cottage as the dog barked viciously. The propane tank stood to my left, overgrown with weeds, save for a blood stained area that peeked above the weed-line. I thought of George as I walked the broken pathway, while the mouths of phantom geese nipped my heels with every step.

Something called out from just around the corner. Somewhere near the clothesline, and the box where Frances used to keep her gardening tools. I wasn't sure if I was being pushed or pulled, I only know that the ghosts of the past dragged me along as they screamed out to be heard.

They screamed, "LOOK! LOOK! SEE WHAT THEY'VE DONE!" as I walked around the bend. And as I turned the corner, I couldn't believe what I saw…

The cottage had been turned into a full-blown grow-house. Its tight confines filled with Marijuana plants that were ready for the market. Five gallon buckets were everywhere. Some empty, and some stacked in rows, while others bore the remnants of last year's harvest. This wasn't good, not good at all. For not only had I trespassed into the lion's den, but I'd also discovered something that could easily get me killed. "Just come home to us," ran through my mind as I back-pedaled toward my vehicle. "Come home to us, Daddy, so we can go to Fordila!"

"HOLY CRAP!" I thought, as I began to run. "I've got to get out of here, NOW!"

As I ran, a tall man emerged from the cottage, who was wearing a wife-beater t-shirt and a ratty pair of sweat pants. At first he didn't see me, but then, as he looked up, he began to shout, while picking up something that looked like a baseball bat. I didn't dare look back, choosing to run for my life, rather than explain what I was doing there.

I had the jump on him, and just enough time to fumble with the keys till the engine roared to life. He swung the bat in an attempt to box me in, but as I skidded sideways with four tires spinning, he leaped out of the way before I turned him into road-kill.

He rolled to his feet, throwing the bat as hard as he could. The bat narrowly missed my window, and as it flew into the trees, I skidded onto the down-slope, as if The Devil was chasing me.

Within seconds I reached the paved road, where I threw the rig into two wheel drive.

"What the hell happened?" was all I could think. "How could that have happened to my fairy-tale world?" There were simply no answers, other than rust never sleeps, and you can never go home again.

The road stretched before me like an unpainted canvas. Leading me far down the mountain, to a place where I truly belonged. "I'm coming home," I said, with a smile. "I'll be home soon, and by daybreak we'll be heading to Florida!"

So I headed down the mountain, on a glorious summer's eve. Toward the loving arms of a child, who considered me a god...

Epilogue

Years of trials had come and gone. And now, there was only darkness, a black cloak where the water and sky blended into a continuous veil that had neither a beginning nor an end. I could feel the warm Caribbean sea pulsing beneath me. Its waters thick and viscous, like a pool of blood on a darkened road where the asphalt hadn't cooled yet.

My team was somewhere below. Somewhere deep in the abyss that seemed a mile away...

I suppose it didn't matter where they were, especially since I'd drifted so far off the mark that finding them seemed utterly pointless. "Does it really matter who shares the sea with you?" I thought. "When you're all alone, while something dark draws nearer?"

I guess not, especially now that the pulse of the thing could be felt between the rhythm of the waves.

And who cares anyway? For after all, there was no one by my side as I stepped into the oily waters of the sound, and no one there when the first of many fell to the ground before me.

So be it, I suppose. It was to be just he and I. There in the midnight water, somewhere between home, and nowhere at all.

Looking up, I could see the stars, as bright as ever on the eve of my final exam. I didn't need to see the shark, for I knew he was there. And as water dripped from his high arching back, I could feel his shape... aAs he drew closer.

I turned to the sky with my back to the darkness below. With each wave my body rose and fell, and as the swells rolled by, something between them moved forward… closing the gap and sealing its fate.

"LET'S DO THIS! I yelled, to the shadow in the waves. "Let's get this over with, and see what comes to pass."

Rolling to face the depths, I looked down in wonder, as a million points of phosphorescent light danced beneath me. "Diatoms," I thought, "countless tiny creatures, all here to watch the final episode of the show."

Reaching across my chest, I drew my knife from its sheath, its blade glistening in the starlight. I held it to the heavens, its razors edge shining like a beacon for all the world to see.

"Follow me," I whispered to the shadow. "Follow me below…"

And with that, I dropped like an angel, into an inky blackness that somehow felt like home. "Follow me, if you wish to die, you nameless, shapeless beast. To a place far below, where I'll stand on solid ground."

You'll fall there, that I know. Just like all the others who've come before you. And it stands to reason I suppose…

For I am… The Master of The Abyss.

About The Author

Lee Ehrlich is an Adventurer/Explorer who is most notably recognized as the World Authority on Underwater Paranormal Phenomena. He is a Paranormal Investigator with over three decades of experience who heads a nation-wide investigative team specializing in hostile and dangerous environments.

His investigative exploits have earned him critical acclaim, which has resulted in numerous radio and television appearances, including a starring role in The Travel Channel's *Legends Of*. On the conference tour, he is a well-known lecturer who brings a unique perspective to the paranormal realm.

Additionally, Lee is an internationally known Scuba Instructor with nearly forty years of diving experience. His unique undersea adventures have been documented in newspapers and magazines world-wide, and he has recently graced the pages of *Skin* and *Scuba Diver* magazines.

Lee lives in Southwest Florida with his wife and daughter.

Other titles from Haunted Road Media:

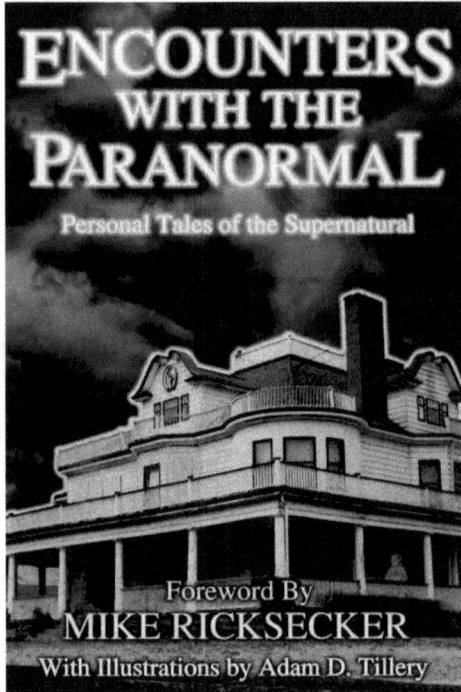

ENCOUNTERS
WITH THE
PARANORMAL
Personal Tales of the Supernatural

Foreword By
MIKE RICKSECKER
With Illustrations by Adam D. Tillery

Almost everyone has a ghost story. Real people. Real stories.

Read about haunted houses and vehicles, experiences during paranormal investigations, visits from relatives that have passed on, pets reacting to the paranormal, psychic experiences, and conversations with full-bodied apparitions.

ENCOUNTERS WITH THE PARANORMAL reveals personal stories of the supernatural, exploring the realm beyond the veil through the eyes of a colorful cast of contributors.

For more information visit:
www.hauntedroadmedia.com